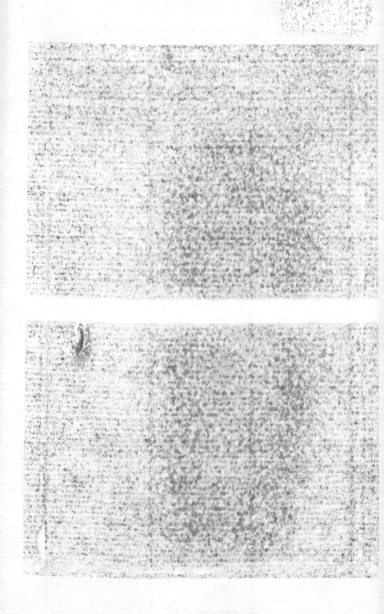

ENGLISH RECUSANT LITERATURE
1558–1640

Selected and Edited by
D. M. ROGERS

Volume 350

THOMAS WORTHINGTON
A Relation of Sixtene Martyrs
1601

A Chayne of Twelve Links
1617

ROBERT PERSONS
A Little Treatise
1620

THOMAS WORTHINGTON
A Relation of Sixtene Martyrs
1601

The Scolar Press
1977

ISBN o 85967 389 8

Published and printed in Great Britain by
The Scolar Press Limited, 59-61 East Parade,
Ilkley, Yorkshire and
39 Great Russell Street,
London WC1

NOTE

The following works are reproduced (original size) with permission:

1) Thomas Worthington, *A relation of sixtene martyrs*, 1601, from a copy in the library of Oscott College, by permission of the President. This copy lacks the first two leaves and the last leaf. In the facsimile these are supplied from a copy in the Community Library, Mount Street, London, by permission of the Librarian.

Reference: Allison and Rogers 917; not in STC.

2) *A chayne of twelve links*, [anon.], 1617, from a copy in the Bodleian Library, by permission of the Curators.

Reference: Allison and Rogers 228; not in STC.

3) Robert Persons, *A little treatise*, 1620, from a copy in the library of York Minster, by permission of the Librarian. In this copy the title-page has been slightly damaged, and in the facsimile the title-page is reproduced from a copy in the library of Lincoln College, Oxford, by permission of the Librarian. Also reproduced from the Lincoln College copy is the cancellandum title-page. In the Lincoln copy the cancellandum is in its original place and the cancellans is before part two of the book: in the facsimile the cancellandum follows immediately after the cancellans at the beginning of the work.

References: Allison and Rogers 632; STC 19410.

A
RELATION

OF SIXTENE MARTYRS:
GLORIFIED IN ENGLAND
IN TVVELVE MONETHES.

VVITH A DECLARATION.

That English Catholiques fuffer for
the Catholique Religion.

AND

That the Seminarie Prieſts agree with
the Ieſuites.

In anſvver to our Aduerſaries calumniations,
touching theſe two points.

Precious in the ſight of our Lord : is the death of
his Sainćts. Pſal. 115.

PRINTED AT DOWAY:

By the VVidovv of Iames Boſcard:

VVith licence. M. D. C. I.

AN ADVERTISMENT TO THE READER,
touching the contents, order, and title of this booke.

INtending at firſt (gentle reader) to make a briefe relation of tenne Martyrs, in the holie yeare; and by the maner of proceding againſt them, to declare that they ſuffered meerly for Religion; I put M. Iohn Rigbie his proceſſe firſt (though he was not the firſt of theſe Martyrs) becauſe I ment to ſet the ſame downe more at large, as being moſt notorious, and moſt amply handled in publique place of Iuſtice. But when I had donne ſo much, and (by reaſon of a iorney that I made) leift it wi.h a freind to publiſh, for the common good; vpon certaine conſiderations, it was not performed as I expected. And in the meane time vnderſtanding that it was opprobriouſly obiected to M. Wharton (as alſo to ſome others, to the offence of manie, and ſcandal of the weake) that the Seminarie Prieſts were at diſſention, and debate againſt the Ieſuites, I thought good, to explicat more fully his anſwer, to that falſe and abſurde ſclander. And hearing alſo, that it hath pleaſed God, to glorifie ſix more Martyrs, I would in nowiſe omit to adde their names herunto. By which occaſions I vvas forced alſo to change the former title, to make it conformable to the whole contents. T. W.

FINIS.

Hunc libellum, cui titulus eſt, Narratio de ſexdecim martyribus &c. cum declaratione quòd Catholici Angli perſecutionem ſuſtineant pro fide orthodoxa; & quòd inter Seminariſtas ſacerdotes Anglos ac Patres Societ. Ieſu benè conueniat; à viris Anglicæ linguæ peritis, pijs & eruditionis Theologicæ nomine celebribus perlectum, nec quicquam depræhenſum habere quod editionem impediat; excudi permiſimus. Actum Duaci, menſe Septembri. 1601.

Bartholomæus Petrus, S. Th. Doct. & Profeſſ.

THE MANER

OF PROCEDING,

AGAINST M. IOHN RIGBIE,

a Catholique Gentleman put to death in
London, this present yeare, 1600.

Mongst other common oc-
currents, which minister
occasion of speach and discourse, in sundrie partes of
the world, it is neither the
least, nor of least importáce
that is dayly reported of
manie Catholiques, put to
death and otherwise afflicted, these late yeares
in England. Whose present hard state, and the
true cause therof, though the best and mightiest
Princes and Potentates of the Christian world
(as also manie others of al estates) do wel see
and knowe, and with compassionable chari-
tie do manie wayes, like the good Samaritan, *Luc.10.*
releue and assist them : yet there be two other
sortes of men, the one not sufficiently wel, the
other very il affected, towards these distressed
Catholiques. For the former seing and not re-
garding their calamities, passe on their waies,
like the Iudaical and carnal Priests and Leuits,
as if it nothing at al pertained to them, either

A 2   to take

to take notice, or to haue care and compassion
of their neighbours miseries. Of which kind of
people, I haue litle more now to say, but hartely
pray God, to make them more mercifull, that
they may find mercie in the time of nede. For
that I am here principally to deale with the last
sort, who more actually persecute Catholiques:
not only depriving them by violence, of their
goods, liberties, and liues : but also accusing and slandering them of hainous crimes,
wherof they are most free and innocent : to
make them odious, or their martyrdom lesse
glorious, amongst the ignorant at home, and
strangers abrode : saing and auouching with
great wordes, othes, and protestations, that
they die not, nor suffer not, for cause of Religion, but for matter of treason against their
Quene and Soueraigne : though in their consciences they can not but knowe it to be farre
oterwise. For why els (besides other proofes)
are they so vnwilling to report, and so loath to
heare, what maner of treason this is, but for
that, when the same is sincerly declared, it easе-
ly and euidently appeareth, to be no other
thing, then mere Religion, and necessarie confession of the Catholique faith ? As hath bene
very often proued, not only by other irrepro-
uable testimonies, and manifest demostrations,
but also by their owne tribunals, in publique
place of Iustice, in the most principal cities and
townes of the Realme : as at London, Yorke,
Lanceston, Chenceford, Lancaster, Winche-
ster,

fter, Durram, Newcaftle, Carlel, Oxford, Dor-
cefter, Glocefter, Wrixam, Warwike, Darbie,
Stafford, Bewmaris, Nottingam, Canturburie, Lincolne, and other places. But for fomuch
as our aduerfries perfift ftil, in auouching and
mantaining their pretended Iuftice in this behalfe, I fhal for the more honour of God, more
manifeftation of the truth, and better information of fuch as be not fufficiently fatisfied, fincerly relate an other example of trial, made in
the caufe of à Catholique gentleman, put to
death in London the 21. day of Iune this prefent holie yeare 1600. In which narration, for
auoiding of al partialitie, I wil omit other
proofes of our Religion, and iuft commendations of the partie (which may notwithftanding hereafter be more largely published) and
fimply in tvvo woordes, touch thofe onlie
points vvhich concerne the neceffarie knowledge of his perfon, and pertained directly to
the caufe of his death: and then fet before your
eies the whole proceffe, as it pafled before manie vvitneffes, in forme and shew of publiq; iuftice. The diuulging wherof in print, no refo-
nable men, and namely the Magiftrats and
others that concurred in this action, can not
diflike, nor poffibly be offended thervvith, except their confciences accufe them, of fome
vniuft dealing againft the perfon, whom they
haue fo publikly apprehended, examined, indicted, iudged, and bereued of his life. Briefly
therefore, his name was M. Iohn Rigbie, one

A 3   of the

of the younger sonnes of M. Nicolas Rigbie of Harrock, in the Countie of Lancaster getleman. VVho coming to yeares, ad vse of reason copetent for that purpose, so sufficietly learned the principal articles of his faith, that continually even to death, he held al the same, to be vndoubtedly true, and necessarie to saluation: as wel appeareth by that which here foloweth. He attayned also the Latin tongue and further proceded not in learning. The rest of his youth he spent partly in his fathers house, partly in seruice: where through humaine frailtie for feare of punishment, and in hope of temporal preferment, ioyned with il example and earnest perswasions, of some worldlie freinds, he yelded so farre to the Protestants Parlament lawes, made for the abolishing of the holie Sacrifice, and other Catholique Rites, and for practice of the new forme of english seruice, as to heare sometimes the same seruice. But being afterwards very sorrowful for having so conformed him selfe, by exteriour act, and personal presence, in the Protestants *Apo. 13* Chruches, (VVhich is there *the note and character of conformitie* to their religion) and therby also depriuing him selfe, of the holie Sacraments, *Heb. 13* and necessarie foode of his soule (*for none may eate of the Altar of Christ, that serue the Tabernacle:* and much lesse, that serue a new Religion, which was never approued in Gods Church) he resolued by Gods grace, to leaue againe that course of life, and so was absolued

from

from his finnes, and reconciled to God, by a Catholique Prieft. And thence forth liued in great peace of his confcience, and alacritie of mind, with zeale and feruour of deuotion : by word and ex mple, drauving fo manie as he could, to the like good eftate, for their foules health. Amongft others (which I may not here omit,though I promifed breuitie) by his earneft prayers, moft dutiful endeuour, and Godlie perfuafions, he procured his owne father to be reconciled to God, in his old age. by which worke of fingular pietie, and by manie others, he dayly prepared the way, to the glorious crowne, that he novv poffeffeth. Wherunto likvvife concurred certaine other occafions, which it pleafed God alfo to permit and to vfe, in bringing him to this bleffed end.

For being (as is wel knowne) in the feruice of Sir Edmund Hudlefton knight, he was fent by his maifter, to Sir Richard Martin Alderman of London, about certaine bufines. Where the young man dealnig fomewhat roundly and fincerly, as it became a faithful feruant in his maifters affaires, this Sir Richard conceiued offence and difpleafure againft him. Which he ftil bore in minde (like Herode and *Matth.* Herodias, wayting opportunitie to be reuenged *14.* of S. Iohn Baptift)til a fit time happened for his *Mar. 6.* purpofe, as fhortly it fel out by this accident.

Maiftris Fortefcue a Catholique widow, and daughter of the fame Sir Edmund Hudlefton, was fommoned to the Seffions at New-

A 4   gate

gate for caufes of Religiō: who being ficke, and
not able to appeare, was to fend one to teftifie
the fame for her in that Court. VVhervpon
this maifter Iohn Rigbie her fathers man, and
hers alfo when fhe needed his fernice, was readie (as God would haue it for his more glorie)
to do this good office for her that day. And fo
going to the Seffions houfe, when Maiftris
Fortefcue was called, he appeared and anfwered, that fhe was ficke, and not able to come thither. The cōmiffioners demanded, if he would
auerre the fame by his oth, he faid he would
fo do. A booke was by and by offered him.
Wheron he was commaunded to lay his hand
(as the maner is) and fo he did: as being readie
to confirme by his oth, that which he had in
cōmiffion to anfwer, according to his opinion
and knowledge. But the commiffioners being
much difcontented, to be thus fruftrat of the
gentlewomans appearance, the forfaid Sir Richard Martin (perceuing him to be the fame mā
that had heretofore bene with him, and had offended him) fuddenly and with choler begaine
to examine him of his owne faith and religion,
before he was otherwife apprehended, or accufed, or had anie cogitation of anfwering for
him felfe. Which neverthelesfe he did with
admirable refolution and corage, to the afto-
nifhmēt of his aduerfaries, and great edification
of manie, as wel prefent as others that haue
fince heard therof, and doubtles alfo of more
yet, vvhich may hearafter heare of it. Our. B. Sa-
niour

niour *geving him mouth and wisdome* (as he *Lue.21.*
promiseth in such case) *which al his aduersaries
were not able to resist and gainsay* . So from this
examination he was carried to prison amongst
theues , and often after examined , and remoued from prison to prison, and at last condemned , and put to death, al in such sorte as now
you shal here read . And that for the former
and greater part , written by him selfe word
by word as foloweth.

*A Copie of my examination the 14. of Febru. 1600.
taken before my Lord mayor of London,M. Recor-
der,Sir Richar Martin,Iustice Dale,with others.*

Comming to the Sessions to take my oth,
vpon occasion (*to testifie that Maistris Fortescue
was sicke and not able to appeare in that place*)
and hauing the oth tendered , and my hand
vpon the booke to sweare , suddenlye spoke
Sir Richard Martin,and said : VVhat are you
that wil sweare ? à papist? to whom taking my
hand backe, I answered, I am à man . but what
more, saith he? at which his replie (not able to
forbeare laughter) I said : Sir what can I be
more then à man? he then said: art thou à Papist, a Protestant, a Puritan or what Religion
art thou of? at which I something staying , he
said presently : wilt thou go to Church, or no? *This is*
to which I said, No . I thought so, said he, he *often*
may sweare what he list, and hath his Priest at *here*
home to absolue him, I warrant you. Sir, said I, *urged.*
I do not vse to make false othes, and if I did, I *I.*
know not anie Priest to geue me absolution

so easely . Then spoke my Lord Mayor , wil

2. you not go to the Church? No my Lord. were you at Church within this moneth? No. were you within this three moneths? No.were you within these twelue monethes? No,my Lord.

3. wil you not go, to the Church ? No. when receiued you the Commumon? Neuer. nor wil you not receiue it ? No my Lord, for I know that to be no Sacrament , and therefore wil not receiue it . O damnable creature , said they! what Religion art thou of? à poore Catholique my Lord. à Catholique said they! so

That is   are we.what is the Catholique Religion? that
the Ca-   which I beleeue . and what do you beleeue?
tholique   That which the whole Catholique Church
faith.   beleueth . what is that? that which I beleeue,
vvhich   my Lord . so I would not be brought from
is bele-   that,by no meanes. I wil warrant you,said Al-
ued at   dermã Martin, he beleueth as his Maistris be-
al ti-   leueth . I pray God I beleue no worse , said I.
mes , in   whose man are you?said my Lord Maior. Mai-
al pla-
ces,by al stris Fortescues,my Lord.how long haue you
er most   serued hir ? these foure or fiue yeares . who
Chri-   preferred you to her ? one Claiton à brother
stians.   in law of myn.is he a Catholique?No,my Lord
Vincen.   à Protestant . vvere you à Catholique vvhen
Lirin.   you came to her ? No my Lord , but alvvayes
ca. 3.   Catholikely brought vp . Hovv chaunced it
that you altered your religion? vvhen I came to riper yeares , my Lord, and considered myn ovvne estate better , I very wel perceiued that course vvherin I thẽ liued, vvas not

the

the courfe vvhere in to be faued. vvherupon,
I altered my Religion. VVhat, said Iuftice
Dale, vvilt thou take the oth of the Supre-
macie ? Sir said I, novv you feeke my blood.
I knovv not al that belongs to that oth. there
be manie can anfvvere you better then I. I
vvil not fvveare. No, said they al at once,
rvhy: VVe haue al taken it, if thou denieft it,
thou art à traitor. To vvhich I anfvvered, I
am no Traytor, my Lord, but à true Subiect.
That vvhich your lordship and others haue
done, is nothing to me, I vvil not fvveare. And
if the Pope should send in forces, to inuade
this Realme, vvhofe part vvould you take,
the Quenes or the Popes ? I anfvveared, the
Quenes my Lord. But if he should come to
fettle the Catholique Religion (as you terme
it) vvhofe part vvould you then take ? Good
my Lord that concerns my life. I vvil not an-
fvver it. vvhat, art thou not à Prieft ? said Sir
Richard. No, farre vnvvorthie so high a calling? Nor a frere? No. Nor taken anie orders,
r or profeffion vpon you ? No more then pro-
feffed my felf, by Gods grace, to liue and dy
in the Catholique Church. VVere you never
out of England? No my Lord. looke if he be
not bald, said Iuftice Dale. No I vvarrant
you, said I. send for à Barber, said my Lord
Maior, and cut of his haire prefently. So vve
refted til the Barber came. Then they set me
on à vvarme ftone, vvhere the Irons vvere in
heating to burne felons vvithal; and the barber
began

began quickly to play his part. But when I
had fitten a litle, the ftone burned through
my hofe, and the fyer vnder burned my legges. VVhervpon I fpoke and faid, I fitt to
hote, my Lord. And prefently they anfvvered al, thou mutt fit hotter yet. Nay then
faid I, put vnder more fyer in Gods name,
vvhearat I heard no one vvord. but, by and
by, they fpoke vnto the barber, and bade
him cut me clofe to the head. VVhereto I
anfvvered, in this quarel, head and al, if it
pleafe you, my Lord. VVhen he had donne
they bade me pay the barber. I faid, No, my
lord Maior should: yet stay faid I, thou fhalt
not take al thefe paines for nothing. So I
tooke forth my purfe, and gaue him three
pence. VVhere at there vvas great laughing,
and I not the leaft merrie, I am fure. Then
my Lord called me againe. Hovv fay you,
4. vvil you yet go to Church? I anfvvered, No
my Lord, this hath not anie vvhitt daun-
ted me. VVhat Countriman are you? A
Lancashire man my Lord, VVhat is your
name? Rigbie. vvhat more? Iohn Rigbie.
vvhere about in Lanca hire? about two miles
from Latham, at a houfe called Harrock
vvas I borne, my Lord. I am more forie, faid
he, for I knovv honeft gentlemen of that name. If there vvere anie honeftie amongeft
them, faid I, I hope in Iefus he vvil graunt
me part by defcent. Then faid Sir Richard
Martin, Sirra Sirra, vvhat prayer doe you vfe
dayly

dayly to fay, for the Pope? Sir faid I, I knovv
not vvhat you meane. Yes faid he, that you
doe, for you fay this daylie praier: and began
to repete certaine vvordes, vvhich vvere
neither English, Latin, French, nor Spanish,
I am fure: but he ment (as it femed) to haue
made Latin of it. I haue forgot it, and fo did
prefently, for except it had bene vvritten it
vvas impoffibile to carrie it a vvaye. Only
the three laft vvords I remember, vvhich
vvere, pro noftra Papa. VVherat not able *That is*
to forbeare laughter, I vfed an oth or tvvo *for our*
faying: by my fai h and troth, I neuer heard *the Pope*
fo fimple a fentence come forth of anie Catholiques mouth: and for myn ovvne part,
though I vnderftand Latin, I do not vnder-
ftand vvhat you faid. VVherat al the bench
laghed vvith me for companie. So my Lord
Maior commaunded the keper to take me
againe to his cuftodie. And I ftood amongft
the fellons til night, and fo vvent to nevvgate
my nevv lodging. vvhere I learned fome neck
tricks, and there refted.

The next day at nine of the clocke when my
Lord chiefe Iuftice vvas fet in his place, I vvas
fent for to the Seffions houfe. vvhere prefently his Lordship asked my name. I anfvvered Iohn Rigbie. VVhat Cuntriman are you?
a Lancashire man my Lord. Hovv long haue
you continevved in thefe partes? fome
foure or fiue yeares, my Lord. vvith vvhom? in
feruice vvith M.is Fortefcue. vvhofe daughter
                                              is she?

is fhe? Sir Edmund Huddlefton his daughter.
vvhere liueth fhe? vvith her faither. VVho
preferred you to her feruice? a brother inlavv
of myn, one Clayton, my Lord. VVhat religion vvere you of, vvhen you came to her? in
hart a Catholique my Lord. but you vvent to
Church faid he. I did my Lord fometimes,
but alvvayes intended by Gods grace to become a Catholique. VVho perfvvaded you to
that courfe, to alter your Religion. No bodie
my Lord, but myn ovvne côfcience. for vvhen
I confidered myn eftate, I found that I
vvas not in the right courfe to be faued. and
therfore I refolued by Gods grace to pro-
feffe that Religion vvherby my foule might be
faued. VVil you not go to the Church? No
my Lord. you liued in Sir Edmund his houfe?
I my Lord. Doth Sir Edmund go to the
Church? I my Lord. And my Ladie alfo? for
any thing I knovv, my Lord. For I tooke
no great heed of any bodies going, but myn
ovvne. Hovv long haue you refufed to go to
the Church? thefe tvvo or three yeares my
Lord. You vvent to the Church once, then
can you not be, as you fay, a Catholique, but
you muft be reconciled. Hovv fay you then
vvere you reconciled or no? vvherto not
knovving vvhat to anfvvere, I ftayed a litle.
and his lordship againe bad me fpeake, then
I anfvvered: my lord to fatisfie your lordship
in this point, I tooke not vpon me, to pro-
feffe my religion vvith out a certaine ground
thereof

thereof , but I had that vvhich belonged to a
Catholique . I vvas in deede reconciled my
lord . vvel said : saith he , and by vvhom ? by
one M. Buckley my lord , vvas he a Seminarie Prieſt ? he vvas a Catholique Prieſt my
lord . vvhere vvas it done ? in the Clinck.
Hovv came you acquainted vvith him ? by a
Lancashire man, a kinſman of myn. VVhere
is he ? dead my lord. hovv many times ſince,
haue you ſenne him , at your Maiſtris
houſe ? Never in my life, neither before nor
ſince . VVhat others haue you ſeene there?
not one my lord ? hovv manie more knovv
you thath are Prieſts ? Not one my Lord .
VVhere is that Buckley novv ? in heaven I
make no doubt . in heaven ! hovv knovv you
that ? he ſuffered Martyrdom for the Catholique Religion . Did you never ſee him
before, and could he perſvvade you ſo fully?
I my lord . for by Gods grace I doubted not
in anie one article of my beliefe . Al vvhich
examination they vvrit dovvne and gaue it me
to ſet my hand to it firſt, for honor ſake, before my lord chief Iuſtice or any of the reſt,
vvhich I did . and then they ſet their hands to
it alſo . Then my lord commaunded the keper
to take me , and to put on me an iron chaine.
vvhich vvhen it came I vvilled him to put it
on, in Gods name, and ſaid alovvd : I vvould
not change my chayne, for my Lord Maior
his great chavne, and gaue the felovv ſix pence
for his paines . By and by my Lord chiefe
Iuſtice

Iuftice fent me vvord to prouide my felfe, for I vvas to be arrayned forthvvith. I bad the meffenger tel his Lordship. I neuer heard fo good nevves in my life before, and fo I vvas commannded to the common Gayle. But (expecting euerie day to be arreigned) the Tuefday folovving, I vvas removed to the vvhit Lyon in Southvvork. and vvas there quiet til the third of March, not hearing anie more vvhat should be done vvith me.

On vvenfday, the third of March in the common Seffions vvith a number of felons I vvas brought to my trial. In the forenone I vvas called and appeared, but nothing vvas faid to me. VVhen the Iuftice vvent to diner vve alfo vvent home to prifon. and benig at dinner Iuftice Gaudie fent his man for me, and I vvent vvillingly vvith my keper . And fo coming to them at Iuftice Dale his houfe vvhere the Iudges dined , Iuftice Gaudie commanded the chamber to be voided , faing there vvere matters of importance to be delt in . Some vvent avvay , but the moft part ftayed. There he called me vnto him , and asked my uame, vvhich I told him. vvere not you committed by my Lord chiefe Iuftice, and examined by him at Newgaae? I my Lord, I vvas fo . You knovv your ovvne hand if you fee it ? I my Lord. fo he shevved me my hand, and I faid: This is my hand. I pray you geue me leaue to fpeake for my felfe. You shal , faid he . I vvel perceiue you haue
thought

thougt better of the matter since , or are growne far more skilfull. This manner of answering for your self before , would haue serued your turne better : but now it wil not. I sent for you to this end. I am told by one of my Lord of Canturburie his gentleman , that you thought you had answered before ignorantly , and are now sorie for that you haue done, and willing to become a good Subiect, and go to Church. If you wil so do , her Maiestie is mercitul , and her Lawes wil take pitie vpon you . How say you , wil you go to Church now ? No my Lord. Good my Lord, **6.** who soeuer informed your Lordship, that euer I did yet yeld , in anie point of my profession, or former answer, was not my freinde, nor euer had my consent therto . I assure you , my Lord, I am a true Subiect, and obedient to her Maiestie and her Lawes, in anie thing which may not hurt my conscience . But to say that I wil go to Church, I neuer did, nor neuer wil. Yea rather, my Lord , then your Lordship should haue anie light suspicion of me , of such a consent, take my first answere , as it *is*, there is my hand, here is my whole bodie, most readie I am , and willing to seale it with my bloode . and I humbly thanck your Lordship, for calling me to answere this point my self. VVhy then, said both the iudges, wil you not go to Church? No, my Lords, God forbid **7.** I should . then we see, said one of them, there is no such matter , as vve vvere made to

beleue . We were told, you were a simple
young man, and willing to recant . but
we fee now, thou art a refolute wilful fellow, and there is no remedie, but law
muft procede . I would be forie, my Lords,
to geue your Lordships anie caufe to thincke
that euer I ment to recant knowing nothing
wherin I haue offended, but only vttered
my confcience . If that be fo great a matter
of offence, let me haue lawe, in the name
of Iefus . Gods wil be done . Then fpoke
Iuftice Dale, a Iuftice of Peace; thou art
a cogging cofening fellow, and getts thy
lining, no man knoweth how, by cogging
and lying . Sir, faid I, for my getting I nede
not much to bragg of it, and for my lying
and cogging vou fpeake of, I wold gladly
you should know, that the Aunceftres of
the houfe, from whence I came, were
gentlemen fiue hundred yeaes before your
grandfather was Iuftice . And fo I ftopped
his mouth . And the Iudges committed me
vnto my keper for that time . The next day
being thurfday we went again to the Seffiõs at
S.Margarits hil. Where about 2 of the clock
in the afternone, I was called to the barr
to be arayned . the Clerck fayd : Iohn Rigbie
hold vp thy hand, where befeeching my
fwete Saviour Iefus, our Bleffed Ladie, and
al the holie companie of Angels, and other
Sainéts to pray for me, I held vp my hand
merily . So the Clerck read the Inditment,
which

which when I had heard, I befech you, my
Lord, fayd I, grant me libertie to fpeake.
anone you shall faid he. So I gaue place, ād the
reft came to the barre, for we were fix arreigned at that time together, fiue fellons,
and my felf. About an houre after I vvas
called again and bidden, hold vp my hand.
which I did as before. my Inditment was read
again, and it was a sharp one. Then my Lord
bad me fpeake, and I anfwered to foure principal poinrs, briefly in this manner.

Firft, my very good Lords, wheras I am
charged in myn Inditment, that I was reconciled, it is very true; to God almightie I fo
was. and I thinck lawfully might be. and as I
remember, it is alfo allowed in your boke of
common prayer, in the vifitation of the fick,
that if anie man find hymfelf burdened in confcience, he should make his confeffion to the
Minifter. Which confeffion manifefteth a
breach betwen God and his owne foule, and
by this humble confeffion he craueth pardon
for his finnes, and reconciliation to God again
by the hands of his Minifter. Secondly wheras I am charged, that I was reconciled from
myn obedience to her Maieftie, and to the
Romish Religion: I wil depofe the contrarie.
For I was neuer reconciled from anie obedience to my Prince, for I obey her ftil. nor
to aine Religion: for although I fomtimes
went to Church againft my wil, yet was I
neuer of anie other Religion, then the Catholique;

lique, and therfore neded no reconciliation
to Religion, vvhich I neuer stood against.
Thirdly, wheras (in my former answers)
I said, I went to Church, it is true, for feare of
temporal punishment I so did, but neuer
minded to fal from the old Religion, and
therfore neded no reconciliation to Religion.
Fourtly and lastly I humbly beseech your good
Lordships, as you wil answer it before God,
to explicat the meaning of the statute to the
Iurie, if the meaning therof be, to make it
treason, for a man fallen into the displeasure
of God, through his sinnes, to be recōcsled to
God again by him, to whom God hath committed the autoritie of reconciliation. If this
be treason, Gods wil be done. Then said both
the Iudges, it was by à Romish Priest, and
therfore treason. I answered, it vvas by a Catholique Priest, who had the libertie of the
prison, and was frie for anie man to come vnto
him, to releeue him: and therfore by the statute no treason. Againe, my Lords, if it be not
inquired of, within a yeare and a day, there can
be no aduārage take aganst me by this statute,
if you wrong me not. Wherto replied one
that sat vnder the Iudges: A! this wil not serue
thy turne, for the Iurie must finde it treason.
and so gaue them instructions, that it must
needs be treason. Nay then Sir, said I, if it
must be, let it be. Gods wil be done. Then said
Iustice Gaudie, Good Rigbie, I pray you
thinck not in anie sorte, I go about to seeke
　　　　　　　　　　　　　　　　　　your

your death . her Maieftie , and her lavves be merciful . If you wil yet conforme your felf, and fay here , before the Iurie go forth , that you vvil go to Church , and fubmit your felf, vve vvil procede no further . My Lord , faid I, if that be al the offence I haue committed, as I knovv it is ; and if there be no other way but going to Church to helpe it, I would not vvish your Lordships to thincke , I haue (as I hope) rifen thus manie fteppes towards heauen , and novv vvil vvilfully let my foote flippe, and fal into the botomleffe pit of hel. I hope in I E S V S , he vvil ftrengthen me , rather to fuffer a thoufand deathes, if I had fo manie liues to lofe . Let your lavv procede. Then faid the Iudge to the Iurie : you muft confider of it , you fee vvhat is faid : you cannot but find it treafon by the Lavv . And fo vvhen the reft vvere arraigned, they vvent forth , and ftood not long to thinck vpon the matter , but came againe , and I vvas called , and bidden againe hold vp my hand. they bad the Iurie looke on the prifoner , whether is he guiltie or no ? and, who fhal fpeake for you ? they al faid: the foreman. I befech you , my Lord, faid I , may it pleafe you to command filence, that I may heare my verdict. vvhich his Lordfhip did . but the foreman fpake fo fofily that I could not heare him. I willed him to fpeake vp, and not to be afeard . Then he faid , Guiltie . To the which I faid , vvith a lovvde voice, *Laus tibi*

8.

VVhere els in the vvhole vvorld, doth the Iudge tel the Inquifiters of truth, vvhat they muft find to be the truthe

B 3 *Domine*

Domine Rex *æterna gloriæ*. And so went from
the barr. When the rest were arraigned, and
iudgement was to be giuen, I was first called.
and Iustice Gaudy said, what canst thou say
for thy self, wherfore thou shouldest not
haue iudgement of death? I answered, if that
which before I said, wil not serue, I can say
no more. Good Rigbie, said he, thinck not I
seeke your death. wil you yet go to Church?

9. No, my Lord. why then, said he, iudgement
must passe. with a good wil, my Lord, said I.
Then he pronounced his sentence, as you
know the manner is. Which when he had
ended, I said, *Deo gratias*. al is but one death,
my Lord, and a flea byting in comparison of
that, vvhich it pleased my svvete Sauiour

Here is IESVS, to suffer for my saluation. I humbly
the pa- thank your Lordship, for your great paines:
tiëce of and friely forgiue your Lordship, and this
Saints, poore Iurie, and al other persecutors in this
vvhich cause vvho soeuer. Wel said, saith he, in dede
kepe the you shew your charitie. and then gaue iudge-
comman- ment to the rest. And vvhen he had done he
dements called vs together, and began his exhortation
of God, perswading vs for our end. vvilling vs to
ãd faith send for a Minister, and prouide for death.
of Ie-
sus. I desired his Lordship to spare my presence,
Apoc. and bestovv that counsail els vvhere. For I
14. hope I am as vvel prouided, as by his exhortation I should be. If you be, said he, it is the
better for you. God spede you vvel. and so
vve parted. I pray God forgeue them al. and
                  amend

amend them, if it be his vvil. Amen.

Christo laudes, & sancta Matri eius honor. Amen.

Thus much he vvrit himself, after he vvas
repriued: and sent it, to a deare freind, vvho
kepeth safe the original. For Iustice Gaudy
vvho pronounced sentence of death against
him the fourth of March, caused him for that
time, to be repriued. and so he continued
prisoner in the vvhit Lion in Southvvork a
boue three monethes more.

On thursday the 19. of Iune, in the Assises
holden at S. Magarets hil in Southvvorke,
(Iustice Kingsmel sitting vpon criminal causes, and Iustice Gaudy vpon ciuil matters
and suites in Lavv, vvho in lent Assises before
had the contrarie offices) M. Rigbie vvas
produced again to the barre, and asked by
Iustice Kingsmel vvhether he vvould yet go
to the Church, or no? And he ansvvered (I
thanck God) I am the same man that I vvas.
It is not lavvful to go to your Church. I vvil   10.
not go to it. Then thou must nedes dye, saith
the Iustice, for longer repriue thou canst not
haue. he answered, my Lord, that is the thing
vvhich I desire, and looke for, but I thinck
my self farr vnvvorthie, to dye for so good a
cause. The Iudge perceuing that he had no
irons on his legges, being a condemned man,
sharply rebuked the keper, and commanded
a fine of fourtie shillings, for that default, to
be set on his head : vvhervpon the keper

brought

brought a ſtrong payre of ſhackells. vvhich
M. Rigbie taking into his handes, kneeling
downe, and making the ſigne of the Croſſe,
kiſſed them, and gaue them again to the keper,
and ſo going vnto the blocke, the kepers man
riuited them on very faſt on both his legges,
and ſo they continued al that day, and the
night folowing. The next day, being friday,
he vvas broght again to the Seſſions houſe in
the forenoone. VVhere after he had ſtoode a
vvhile the irons fel from of his legges vpon
the grounde. vvherat he ſmiled. the keper
demanunding vvhy he ſmiled, he told him,
his ſhackles vvere fallen of, and bad him ri-
uite them on faſter, vvhich he did as he
thought very ſure: but vvithin a litle ſpace
they fel of again, vvhervpon he called again
vpon his keper, and vvilled him to make
them faſter. For I eſteme them, ſaid he,
Iewells of to great pricè to be loſt. The
kepers man, that had put them ontwiſe before
being much amazed, refuſed to do it againe.
I wil faſten them no more, ſaid he, for I
thinck it is not Gods vvil you ſhould vveare
anie irons. in ſo much that the keper commaunded an other of his men to do it. And
then Maiſter Rigbie remembring that à Catholique maide in the priſon, called Mercie
had that morning told him, that the night
before ſhe ſaw in her dreame, as ſhe thought
his irons fal of from his legges, ſaid to his
keper, novv the maides dreame is found to be
                                        true.

true. and sent alſo vvord therof to the maide
from the Seſſions houſe. Moſt men that ſaw
it, or haue heard of it, vndoubtedly thinck
it to be miraculous. VV hat the Iudges vvith
the reſt of the bench, and others in authoritie
thinck of it, is hard to iudge. They knew not
belike them ſelues what to ſay. and therfore
neither that day, nor afterwards ſpoke at al to
the priſoner. but conſulted amongſt them
ſelues, and vvith much difference of opinions,
and often altering of ther purpoſes, at laſt one
concluded, that which otheis misliked, that
he muſt dye. In the meane time, returning
that euening with his keper to the priſon, he
vvas permitted to lodge in his accuſtomed
châber. vvhere manie had before viſited him,
being much delighted with his milde and
ſwete conuerſation. And now manie more re-
ſorted vnto the priſon to ſee him, vpon the reporte of his irons ſo ſtrangely falling of his
legges. Amongſt other things, a Catholique
priſoner in the ſame houſe, demâded of him,
what hethought of that failing of, of his chaines.
He anſwered, that he hoped, the bandes of his
mortalitie ſhould ſhortly be looſed. as in dede
it proued. An other, conſidering that often-
times men of excellent corege, and reſolution
of mind, do notvvithſtanding ſuſtaine great
conflicts, betwen the ſoule and the bodie, be-
twê reaſô and the ſenſual part, asked him, how
he felt him ſelfe? I am ſaid he, I thâke our Lord,
in very great côforte, and côſolation of mind.

B 5   The

the refidue of his time he fpent likevvife in
vertous exercifes, vvith great deuotion frequent prayer, much abftinence, watching and
fafting, more and more, as his end drew neeer.

On faturday in the morning vvord vvas
brought him, that he should dye that day. he
anivvered very cherfully: *Deo gratias.* It is the
beft tydings that euer vvas broght me, of anie
thing fithence I vvas borne . fo vvillingly he
beleued that vvhich he defired. though moft
men did not yet thinck it probable, for the
reafons aforefaid. For it is vvel knovven,
and reported by fuch as could tel , that the
Iudges put his name twife in the Calendar
of thofe that vvere to dye , and tvvife out
againe the fame day, before he vvas executed.
For Iuftice Gaudie endeuoring to repriue
him lo᷒ger, Iuftice Kingfmel vrged, and vvould
nedes haue him to dye . And in fine Iuftice
Gaudy feenig his intétio᷒ croffed by Kingfmel,
vvho the third time put his name in that calendar agane, and fo deliuered it vp amo᷒gft thofe
vvhich should dye, turned himfelf from the
companie , and vvas by fome fene to vvepe.
This vncertentie , efpecially the Calendar
being brought to the keper , his name left
out , after it had bene tvvife fent for , and
altered, deceiued manie of his frends, vvho
had a purpofe , to haue bene prefent at his
death , had they not thus bene perfwaded to
thinck vndoubtedly , that he vvas againe repriued.

The

The fame day the Minifter of Saint George his Church, adioyning to the prifon, cõming to Maifter Rigbie, he curtously faluted him and asked vvho he vvas. The Minifter faid, I am parfon of Saint Georges parish: and hearn'g you are this day to dye, am come by commandemenᵗ to conᵉer vvith you, and to inftruᵗ you. I thanke you, faid M. Rigbie, for your paines. but vve tvvo are oppofite in Religion. Therfore I am not to conferre vvith you in matters of faith. I haue long looked **for** for death, I am prepared, fully refolued, and moft readie to offer vp my life for fo vvorthie a caufe. The minifter benig hervpon about to depart, Maifter Rigbie tooke him by the hand, and very courtously toke leaue vvith him faing: Fare you vvel Sir, I pray God make you a good man.

Betvvixt fiue and fix of the clocke in the afternone M. Cheeke, one of the vndershrifs ófficiers, comming to the prifon, called for M. Iohn Rigbie, faing they ftaid for him. He anfvvered, I am readie for you, good M. Cheeke. May it pleafe you to ftay but a very little vvhile, and I come. Ad fo haftening he vvent moft fweetly and curtously to falute, and take his leaue of his felovv Catholique prifoners, and other fredes then prefent vvith him: vvho al vvith great refpeᵗ (as to one going to poffeffe a Kingdom, for revvard of his faithful feruice) euerie one humbly kneeled vnto him, and he vvith like refpeᵗ to

them,

them, as to Gods defigned Martyrs, alfo kneeled: and to their great confolation imbraced,
and faluted euerie one of them with a kiffe
of peace. In which deuout manner leauing
them, and defiring their charities, to affift
him in this his iourney, tovvards his owne
country, with their deuout prayers, promifed them that he wold remember them (as
they requetted) in his affuredly. Then going
downe into the yarde, he found the hurdle at
the ftayers foote redie prepared. Where
he kneling downe, and firft figning himfelf
with the figne of the Croffe, framed himfelf
to fay fome prayer. but prefently one Maifter
More, the vndershrifs deputie, interrupted
him. and he rifing fmot his hand vpon the
horfe, merily faing, Go thy vvayes, this is
the ioyfuleft day that euer I knevv. And
figning himfelf again with the figne of the
Croffe, laid himfelf gently downe vpon the
hurdle, vvith great alacritie of minde, as
wel appeared by his fvvete Angelical conte-
naunce. vvhich the ftanders by curiously ob-
feruing, fome asked him, if he laughed from
his hart, he anfwered? yes verily from my
hart. And beare vvitnes vvith me, al good
people, that I am now forthvvith to giue
my life only for the Catholique caufe. Maifter
More taking exceptions faid, No Maifter
Rigbie, you dye for treafon in the higheft
degree, for being reconcilid by a Seminarie
Prieft:

Prieſt . Yes Maiſter More , ſaid he again,
for neither can that be treaſon. nor yet I
dye not for that only. For as you knovv
the Iudge offered me oftentimes to ſaue my
life , for only going to Church . Then pulling his hat downe to ſhadovv his eyes, bad
them , In the name of our Lord go on;
and ſo ſetled himſelf to his deuotions.
But they making a litle ſtaye, he ſaid merily : vvhen go you ? I think your horſe
is not able to draw me . At vvhich vvords
they vvent forvvard , and he fel vnto his
prayers.

In the vvay tovvards the place of execution, called S. Thomas Watering, came ryding
as was thought two courtiers . but ſhortly
one of them was knowne to be the Earle of
Rutlãd, and the other was Captaine Whytlock
in his cõpanie . they cõming nere the hurdle,
and viewing the priſoner, the Captaine demaunded of him, vvhat he vvas , of vvhat
yeares , and what might by the cauſe of his
cõdemnation to this kind of death? M. Rigbie
looking vp , and hearing ſome name the Earle
of Rutland, ſuppoſing the Captaine to be the
Earle, tooke of his hat and deſired his honor
humbly to pardon him , in being ſo vndutiful
as to haue bene couered in his preſence, for I
knew not(ſaid he)of ſuch honorable aſſëblie.
and to your queſtiõs may it like your honour,
my name is Iohn Rigbie, a poore gentleman, of
the houſe of Harrock in Lancaſhire : my age
about

about thirtie yeares , my iudgement and condemnation to this death , is only and merely
for that I anfvvered the ludge,that I vvas reconciled ; and for that I refufed to go vnto
the Church , to heare the Englith seruice.
Wherat the Captaine feemed to meruel:
and faid, fure it is very ftrange, that anie man
should be put to death for that. vndoubtedly,
faid the prifoner, it is for no other caufe , I
doe affure you . The Captaine vvished him
12. to doe, as the Quene vvould haue him (that is
to go to the Proteftants Church) and turning
to the Shrifs deputie, conferred vvith him
about the matter . After a little fpace the
Earle and the Captain rode againe to the
hurdle , and caufing it a little to be ftayd,the
captaine faid, are you a maried man, or no?
No fir,faid he,I am a bacheler; and (in fmiling
wife) more then that , I am a maide . that is
much , faid the Captain , for a man of your
yeares , you haue it feemeth ftriuen much
againft your owne flesh.M. Rigbie anfvvered,
I vvould be loath to fpeake anie thing contrarie to the truth, I am in dede a maide.
and that is more then I neded to fay. The
Captain concluded : Then I fee, thou haft
vvorthily deferued a virgins crowne . I pray
God fend the the Kingdō of heauen,and that
thou maift do vvel : I defire thee , pray for
me. and fo they rid to the place of execution,
not fpeaking anie more to him.and vvhen the
officiers vvere readie to turne him of the
cart

cart, the Earle and the Captain posted avvay, much astonished at his courege and constancie.

The Captain often related these particulars, and vvithal added that he had seene manie dye, but neuer had, nor should see the like to him : for modestie, patience, and vndoubted resolution in his Religion. And that it vvold not be good for our state, to put such men to death.

Novv the prisoner being in place, to end this tragedie, the officiers brought him frō the hurdle to the cart. vvhere he kneled dovvne and said the Pater noster, Aue Maria, Credo, and Confiteor al alovvde, vntil he came to those vvordes, *the holie Apostls S. Peter and Saint Paule*, wherat the ruder sort of the people exclamed, that he prayed to Saints. and so he vvas not permitted to come to the end. The executioner helping him vp into the cart, he gaue him an angel of gold, saing: here take this in token that I friely forgiue thee, and al others, that haue bene accessarie to my death. Thou shalt haue more, a poore sute of fustian, and a new shert vvhich I put on this morning. I vvould it vvere better for thee. Then taking of his hat, he threw it from him. And making the signe of the Crosse, he vewed the multitude (vvhich vvas very great) rovvnd about him. And vvith cherful contenance holding his handes before his breast, vvith his eyes closed, he meditated a litle while.
                                                        And

And after looking vp, femed to make countenance to fome of his freinds in the preſſe. The executioner in the meane time vntied his garters, himfelfe vntruffed his points. and that fo nimbly, as the beholders merueled, to fee a man in fuch cafe, fo quick and actiue, and nothing difmade for death fo nere approching. Taking alfo his falling band from his neck, he rowled it on a heape, and caft it from him, as farre as he could. Wherupon fome faid: that wil be taken vp for a Relique. His clothes being taken of al to his shert, the hangman offered to put the halter ouer his head, which he ſtayed, taking it betwixt both his handes, fo kiiſed it, and gaue it to him againe fayirg: Now do your pleaſure with it. And prefently he put it ouer his head. Beginning then to ſpeake to the people, More the vndershrifes deputie bade him pray for the Quene, which he did very affectionatly, as might appeare to come from a charitable, and loyal hart. The deputie asked him: What Traitors knoweſt thou in England? if thou knoweſt anie reueale them. God is my witnes, faid he, I know none. VVat! faith the deputie again, if he vvil confeſſe nothing, driue avvay the cart. VVhich vvas donne fo fudainly, that he could neither ſpeake to the people: nor recommend his foule againe to God, as he vvas about to do. Again the deputie very shortly commanded the hangman to do his dutie: meaning that he should cut the rope,

rope, and let him fal downe, vvhich vvas
so incontinently done, that he stood vpright
vpon his feete, like to a man a litle amazed,
til the butchering fellovves clasping about
him, by maine force threvv him on the
ground. Where coming againe perfectly to
himselfe, he said alovvd and distinctly:
God forgene you. Iesus receiue my soule.
And immediatly an other cruel felovv standing by (who was no officer at al, but a
common porter) set his foote vpon the Martyrs throte, and so held hi n dovvne, that
he could not speake anie more. VVherof
the same felovv made great vaunt, and bosted
aftervvards, vntil some of the more ciuil
people, reprehending him for his bad mind,
and hard hart, he began to be ashamed of
his fact, and denied it to others, that charged him thervvith. Others held his armes
and legges whiles the executioner dismem-
bred, and vnbovveled him. And vvhen he
felt them pulling out his hart, he vvas yet
so strong, that he thrust the men from him,
which held his armes. Finally they cut of his
head, and diuided his quarters, disposing of
them in seueral places about Southvvork, as
is accustomed. The people going avvay mutte-
red much at the crueltie vsed in the executiõ.
And generally al sortes bevvayled his death.

Thus you haue a plaine and sincere narration of this mãs death, and of the cause therof.
Which vvas, as you see, for being reconciled

and for

and for refusing to go to the Protestants Church. For he vvas in dede condemned for the one, and executed for the other. Now whether either of these, or both together be treason; or may truly be so called; is the principal question of controuersie, touching this mans and other Catholiques suffering in our conutrie.

For resolution wherof, if but in England it selfe, the greatest number of voices of al English persons (supposing that al durst and would speake that they think) might decide the matter, there were no great doubt, but the verdict would be clere and absolute, for the Catholiques in this behalfe. For not onlie Catholiques themselues, which (God be thanked) are a very great number: but also most Protestants, and in maner al Puritanes, and some others of diuers other sects, take these facts of Catholiques to be mere matters of conscience, and voide of al treason: and but those few onlie, in whose handes the gouernment of the Realme now specially consisteth, with a few more that folow the sway of authoritie, do hold or professe the contrarie opinion. Or els if the whole state of the land, of former times, from our first conuersion to Christ, to these late yeares: Or finally if al the whole Christian world, both of times past and present might be Iudge (as by al reason it should) then sentence would easely be for vs, and al further dispute
would

would be nedles. For neither in England
before our dayes; nor els where before nor
as yet in al Chriftendom; no not in thofe
other places which are alfo diuided from
the Roman Church,is there anie fuch opinion
holden nor fuch lawes made, that to be reconciled, or abfolued from finnes by a Catholique Prieft,fhould be treafon,but only in England,within thefe laft 40.yeares. For albeit
in Geneua, and in fome parts of Germanie, as
alfo in Holland, and fome other like places,
they punish with leffe penalcies, fuch as go
to Confeffion,heare Maffe, or otherwife practife the Catholique Religion : yet none fuch
are in anie of thofe places eftemed nor iudged
Traitors,nor bereued of their liues for the fame. Neither are anie punished at al,but oly in
England for refufing to fweare,that they think
in their confcience that the King, Quene, or
Prince, is and ought to be fupreme head, or
fupreme gouernour of the Church,immediat-
ly vnder Chrift, in al caufes as wel fpiritual
as temporal. For asking, or receuing anie
maner of difpenfation, indulgence, or other
grace of the Sea Apoftolique. For hauing an
Agnus Dei, Beades, Graines, Croffes, Me-
dails, Images, Pictures, or other things,
bleffed by the Bifhop of Rome. For per-
fwading anie perfon to be a member of the
Catholiq; Roman Chruch. For hauing authoritie fubordinat to the fame Roman Chruch,
to abfolue from finnes. For being made

C 2   Prieft

Prieſt in anie Engliſh College or Seminarie
without the Realme, and ſo returning into
their countrie. And for the like things enacted
and made as heynous crimes by new Parliament lawes. Al which pertaine directly,
and euidently to Gods ſpecial Seruice, Sacrifice, Sacraments, ſpiritual regiment, reliefe
and health of ſoules. And ſo are matters of
Religion, moſt really diſtinct in nature and
ſubſtance, from matters of temporal ſtate;
and much more from treaſon, and from al
diſobedience to temporal Princes. Whoſe
Soueraigntie, and ſecuritie both is and alwayes hath benne moſt ſpecially maintained
and neuer oppugned by the Catholique Religion. For euen as Chriſt him ſelfe and his
Apoſtles, and their perpetual Succeſſors
yelded, and taught al men to yeld tribute,
obedience, and al dutifid honour and ſeruice
to temporol Powres and Princes, and diligently to pray for al ſuch both publikly and
priuatly: ſo al Catholiques in England, and
euery where continually do the ſame. And
namely this holie Martyr (as appeareth before) acknowledged and yelded al temporal
powre, and authoritie to the Quene, ſtil pro-
feſſing and behauing him ſelfe as a faithful
and loyal ſubiect, ſeruing her, and praying
for her, and euen to death denying and de-
teſting al treaſons and traytors. How wrongfully therfore he was condened to death, may
ſufficiently appeare by that which hath benne
here

(margin notes) Matt. 22. Rō. 13. 1. Pet. 2. 1.Tim. 2. Pag.52

here said.Firſt becauſe the Lawes or ſtatutes
pretended againſt him, are not ſufficient Lavves, wherby to condemne him, depending
wholly vpon falſe and vnlawful groundes,
if in dede he had benne of an other Religion
before, and afterwards reconciled to the Catholique. Secondly becauſe his proper caſe
was ſuch, that by the ſame ſtatutes he could
not be conuinced, as him ſelfe very wel declared at his arraigomem. Neither by the ſtatutes
againſt reconciliation, for that he was alwayes
in faith a Catholique, and therfore neded
not reconciliation to anie Religion, ncr was
ſo reconciled, but only abſolued from his
ſinnes committed of frailtie. Nor by the
ſtatute aganſt receiuing or releuing Catholique Prieſts ; becauſe the Prieſt that abſolued him, had at that time ſo much libertie in priſon, that al men that vvould might
come to him and releue him. And much leſſe
is there anie thing at al in that ſtatute prohibiting anie man to be temporally or ſpiri-
tually releued by him. But al their accuſations and proofes failing, the Iudges alſo and
the whole bench being ſilent, and moſt men
expecting that the priſonner ſhould be quit,
and frie from ſentence of death, then came in
the comon vnderſong (*the fauburden of ſuch
tragical pagents*) from a companion that ſat be-
neth, ſaying ; *Al this wil not ſerue thy turne ; for
the Iurie muſt finde it treaſon. If it muſt be* (ſaith finally the happie martyr) *let it be.* *Gods wil be*

An.reg.
Eliz.
5. 13.
& 23.

An.27.

Page
20.

C 3   done.

done. And fo I wil fay no more in a matter fo clere, touching the pretenfed caufe of his condemnation to death.

It refteth only, to fpeake a vvord or tvvo more of his refufal to go to the Proteftants Church. Which as it vvas the particular caufe, that the faid fentence vvas geuen, fo vvas it alfo the principal caufe that thefame vvas put in execution: for othervvife either it had not bene pronounced, or had bene remitted or annullated, if at anie of tenne or twelue times, vvhen it vvas publikly vrged vnto him, he vvould haue yelded therto.

And firft it is a thing certaine and euident, that this refufing or omitting to be prefent, at the publique Seruice of a contrarie Religion, is novvhere els fo greuoufly punifhed, as now in Englãd. For the Catholique Church to beginne vvith al (becaufe her aduerfaries count her very feuere) is fo farre from vrging or forcing, thofe that be not Catholiques, to be prefent at Maffe, Matines, or at anie publique Office in the Church, that she aloweth none fuch at al to enter in, nor to abide there, though they should defire it. And hath for this purpofe a fpecial Order of Clergie men, vvho are called *Oftiarij*; vvhofe office is to admite only the obedient children of the Church, and to kepe out, or driue out al others. And if by ignorance, force, or othervvife, anie that ought not, happen to be there, incontinently as the fame is perceiued, the

Sacrifice

Sacrifice, and al other publique Offices do ceafe, til they be got out againe. In other places, efpecially in the moft partes of Germanie, ftraict Lavves be ordayned, that none shal be côftrained to anie practife, or outward conformitie in anie other Religion, then them felues like and alow of. and that al perfons may friely, vvithout impechment or moleftation, vfe that Religion, vvhich in their confciences they hold to be beft, and moft aualable for their foules health. Wherby innumerable perfons of diuers Religions, notvvithftanding their diuerfitie of opinions in matters of faith, and their daylie frequenting of diuers Affemblies in diftinct Churches, liue and conuerfe together, ech one according to his profeffion, trade, and traffike, in al peaceable and quiet maner. Only in England, and in few other places, the Catholique Rites, Offices, and efpecially the Sacrifice are prohibited: and a certaine conformitie, or external shew, is required and exacted (in euerie prouince, countrie, or kingdom diuerfly, as their doctrines be diuers) vpon fmaller, or vpon greater penalties. Which in England are more and more augmented thefe later yeares. For vvheras in the beginning of the Quenes raigne, it was prohibited to fay or heare Maffe, vnder the paine either of paying an hundreth Markes, or els of fuffering fix monethes imprifomnent: in a latter ftatute, the price or penaltie is increafed; that vvho

An. reg. Eliz. 1,

An. 23.

C 4   foeuer

foeuer heareth Maſſe , muſt both ſuffer a vvhole yeares impriſonment , and alſo pay an hundreth Markes . And he that ſaith Maſſe muſt be committed to the next Gaole, for a vvhole yeare , and alſo pay tvvo hundreth markes; or els remaine in the Gaole , vntil *An 27.* he ſhal pay it . And if he be a Ieſuite, or a Seminarie Prieſt , then both he , and thoſe that intertained him, muſt al dye for it . The Prieſt as a traitor,the other as fellons . Again vvheras in the ſaid former ſtatute , al perſons aboue the age of *xvi.* yeares are commanded to be preſent at their new forme of ſeruice *(brought in place of the Catholique Office , and Sacrifice at the ſame time aboliſhed)* euerie Sunday and Holie day , vpon paine of paying xij pence for euerie dayes abſence : the ſame is not only augmented in the other ſtatute (to a farre greater price , then Chriſtians pay for vſe of their Religion in Conſtantinople) to xx. poundes for euerie monethes abſence from their Church : but alſo vvithout ſtatute, Chriſtians in a Chriſtian Realme (vvhich is much to be pitied and iuſtly vvondered at) are finally perſecuted to death , for not committing an act , and a ſinne againſt their conſcience . As vvas manifeſt in this bleſſed Martyr, and in manie others . Who if they would but haue yelded in this one point, ſhould not haue dyed, for al their other ſuppoſed treaſons.

But if anie man wil yet doubt, or ſeme to meruel

meruel, why this Martyr (and the like of
manie others) would not in al this longe
combate, being fo often and fo earneftly
vrged therto, faue his life by once faying he
would go to the Church: himfelf plainly
and publikly anfwered the Iudges, and the
vvhole vvorld, that he could not do it, becaufe he fhould by fo doing, *not haue faued*
but haue loſt his life. and therfore *he loſt it in*
this world, and fo found life euerlaſting. Rightly
confidering that better it was, to fal into the
cruel handes of men, then into the iuſt
vvrath of God almightie. Who is a ieloufe
God, that neither vvil fuffer his people to
ferue other gods, nor him felfe to be ferued
in other maner, then by Moyfes, and by his
other high Prieſts he hath apointed. VVherof
(befides manie others) vve haue a moſt ter-
rible example in the people of the Iewes,
that did not feuer them felues, from the
Tabernacles of the impious, as they were
commanded, but yelded to the Oppofites
of Moyfes, and vvere invvrapped in their
finnes. And fo not only Core, Dathan,
and Abiron, the heades and ringleaders,
vvith their vviues, children, and their re-
tinewes, vvere fwallowed vp in the gaping
earth, defcending aliue into hel; and their
tvvo hundreth and fifteie complices and
cooperators, al deuoured vvith fire from
heauen: but alfo their other adherents,
and partners in the fchifme, to the number

Mat.
10. &
16.
Ioan.
12.

Dan.
13.

Exo.
20. &
fequent.

Nu.16.

C 5   of fourtene

of fourtene thousand seuen hundreth of the
people , perished in like sorte by the same
fire : vvhich ceased not deuouring those that
had anie way participated in the same reuolt,
til Aaron sent by Moyses , had apeazed the
vvrath of God , vvith Sacrifice and other
prayers. And shal we think that the same
God vvil not as iustly and seuerly , either in
this vvorld, or in the next, punish vs Christia-
nes, if vve ioyne our selues in profession , or
practise of a contrarie Religion, to that which
Christ, and his Apostles, and their Succes-
sors taught and obserued , and vvhich our
countrie vvas first conuerted vnto ? No assuredly. For he is the same iust God stil , to
Iewes and to Gentils , to Israilits and Chri-
Heb.   stians; *Iesus Christ yesterday , and today, the same*
13.   *for euer.* Who commandeth vs, not only not to
Mat.   beleue those that shal say: *Loe here is Christ or*
24.   *there:* but also *not to go out,* of the felowship
of al nations christned , into one corner,
Augde tovvne, or countrie: as S. Augustin vnder-
vnit.   standeth that place . And the Apostle admo-
Eccle. nisheth vs the same, more at large: *No societie*
c. 13. (saith he) nor felowship: *no agreement, no par-*
2. Cor. *ticipation , no consent* can be betvven Christ and
6.   Belial ; and none ought to be, in the publique
prayers, nor in assemblies for the seruice of
God, betvven Catholiques and vvho so euer
of contrarie Religion . *Go out of the middes of*
them, and separate yourselues: saith our Lord ,
and touch not the vncleane , and I vvil receiue you.
                                                    And

And contrariwife at the laſt day, he wil bring *Pſal.* thoſe that decline into obligations (for loue or *124.* for feare of the world) with the workers of iniqui- tie, as teſtifieth the Royal Prophet. Who like- vvife admoniſheth vs in an other Pſalme by his owne example , or rather in the perſon of euerie faithful ſoule, ſaying : With *Pſal.* them that do vuiuſt things, I wil not enter in . I haue *25.* hated the Church of the malignant: and with the impious I wil not ſit. And the Prophet Elias crieth vnto ſuch as vvould ſerue both God *3. Reg.* and his enimie : How long hatt you on two wayes; *18.* if our Lord be God, folow him: but if Baal, folow him. Good Tobias a youth in captiuitie, *Tob. 1.* vvould not go (as manie did) to Ieroboams golden calues , but fleeing their compagnies vvent to Ieruſalem , to the Temple of our Lord, and there adored. The three children Sidrach, Miſach, and Abdenago in the like captiuitie , fearing God more then men, anſvvered boldly, Be it knowne to thee ô King, *Dan.3.* that we worſhip not thy God , and we adore not the golden ſtatue, which thou haſt erected. Old Eleaza- *2.Mac.* rus would not eate, nor ſeme to eate ſwines *6.* fleſh , aganſt the law; but rather choiſe a glo- rious death, then a weriſome or hateful life, if by diſſimulation in ſo religious a cauſe , he ſhould haue procured damnation to his owne ſoule, and alſo eternal ruine of manie more by his example . Read alſo the hiſtorie of the *ca. 7.* mother and her ſeuen ſonnes, al martyred for the ſame cauſe. And generally the Iewes did *10. 4.* not con-

not conuerse, nor communicate vvith the
Samaritanes in spiritual affayres ; vvhose
cuſtome herein our Sauiour approueth, and
geueth expreſſe ſentence for the Ievves in
this behalfe; and that the right adoration,
and ſaluation was of the Ievves part. Becauſe
they had good ground for their Temple in
Ieruſalem, and the Samaritanes none at al,
for their worſhiping in Gariſin. An other

Mat.
12.
general rule our Sauiour geueth, *He that
is not vvith me, is againſt me; and he that gethereth
not vvith me ſcatte.eth.* VVherupon S. Ierome

Ep 58.
Damaſ.
proueth, that al they do ſcatter, that gether not vvith the reſt of the Church, and
particularly that gether not vvith the chiefe
Paſtor therof, ſucceding Sainct Peter. To
the ſame effect the Apoſtle ſaith: *you can not*

1. Cor.
10.
*drink the Chalice of our Lord, and the Chalice of
diuels : you can not be partakers of the table of our
Lord, and of the table of diuels.* And to ſuch
Neuters as vvould ſerue al turnes he crieth:

2. Cor.
6.
*Beare not the yoke vvith infidels. for vvhat partici-
pation hath iuſtice vvith iniquitie, vvhat ſocietie is
there betvven light and darknes;* finally, *What
agreement hath the Temple of God vvith Idols?* And

In oſee.
11.
Amos.
8
Hab. 2.
Soph.
1.
vvhat be the Idols that novv moleſt the
Church (ſaith S. Ierome) but Hereſies ?
VVherfore al that looke to haue feloſhip
vvith Chriſt and his members in his bodie
and blood, muſt flie from the feloſhip of
al infidels, and abſtaine from al partiṛici-
pation in cauſes of Religion, vvith thoſe
                                        that

that haue erected an other Altar or table, or that haue erected a contrarie forme of feruing God, againft the Altar and Sacrifice of Chrift, and his Catholique Church. And in novvife conforme them felues to thefe nevv procedings, by going to their Chur-ches, vvhich is *the proper marke of their focietie.* ^{Apoc.} And therfore moft conftantly refufed by this ^{13.} glorious Martyr, fo manfully fighting this good fight. wherby himfelfe hath ioyful-ly received a Crovvne of glorie; God al-mightie is fpecially glorified; his Saintes highly honored; Catholiques much edified, and comforted; and the Proteftants greatly ashamed and confounded. *Our Lord graunt al* ^{Pfal.} *thofe, may be* frutfully *ashamed,* happilly *con-* ^{69.} *founded, and* quikly *turned back, that* novv ^{128.} *hate Sion.* Amen.

A. BRIEF

A. BRIEF MENTION OF
NINE OTHER MARTYRS, AND
certaine other Catholiques persecuted for the same cause, this same yeare, With an answer to our Aduersaries obiection, of discord amongst Catholiques.

AT York in Lent last was arraigned M. Christopher Wharton Priest, Maister of Art of the Vniuersitie of Oxford, suspected and accused to be a Seminarie Priest . and therupon indicted of hiegh treason, for returning into England, contrarie to the statute made in the yeare of our Lord, 1585. Who was in dede made Priest at Rhemes by the Cardinal of Guise (of Blessed memorie) the last day of March. 1584. (As also 30. other Englishmen receaued holie Orders the same time with him: of which diuerse be now also Martyrs) Neuertheles he confessed no more but that he was a Priest, before the said statute was made : leauing it to his accusers to proue when he was made. For he being about the age of three core years, might wel (by dispensation) haue bene made Priest in the reigne of Q. Marie, or before the feast of the Natiuitie of S. Iohn Baptist, in the first yeare of this Quene, and so out of the danger of this new statute. Manie odious things were obiected and amplified (as their custome is) against the Pope, Cardinals, Archpriest of England, Iesuits and Seminarie Priests, charging them with Idolatrie, Superstition, much false doctrine; with Treason against the
                                                                                  Quene

An. Reg. Eliz. 27.
M. Robert Anderton. Io. Sands. W. Tomson. Ro. Debdal. Ed. Burden. Hugh. Tailor. Thur. Hunt, &c.

Quene and Realme, and with diſſentions alſo
betwen Ieſuits and Seminarie Prieſts. al falſe
and impious ſclanders; as he plainly told them;
nothing at al pertaining to the Indictmḗt (wherupon his lieſe depended) about the time when
he was made Prieſt. Concerning which point
after a few vncertaine coniectures were alleaged
which agreed il, and proued nothing againſt
him: vpon the onlie teſtimonie of M. Sauil,
Baron of the exchequer (who was alſo his Iudge) affirming that he knew him in Oxford,
ſome years after the time mentioned in the new
ſtatute; and then not taken for a Prieſt: he
was denounced, Guiltie, and condemned to
death as for hiegh Treaſon. And a graue Catholique Matron was alſo indicted of felonie,
and condḗned to death, for receiuing him into
her houſe. As if ſhe alſo had knowé him in Oxford to haue bene no Prieſt, and afterwards made Prieſt; who knewe him not at al, but a ſmal
time before he was taken in her houſe. Finally
after earneſt perſwation to go to their Church,
which ſhe vtterlie refuſed, ſhe receaued her
Croune of Martyrdome, according to the Goſpel, whoſoeuer *receaueth a prophet, in the name of
a prophet, ſhal receaue the reward of a prophet.*

And albeit there ſemed leſſe probabilitie to
peruert the venerable Prieſt, yet they omitted
not to vrge vnto him the viual tentation; that
if he would go to their Church, he might inioy
both lieſe and libertie; and be præferred alſo
amongſt them. Al which he conſtantly con-
temned

temned in respect of Gods honour, his ovvne
saluation, and edification or destruction of
manie by his example. And so in Easter vveke
the 28. of March he also receiued his glorious
croune. And to their other impertinent talke
(both before and after his sentence) he also ansvvered briefly, that in the Catholique Romane Religion (which he professed, and for
vvhich he was readie to dye) there is neither
Idolatrie, nor Superstition, nor falshoode, nor
contrarietie of doctrin. And though there be
dissentions som_imes amongst Catholiques,
either Priests or others, yet those differences
are not in Articles of their faith, but in other
matters, of some particular Iurisdiction, right
or title, (spiritual or temporal, and the like. And
that for his ovvne part he had no such controuersie vvith anie Catholique, nor breach
of charitie vvith any person liuing vvhosoeuer.

Which was for him, at that time, a very sufficient answer. And much hath bene said,
and vvritten also these late yeares, of the pu-
ritie and vnitie of the Catholique doctrin.
Neuerthelesse here it shal not be amisse (gentle
reader) to adde somwhat more in explication
of his answer, touching the differences rissen
amongst some English Catholiques, vvhich
our Aduersaries so reprochfully obiect to al.
For albeit, the perfect are neuer scandalized;
yet the vveake often are; and some do mistake
the case; and some doubtles are guiltie of great
fault, in making or in nourishing this debate.
Al which

Psal.
118.
v.165.

Al which wil be more clere ; if first calling to mind the state of Catholiques , before this controuersie begane ; vve then consider vvhence it proceded ; vvherin it consisteth ; and betvven vhom it is.

And to this purpose it semeth necessarie, that
we beginne from the last general reuolt , from
the Catholique Religion in our Coūntrie ;
Which vvas in the first yeare of this Quenes
raigne . For she comming to the Croune in
the end of the yeare 1558. vvithin few monethes after a Parliament vvas called , vvherin
vtterly aganst the vvilles of al the Lords
spiritual (auouching that they did not ; nor
vvould not consent to change the state of Religion) the Lords temporal and Commons
tooke vpon them , and *de facto* pretended, to
abolish al authoritie or Iurisdiction of the
Bishop of Rome in England : abandoned
the holie Sacrifice of Masse , and other Catholique Offices : and in place therof restored
the nevv forme of Seruice instituted, in the
second yeare of K. Edvvard the sixt , but
augmented , *altered, and corrected* (for so they
speake) and further in most peremptorie and
arrogant manner , did *in Gods name* (but vvithout commission from God) *earnestly require
and charge al the Archbishops Bishops and other Or-
dinaries* , that they should indeuour themselues , to the vttermost of their knovvledges ,
to see the same put in execution ; threatening
them vvith Gods vvrath and punishment ,

D   *if thĕ*

if this good and wholsome Law (for sooth) *were neglected.* Al which holie Bishops obeying God, rather then men; vvere presetly depriued of their Bishopriques, and al other constant Clergimen of their spiritual liuings, and benefices; Heretiques, or such as yelded to the parctise of Heresie, put in their places. And diuerse also of the Laitie sharply punished, for not conforming themselues to these nevv procedings. In which state though the same Catholique Prelates stil kept their titles and right, al vvel of their dignities, as of their holie functions (which could by no meanes be taken from them) yet did they not exercise any publique Iurisdiction; but expecting better times, al the Bishops, and most of the old clergie haue ended their liues in prison, banishment, or in other poore state, al more or lesse restrained and persecuted. Wherby the Ecclesiastical Ierarchie of the Church of England, for lack of succeffion of ordinarie spiritual Pastors, did vvholy decay and ceafe; yet continually there remained some constant Catholiques, and some few Catholique Priests, which ministred the holie Sacraments, and supplied in priuat and secret sorte, other necessarie Offices vvithout anie subordination of one to an other vvithin the Realme; the Sea Apostolique graunting facultie, to the worthie Confessor, the Bishop of Lincolne and others, to subdelegate such as vvere found fit to heare Confessions, and
to absolue

to abſolue, alſo in Caſes reſerued, as nede
should require. And furthermore this good
ſeede of Catholique Religion conſerued by
Gods goodnes, vvas alſo vvel vvatered, and
proſpered much by ſundrie good bookes,
written by diuerſe learned and zealous men,
in defence of the Catholique faith. wherby
not only theſe Reliques vvere confirmed and
ſtayed therein, but ſome alſo conuerted from
ſchiſme and hereſie. But in the firſt tene years
moſt men ſtil hoping of a change, or tole-
ration, litle induſtrie vvas vſed, for making
more Prieſts, to ſerue our countrie in this
greate deſolation: til the renovvmed Doctor
Allen, (aftervvards Cardinal) moſt prudent-
ly foreſeing the great defect of a ſucceſſion
of Prieſts, vvithout vvhom no Sacrament
could be duly adminiſtred, no Sacrifice offered, and conſequently no Religion long remaine, but al turne to Hereſie, Apoſtaſie,
and Atheiſme, found meanes (by Gods ſpecial prouidence) in the yeare of our Lord
1568. to erect in the vniuerſitie of Doway
with the approbation of Pius Quintus, a College of English ſtudents; vvho by yelding
themſelues to Collegial diſcipline, and to a
ſet forme and courſe of ſtudie, with publiq;
exerciſe, might attaine more vertue, zeale
and knovvledge, and ſo be made Prieſts, and
returne into their Countrie; as aboue foure
hundred haue ſince donne, to the infinite
good of manie thouſand ſoules, from this

one Mother

one Mother College , not only the firſt of
the English nation , but (as vve take it) the
firſt in Chriſtendome , inſtituted after the
forme of Seminarie Colleges , appointed to
be erected, by the holie Councel of Trent,
in al Catholique Prouinces , for the better
education, and perpetual ſucceſſion of Cler-
giemen

The good reporte and euident proofe of
vvhoſe profitable indeuours eaſily moued our
holie father Pope Gregorie the thirtenth, to
indue the ſame College, vvith a monethlie
exhibition or penſion , in the yeare 1575. For
before that time, it had no other Reuenevves
but the ſtipend of Doctor Allen their Preſident
and Founder , being one of the kings Profeſſors of the Vniuerſitie , and vvhat more
he procured of other Benefactors . Which
ſo continued , til the tumults of the Lovv-
countries , and povver of the Rebels did
grovv ſo great , that in the yeare 1578. by the
vvorking of the Quene and Counſel of England , with the Prince of Orenge , and his
confederats, the ſaid College vvas driuen from
Dovvay , and ſo remoued to Rhemes in
France . VVhere ſtil it proſpered , much
contrarie to the expectation of their per-
ſecutores . Yea moreouer (marke ye here
the great mercie of God tovvards the afflicted of our Nation) the ſame yeare our ſaid
holie father Pope Gregorie founded an other
English

English College in Rome; that there might
be tvvo fuch nourceries of Clergimen for
our Countrie, committing the gouernment
therof, to the moft exquifite Order, that
the chriftian vvorld novv hath, for education
of youth (efpecially for fuch an Apoftolical
purpofe as this is) to the holie Societie of
I E S V S. VVhich charge fo laid vpon them,
vvas to the fingular fatisfaction and confolation, not only of manie zelous and vertuous
youngmen already affembled in Rome, to
inioy the benefite of this College, hearing
of his Holines intention before, but alfo of
al other fincere Catholique Englishmen,
which fought the good of their countrie,
before their ovvne priuat. The firft Rector
of this College vvas father Robert Parfons
of the fame Societie, a man vvithout manie
vvoordes, commended abundantly by his
vvoorkes. And shortly againe in the yeare
1580. at the inftance of M. D. Allen in the
name of English Catholiques, father General
of the fame Societie, agreed alfo to fend
English Iefuits into this harueft, and prefently fent the fame F. Parfons and father Campion, both men of moft excellent good talents. And the next yeare very notable men
alfo, F. Heyvvod and F. Holt, and fo continually the like miffions are maintained ftil. Then
the Seminaries and the Societie, with other
Priefts remaining of the old ftore, labored
iointly and merily together, for the conuer-

D 3   fion

fion of our countrie *vnamines in domo Dei*. There were in England before this yeare, of the College of Dovvay, about feuentie Priefts, (vvhich vvere not for euerie shire tvvo) and as yet none of the College of Rome. But this yeare 1580. entered the Realme, of both the Colleges, and of the Societie, and other Priefts, that had liued before in Rome, and els vvhere priuatly, nere fourtie. And the next yeare aboue fourtie more. Which great increafe of vvorkemen, and efpecially the comming in of Iefuites (Whom the Heretiques litle expected, and leffe vvished) vvrought diuerfe effects. Some ftormed, others admired; fome fought to intrap them in fnares; others to be inftructed, and fpiritually releued by them; fome imagined to difpatch al Iefuites, and Seminarie Priefts, out of the Realme againe, by publique Proclamations and more feuere parliament Satutes, and greater perfecution of al Catholiques. But no malice being able to ouerthrovv the vvork of God, ftil Catholiques increafed in number, and in corage, and more vvere willing to fuffer and to die for their faith, then before; more and more vvere incenfed vvith defire to go to the Seminaries; and fome immediatly to the holie Societie, that fo they might enter into the fame vvorke, and be participant of the fame glorious revvard. Of which forte fome be already in heauen, others yet laboring in the vinyard. By occafion

of thefe

of these nevv lavves, and of more preaching writing, and persecution follovving, manie poore soules sleeping in sinne and ignorance, in diuerse parts of the Realme, heard of these heroical attempts, of men that had dedicated and consecrated their liues, to saue the soules of their deare contrimen. And that not only tvvo great Colleges of Englishmen did dayly send Priests amongst them; but also the Societie of IESVS, which continually sendeth such men into the furthest parts of the vvorld, to conuert Infidels, doth also send into England, to conuert their countrimen from Schisme and Heresie. Al these brutes did exceeding much good, and much more the often preachings, svvete conuersation, most exemplar liefe, continual praiers, and daylie offering of the dreadful Sacrifice, made manie to open the dores of their soules, *and out of manie harts cogitations were reueled .Luc 2,* And no meruel, that manie merueled to see and heare these things, for so it happeneth vvhensoeuer such men come into anie countrie to preach Christ and the Catholique doctrine. As Sainct Augustin the Monk our Apostle, brought al England into admiration when he came vvith his felovves, and taught vs the vvay to saluation. Al the hil-countries of Iurie merueled, hearing so admirable things, at the Natiuitie of S. Iohn Baptist *Luc 1,* the precursor of Christ. And al England merueled vvhen they vnderstood of these

D 4   mens

mens Apoftolical comming to reftore the faith, which at the feaft of the fame S. Ihons Natiuitie, iuft tvventie one yeares before, vvas abandoned. Manie vvith great furie and malice, fpecially fome Minifters cried treafon, fedition, confpiracie aganft the Quene and the Realme. And albeit the vvifer fome knevv vvel ynough thefe men meant no treafon, but faluation vnto al; yet treafon it muft be called for pollicies fake, and crueltie muft be vfed, to trie if they might fo fuppreffe this zeale which they could no more do, then the Ievves could quench the zeale kindled firft in the holie Apoftles vpon whitfunday. For vvhy? Chrift our Sauiour had faid before that time, which he performeth to the vvorlds end, that he *came not to fend peace* (to vvit a blind peace in finne and error) *iue the fvvorde, and feparation.* I came to caft fire on the earth; *and what wil I elfe* (faith our meeke Lord) *but that it be kindled,* and burne? The fmoke of which fire fo trubled the eyes of the Ievvish counfel, that it made Gamaliel geue no il aduife, to let the Apoftles alone, and fee vvhat iffue their attempts vvould haue. Some of the Quenes counfel shevved them felues of the fame opinion, in this cafe. iudging it vaine to kil Priefts in England, fo long as more come after them, from the Seminaries, and from a Religious Societie that dieth not. And amongft others, one M. Fletvvood a Iuftice

Mat.
10.
Luc 12.

Iustice of peace in his countrie, and a hote proteſtant, when ſitting vppon cauſes cf Religion, he heard that there vvas one M. Laurence Iohnſon a young man, and a Seminarie Prieſt (aftervvards a Martyr) commen into the ſame Prouince, *Nay then* (ſaith he) *we ſtriue in vaine, we hoped theſe old Papiſtical Prieſls dying, al Papiſtrie ſhould haue died, and ended with them; but this new broode wil neuer be rooted out, it is impoſſible euer to be rid of them, nor to extirpat this Papiſtical faith out of the land.* And much more manie Heretiques deſpaired of euer effectuating this their deſire, to abolish the Catholique Religion in England; vvhen they ſavve this nevv fire of the Societie of I E S V S ſeaze vpon Engliſh harts. Wherupon manie of al other ſorts of people, and ſome alſo of their Rabbins and greateſt Doctors diſvvaded, ſo much as they could, from rigorous perſecution of Ieſuits, Seminarie Prieſts and of al other Catholiques; for that the more they ſhould blovv this fire, the more it vvould burne. As namely Doctor Humfrey of Oxford, did ſo much diſlike the putting to death of father Campion, that he could not diſſemble his counſel and opinion (no not after the Martyrs death, vvhen it vvas to late to recal him to lieſe againe) but in his booke intituled: *De praxi Romanæ Curiæ* bevvailed the ouerſight of thoſe that cauſed his death; affirming that the common Prouerb,,

Mortuus

Mortuus non mordet, vvas not true in Campian.
Campianus enim mortuus adhuc mordet. For *Cam-*
pian (faith he) *being dead doth yet bite.*
Wherby, and by innumerable other examples and teftimonies, al the vvorld doth fee
(though fome of mere malice vvil not con-
feife it) that the Catholique caufe is meruelous vvel amended by the coming of zealous
Seminarie Priefts, and of Iefuites. That by
their abode the fame good is dayly augmented
and multiplied. And therfore the parting à
way of either forte (which God forbid)
muft nedes be an intolerable loffe, and hin-
deráce to the cóuerfion of our countrie, how
foeuer fome few catholiques, thefe later yeares
falling into faction, wish al the Iefuites and
manie others to be remoued from this worke
both within and without the Realme.

But how much more neceffarie it is, that
thefe fevv difturbers of the common good, be
corrected, or remoued, shalbe eafie to iudge
if vve examine from vvhat roote, this ftir-
ring of theirs procedeth, and vvhither it ten-
deth. For euident it is, by this litle I haue
novv faid, that fometime al ranne vvel, al
fovved good feede, al labored in peace, vnion
and mutual loue.

Whence then came this il feede, this diflike, this diffention, this debate, vvhich novv
appeareth? *The enimie man hath fovved it,* and it
is a maflin of manie vvedes. Old Satan feing
infinite good fruit fpring and profper, in the
fertil

Mat.
13.

fertil English filde, of mere enuie (for that
is his propertie) so bevvitched some by ambition, vaine liking of themselues, and desire
to be estemed, and preferred before others;
that seing other men do more good, haue
more credite, and be more estemed then
themselues, begane to repine and disdaine
at others more estimation; and not being able
othervvise to excel, nor yet match them; fel
into that bad sinck of emulation, and anger
against those of better talents and vertues,
that they could not abide to heare others
more commended then them selues. As shortly appeared by their rustie *Raca*, and mutte-
rings. For vvhen they chaunched to read,
or heare other mens greater praises, streight
auerting their countenance, insinuated as in
clovvdes, or in general termes, as if they
knevv these men not to be so good, nor so
lerned, nor vvise, as they vvere reputed;
and so proceded from degree to degree into
open detraction, false sclandring, malicious
accusing, scandalous publishing, and into
most absurde and impudent auouching of
faults, deuised by them selues, or wrasted
from other mens fovvle mouthes, and made
worse and agrauated, against their brethren,
for no other true cause, but for that they
are estemed their betters, and to bring them
selues therby to more equal balance, and so
to be thought as good as they.

To these vices, other the like did also
concurre

concurre, as seruants and copemates, which stil made the persons more and more different, and vnlike in qualities. VVherby also the emulation vvas more increased. As the more loose and idle life of some, made them dislike the better discipline and greater diligence in others. Also hastines of nature pronnes to anger, vvith litle mortificacion of inordinat passions, much impatience and the like il behauiour, made some Priests lesse desired of other Catholiques, and herevpon again did often grovv false suspicions, sinister surmisses, and rash iudgments, that they were cast out of fauoure, or disgraced by those vvhom they did emulate. Where as in deede there vvas no other cause, but their ovvne il cariage, and especialy their il tongues against good and innocent persons, vvhom for their more credite, they could not brooke. Vpon these strings, and the like the subtile serpent plaid his part, and the diligence of Heretiques toke hold of the occasions, to nourish and egge forvvard these humurous phantasies, and animosities of busie heads, fraight vvith ambition, and desire to rule others, vvho haue neither vvel lerned to rule themselues, nor to be ruled; being voide of that charitie, by vvhich they ought to build, to the increase of the vvhole bodie, and not to diminish the same bodie, nor to hinder, nor pul dovvne that which others build.

And

And al this principally becaufe they favve our
late good Cardinal in his time, and others with
him, efpecially the Iefuits, both then and after,
to be more in credite and fauour vvith great
Princes, and other great or rich perfons: which
they often obiect for a great quarrelle; not
mentioning that they ate more eftemed vvith
the meaner and poorer forte alfo. But I pray
you (deare brethren and freinds) that vvould
be more eftemed then you are, tel me vvhat
fault is in the fathers, or in other men for
this? Is not honour and eftimation the revvard of vertue? efpecially amongft good
men: fuch as you can not denie thefe Catholiques to be, vvho ordinarily prefer Iefuits before you? vvil you blame them for being more
vertuous, and for deferuing better then you?
for if they did not deferue better, fo manie good
men vvould not more efteme them. Or els
vvil you blame the vvhole Catholique vvorld
and al other countries, that beginne, or returne to be Catholiques, for embracing the
Iefuits labours more then yours? vvil you
barre mens iudgments in making their ovvne
choice, by vvhat fpiritual men they vvil be
chiefly directed? Or vvil you abridge their
liberties, and force them to leaue the Fathers, vvhofe conuerfation, and difcretion
they like better then yours; and to be directed
by you, of vvhom they haue not fo great an opinion? Is this the libertie you talke of, and which
you

you promise, if you may haue your wills, that ghoſtly children ſhal firſt forſake their gloſtly fathers whom they moſt deſire, and then be bond to thoſe which you like beſt? Truly moſt men thinke, that nevv ones of your appointment, vvil not be ſo good. You vvil ſay, they ſhal be better and fitter. you can ſay no leſſe. for vvhy ſhould they change but for the better? And yet we tel yov ſtil, that moſt men think, they vvil not be ſo good. You ſay there is no iuſt, nor reaſonable cauſe, VVhy Catholiques ſhould entertaine Ieſuites before you, folovv their counſels rather then yours, aduenture al they haue by receuing them, then by receuing you, commit to their diſcretions, the diſtribution of their almoſe and charitable beneuolences, more then to yours. Theſe be the blocks you ſtumble at. And you can no more condemne Ieſuites, for condeſcending to ſerue good Catholiques in theſe and the like things, then you condemne your ſelues for al that you do to the liking of your ghoſtlie children.

Perhaps you vvould haue them, vvhen they are vvilled to do ſuch good offices, to refuſe to do them, and to ſend them to you; as though al ſuch affayres depended vpon your vvills, vvho ſhould manage them; and as though the requeſt of the partie, vvere not ſufficient vvarrant, for euerie one, to do the good he can, in order and ſubordination to his Superior. Yet ſuppoſe the fathers ſhould direct

direct such persons to you, as come to them;
thinke you that the parties vvould forthvvith
repaire to you? intertayne you? folovv your
counsel? commit much to your discretions?
No surely, in this they vvould not folovv the
fathers counsel: For those that seke first and
principally, to direct their liues and actions,
by aduise of the Fathers of the Societie, do
secondly desire to be directed by such other
Priests, as most imitate the Fathers in manner of liese, such as loue them best, and best
agree vvith them. And the cause of this
better liking, which so manie haue to be
assisted by Iesuites (besides the particular vertues of euerie one) must nedes be some important good and conspicuous things, in the
Order it self, which are not in our vocation.
As particularly, their Religious profession,
their stricter discipline and set rules of life,
their renounciation to al dignities, and proprieties in this vvorld, and the resignation
of their ovvne wills, liuing alvvayes in obedience to a Superiour; vvho taketh due
account of their behauiors, of their labours
of their fruites, and of their talents, what
they are able to do, where and wherin they
may do most good, and so the same Superior imploieth them. If they haue imperfe-
ctions, they haue special approued remedies
to amend the same: and if they correct not
themselues the sooner; this Superior in the
meane time hath care to cure euerie one, and
is readie

is readie to anſvver for his ſubiect, vvherſo-
euer he abides, which is a good vvarrant;
for their hoſt, and vvhoſoeuer dealeth vvith
them. And ſpecial care is alwayes taken, to
haue them very fit for miſſion, before they
be ſent, and at al ſeaſons they are readie to
be changed from their imployments. Wher-
ſoeuer they go, they are ſtil in a ſtrong
caſtle, defended with ioined forces of expert
ſoldiars, firme vvals, good armour, and al
neceſſarie furniture; which make not only
themſelues more ſafe, from the aſſaults of
the ſpiritnal enemie, but alſo by hovv much
they are better guarded and furniſhed, ſo
much more able are they, to aſſiſt, guide,
and lead others ſaſly. Whereas vve of the
other vocation (though Eccleſiaſtical and
Clergimen) are abrode in the vvorld, hold
our intereſts, proprieties or poſſibilities, in
the vvorld. vve are more at our ovvne li-
herties, and make not ſo often account of
our baylivvickes, nor yeld ſo freqent rea-
conings, vvhat profite vve make of our talents, nor vvhat fruit anie reape by our labours; vve vvander abrode as ſingle men in
open filds, or vnfenſed villages, ſo much
more ſubiect to tentations, as vve are more
intangled in the vvorld, and the leſſe able to
reſiſt, becauſe vve haue not renounced the
vvorld, nor our ovvne vvils. And vvhy should
vve then meruel, that men are more afeard
to be guided by vs, then by thoſe they finde
                                                  more

more like to guide them aright? And what wrong is donne to vs, by other mens seeking ther owne secucitie? Thus vve see briefly vvhence this controuersie sprong, and hovv this il seede came into our fild, vvhere first none but good vvas sovven.

Now vve are to consider vvherin it consisteth. Which is not (as our aduersaries vvould haue it, and falsly reporte) in anie point or article of the Catholique faith; for vvhosoeuer obstinately defendeth anie such error is an Heretike and no Catholique; but it consisteth in the varietie of opinions, desires and endeuors, about the persons, that are specially to direct others as guides or heades, and about the maner of proceeding in our common vvorke, for the reducing of our countrie to the Catholique Religion. And thus farre vve al agree, that some fevv, or rather some one, ought to be chiefe leader of al the rest, because manie heades hauing or arrogating equal autoritie, must nedes make confusion. And at the begining, al that entred into this holie vvorke either gaue thé-selues vvholy to the direction of D. Allen (and that long before he vvas Cardinal) or els concurred vvith him, in al their actions tending to this purpose. not anie one Catholique man of our nation opposing against him, from the time of erecting of Dovvay College til that about the yeare 82. three or foure gentlemen in Paris began the first contra-

E diction

diction againſt the ſaid D. Allen and againſt
F. Parſons. Sir Frances Inglefild. M. Hugh
Ovven, and al other agreing vvith them. For
theſe men neither vouchſaſing to folovv the
high and ſtraight vvay, alredy vvel found out
and very vvel proceded in, nor to ſit quiet
and at reſt, deuiſed other byvvaies, caſt nevv
plots, which neuer had good effect, but much
hindred and ouerthrevv diuerſe good things
intended, as is vvel knovvne. They thought
it reaſon to exclude D. Allen, by the title
of *a Breuiarie man*, from dealing any further
in helping of our countrie, but only by his
education of ſchollers to be Prieſts. For
theſe men vvould geue them inſtructions,
hovv to behaue themſelues tovvards the
ſtate of England. And ſo they vvould bring
D. Allen and al his, into their countrie: as
one of them was not aſhamed to bragge
and that in D. Allens ovvne preſence.

In like ſorte they excluded F. Parſons,
from their counſel, and from knovvledge of
their deuiſes, becauſe he is a religious man:
as though he vvere not more fit, and no vvay
leſſe fit for that. For vvho is ſo meete to
geue aduiſe, in ſpiritual or in vvorldlie affaires
as thoſe which haue renounced al priuat in-
tereſt and proprietie in the vvorld? Doth
not our Sauiour ſay, that thoſe which haue left
a' in this vvorld, *ſhal ſit vvith him in iudgement, and
iudge the vvorld?* Doth not S. Paule hervpon
inferr, that ſeing he and other Apoſtles, and
Religious

Mat.
19.

Religious men *shal iudge the world, and the A-* 1. Cor.
postata Angels; much more it is conuenient, that they 6.
shal iudge secular affaires?

They excluded Sir Frances Inglefild, because he had bene long forth of the Realme,
and novv ignorant (as they supposed) of the
state of things there; as though he that had
bene of the priuie Councel to Q̄ Marie, vvere
not more able both for his vvisdome, sin-
ceritie, and long experience, to be a Coun-
seiler, then anie of them? or that he had
not as particular knovvledge, as anie of them,
hovv things stood in England? They excluded M. Hugh Ovven, M. Thomas Fitzherbert,
and aftervvards sir Charles Arundel, and al
others, that agreed vvith. D. Allen, because
they vvould not leaue him, and the vvhole
nation, and hang vpon them. For the same
cause they could not abide sir William Stanley, finding him to agree so wel with D. Allen, sir Frances, F. Parsons, F. Holt, M.
Ovven, and others; and also because he is
a soldiar, and they better statesmen, in their
ovvne conceipts; as though he being so renovvmed a soldiar, vvere therfore lesse fit, to
geue his aduise hovv our countrie may be
brought againe to the Catholique faith, being
othervvise a man of as found iudgment, as
any of them, and (as al that knovv him and
them can vvitnes) as farre more sincere,
more vertuous, more studious, more laborious to help his countrie, and al his coun-
E 2 trie

rie men, as he is more valient in the wars
then they are, which is no smale difference.

They admitted the Earle of Westmer-
land to their Partie, so farre only as he vvould
concurre vvith them, to oppose against, and to
ouerthwart other mens good labours: but
by no meanes vvould they take him for their
chiefe. Thomas Morgan vvas the beginner
of al; wherof it is called *Morgans faction*. but
M. Charles Paget vvas chiefe commander:
the Lord Paget vvas content to be ruled by
them. wherupon they complained the more,
that the Earle of vvestmerland vvould not be
ruled also; thus this contradiction began.
And vpon this ground they haue continued
the same, entertaining and imploying al mal-
contents they could get, to yeald to their
bend. So far forth that vvithin tvvo or three
yeares, they seduced tvvo Seminarie Priests
to treate vvith them, and to be imployed by
them, yea one of them at least to treate vvith
Secretarie Walsingham. And aftervvardes
induced the same tvvo, to write tvvo bookes
the one against F. Parsons and al Iesuits; the
other against the Cardinal. Especially against
his Epistle vvritten in iustification of Sir
William Stanley his rendring the Citie of
Dauenter to the right Lord therof, the
king Catholique. Which fact vvas not only
iust, lavvful, and necessarie by the lavves
of God and Nations, in respect both of the
place, and of himself; but also he had a
                                   particular

particular licence for his perſon, of the Earle of Leceſter to depart from that ſeruice, and to repaire vvhere he vvould, for his better contentment. which licence hath bene ſeene by ſome English Proteſtants: Agents ſometimes in Flanders, and is to be ſhevved vvhenſoeuer occaſion ſhal require. As yet this faction vvas but ſmale and greene amongſt Catholiques in England; for the tvvo foreſaid Prieſts very ſhortly retired thence, and verie fevv durſt breake openly vvith their brethren, nor with the Fathers, ſo long as the Cardinal liued. But preſently vpon his death, ſome other vnquiet ſpirits, though priſoners for their faith (hauing long exerciſed their good felovv priſoners with much patience) more openly ioyned themſelues vvith the ſame trubleſome, withwhom they had ſecretlydealt before. And ſo did alſo manie of the ſcholars in Rome, againſt the Protector himſelfe, and their other Superiors. Sodeinly becomming great ſtates men, as then they thought themſelues. For the better appeaſing of which diſſentions, and preuenting the like, al Catholiques generally deſired to haue ſome Superiors, and Subordination in the English Clergie.

But for ſo much as al former Subordination vvas vvholy interrupted vvithin the Realme, it could not otherwiſe be reſtored but by the Sea Apoſtolique, or by ſpecial commiſſion geuen by his Holines for this purpoſe. For novv in

our coun-

our countrie vve had neither Primat; nor
other Bishop, nor Ordinarie of anie one
Diocese; nor anie Archpriest; nor Vicarge-
neral; nor Archdeacon; nor Deane of anie
Chapiter; nor anie Chapiter; nor other Ecclesiastical communitie at al; nor so much as
an ordinarie Pastor, nor Vicar of anie parish;
but only priuat Priests, vvho had subdelegat
faculties in court of conscience only, for ad-
ministration of Sacraments, and some other
spiritual functions.

But these vvere no more a mystical bodie,
then certaine prouision of stone, lime, and
timber, are a house or a church, before they
be compact together, and formed vvith vvals
and roofe: for euen so vve were a certaine
prouision of Priests ordained, for restaura-
tion of our decaied Hierarchie, but vvere not
disposed of in anie subordination vnder a
head. And so had no possible meanes in our
ovvne nation, to make anie Prouincial Concel
Synode, Conuocation, or Chapiter, nor had
anie electiue, or decisiue voices or suffrages,
to choose supperior or other officer, nor to
determine anie thing iuridically. And therfore for the due ioyning of Clergie men to
make a Hierarchie (none of them hauing
further autoritie) diuerse of the chiefest and
eldest sort asvvel in England, as in banishment humbly proposed this our case and desire to his Holines, vvith such suggestions as
to them semed most mete. Manie thougt
it conue-

it conuenient to haue fome Bifhops confe-
crated, for the better gouernment of our
Church, and moft fpecially for adminiftring
the holie Sacrament of Confirmation; though
our Cardinal in his time, vvas not of that
minde; for if he had, it had bene done. Finally, after mature confultation, his Holines
refolued to make an Archprieft vvith tvvelue
Affiftants, to gouerne the reft in England.
And vpon the particular information of the
fame chiefe and eldeft forte of English priefts
teftifying the fingular good talents, vertue,
learning, vvifdome, zeale, difcretion, and
other good parts, and confiderable circum-
ftances, concurring præeminently in the perfon of M. George Blackvvel, this autoritie
of Archprieft vvas laid vpon him; to the
great ioue and fingular liking of al, except
a very fevv, efpecially thofe that afpired to
haue bene promoted themfelues. Who hearing by our Protectors letters, that this Archprieft vvas conftituted, and tvvelue Affiftants
appointed, deferred to fubmit themfelues,
til they might fee further confirmation therof
from his Holines. And shortly they fent tvvo
meffengers to Rome, not fo much to learne
his Holines true meaning and intention (for
they knevv it already, but thought they vvere
not bound to acknovvledge it) as to trie, if
they could procure this autoritie to be recal-
led, or altered; and fpecially to be remoued
to fome other perfon; alleaging againft their

E 4 appointed

appointed Superiour, nothing but meere falf-
hoods, and that he agreeth too vvel vvith
the Iefuits, and fpecially vvith F. Parfons.

So the controuerfie is novv come to this fpecial point; whether the R. R. Archprieft be
a fufficient and fit man for the place he is in,
feing he agreeth vvel vvith the Iefuits, and
namely vvith F. Parfons; and concurreth vvith
them to gaine foules; or that he shoud be remoued, and fome other put in his, or in fome higher place, that diffiketh of F. Parfons,
and other Iefuites; and that the Iefuites should
alfo depart out of England, and be remoued
from the gouernmét of al English Seminaries,
euen from thofe which they haue procured?
Al vvhich is fo abfurd and barbarous an attempt
that it needeth no further confutation. Euerie childe, and fimple man or vvoman doth
knovv, that it is a good thing to build a Church
or a College, and to gaine foules: and that
pulling dovvne, and hindring of fuch vvor-
kes is very naught and wicked. Againe, it is a
moft knowen thing (and none of the malcon-
tents can poffibly denie it) that F. Parfons, for
his part, hath moft painfully and frucfully laboured to helpe his countrie aboue tvventie
tvvo yeares already, that is, fince the English
College in Rome vvas founded. In procuring
vvherof his part was not leaft, vvith D. Allen, and D. Levvis, agreing in his intention
with vvhofoeuer vvas moft fincere.

In England he did more good in tvvo
                                            yeares

yeares, then I thinke anie of his emulators
haue donne in tvventie; or are like to doe in
al their life. For one example; let his lerned
and vertous bookes teſtifie vvritten againſt
Hanmer and *Charck*, and in *detection* of *Iohn Nicols*,
and *the reafons*, vhy Catholiques refuſe to goe
to the Proteſtants Church. And eſpecially
the *Chriſtian Directorie*, firſt ſet forth vvith the
title, of *Refolution*, ſo often printed ſince, and
ſtil deſired. A vvorke worthie to be in al
languages, and in al mens hands. By which
innumerable Catholiques, haue ben, and daily
are much confirmed, conforted, and edified;
Schiſmatikes and Heretikes continually conuerted; as very manie doe daily reporte of
themſelues, that they vvere conuerted by
reading F. Parſons booke of Refolution. After his going out of Englãd, which vvas dout-
les (as manie good effects haue ſhevved) by
Gods ſpecial prouidence (as vvas D. Allens
going thence alſo, vvhen he had donne much
good) he firſt got tvvo thouſãd ducats of gold
(which do make ſix hundreth pounds ſtarling)
euerie yeare to Dovvay College, then reſi-
ding in Rhemes. He procured alſo a College
for English children in Evv. Aftervvards
tvvo more notable Colleges for English
ſcholars, and tvvo other reſidences for English Prieſts in Spain. An other College likevviſe in Flanders, vvhen by reaſon of the vvar-
res in France, that of Evv ceaſed. And (which
may haue place vvith the greateſt and moſt

difficult vvorke of al) he hath reduced the
College of Rome, to a mirrour or spectacle
of right Collegial peace, mutual loue, great
vertue, and of much increase in learning,
which a few yeares agoe, vvas fallen into
extreme danger of vtter ruine, by dissolu-
tion of the members, and tumultous con-
tempt of superiors and good orders. I omit
here his redeming of manie English captiues from fire, gallovves, and gallies, vvith his
charitie in procuring them reliefe, and manie
of them sufficient meanes to liue ; and manie
other good deedes, both in general to his
vvhole nation, and to innumerable particular
persons. By this that is already said, euerie
one may sufficiently see, vvhether it be good,
that the chiefe of our Ecclesiastical Hierarchie
in England, and his freinds and subiects should
agree vvith this father, and al the Societie ; or
that they should picke quarels, and make
vvarrs against them, contemne and abandon
al the good vve haue, and may haue by them.
Which in dede vvere to hinder the best meanes
of increasing the Catholique faith in our Countrie, and consequently to hold heresie there
the longer ; an so I end this point, and come to
the last.

In vvich I am to declare, betvven vvhom
this controuersie remaineth. And this also is
partly donne alreadie. For seing the special
drift of this contention is, to haue the
Archpriest remoued from his office, and the
Iesuits

Iesuits out of England , and from al English
Seminaries; it is euident that the controuerfie
is betvven the Archprieft , vvith al afvvel Iefuits as other Priefts, and Catholiques, that
alovve or like of the Ecclefiaftical fubordina-
tion lately reftored in England ; and the mal-
contents vvith their partners, that oppugne or
diflike the fame : and not betwen the Iefuits,
and the Seminarie Priefts . vvhich can in no
other fence be iuftified , then one may fay
an Egyptian is white, becaufe his teeth are vvhite.
At leaft , it is as falfe as vvas the report made
to king Dauid, that *al his fonnes were flaine:* vvhen
only Amnon vvas flaine , and no more . As I
vvil novv further demonftrate , that the truth
may appeare, and the Seminarie Priefts (fpeaking abfolutly of the chiefeft beft and farre
greateft part) from the begining of the firft
Seminarie to this day, may be clered from
this iniurious fclander .

2.*Reg.*
13.

Firft therfore when D. Allen began this holie
vvorke , he had a chiefe care to haue his College vvhere ther vvas alfo a College of Iefuits
that therby he might the better haue their
continual confel and help , fpiritualy and temporally in al his affaires . And namely that the
ftudents might frequent the holie Sacraments
and fome leffons in the fathers College . which
they did continually, til both they and the
Iefuits were driuen from Doway by the pro-
curement of heretiques, for their more zealous profeffion of the Catholique Religion ,
then the

then the vulgar forte of Catholiques commonly shevv. Which wel shevveth the good agreement, betvven the Iesuits and the Seminarie at that time. The fame is also manifest by that D. Allen in his returne from Rome, before he had yet begunne his College, so gladly ioyned himself in companie, vvith F. Maximilian de Capella of the fame Societie, Doctor and Reader of Diuinitie in their College in Dovvay: whose good aduises, and special commendations to diuerse charitable men much furthered the fame good beginings.

Aftervvards F. Antonius Possiuinus, and F. Oliuerius Manereus most affectionatly concurring vvith their informations to their General, and he and they commending the state of the English College to Pope Gergorie the thirtenth, obtained his monethly pension for them. After this againe, the Catholique kings pension (which is greater then the Popes) vvas not only procured, by F. Parsons commendations and trauel (as is noted before) but also by his industrie most especially, or by F. Creswels, or some other of the fathers, it is stil payd. which vvith manie other notorious examples of greate benefits, which D. Allen, and his Seminarie haue receiued of the Fathers, do vvel declare the mutual liking, sineere loue, intire affection, and confident dealing betvven him and the Societie, and betvven al his and al their true folovvers and freinds.

The fame is vvel testified also on the Cardinal
his part,

his part. for though he vvas not able to requite
them in other good turnes, yet he euer grat-
fully acknovvleged the great good our countrie reapeth by the holie Societie; as is to be
seene in most of his printed bookes. specially in
his *Apologie of twelue Martyrs*; in his *Answer to the
pretensed Iustice of England*; and most particularly in his *Apologie*, written by him iointly in
defence of the charitable indeuors *of the Societie,
and of the Seminaries*. In which elegant booke,
next to the worthines of Gods cause, he most
amply commendeth good Pope Gregorie the
thirtenth, and the holie Societie of I E S V S.
Moreouer touching his most gratful affection
towards F. Parsons, omitting other innumerable proofes, his letters written shortly after
he was made Cardinal, to M. Thomas Bailey,
his substitute in the College at Rhemes, do
sufficiently testifie in these words; *you are al glad
and reioyce* (saith he) *for my promotion. God graunt
it be, as I trust it is, to his more honour, and good of our
Countrie, for else I had rather haue kept my black
cappe stil. But how much soeuer you haue cause to reioyce
in this behalf, so much more, al you, that loue me so
dearly, are bound by a new obligation, to loue, and
be gratful to the whole Societie, and namely to our own
special good Father, and chiefe cooperator. For next
vnder Heauen F. Parsons made me Cardinal.* And
more to the same effect in the same letter.

And that he continued the same affection,
and sincere correspondence with the fathers,
his owne good Nephew M. Thomas Allen,
and sundrie

and sundrie of his letters doe testifie. amongst
which one vvas vvritten not long before his
death, to one that then began to be malcon-
tented, and since hath ioyned vvith others.
yea and (as is more then probable) dravvne
others vvith him. This then being clere touching the Cardinal, the same muft alfo needs
be true, in al that sincerly loued, and agreed
vvith him. For othervvife in breaking his ex-
preffe commandement, in that verie point,
vvherin they pretend to agree vvith him, they
erre as farre from the truth, as *he that saith he*
loueth God and breaketh his commandements. In so
much that during the Cardinals time, not
aboue foure or fiue in England, besides flat
Apostates, durft shevv the contrarie; though
after his death more appeared: therby be-
vvraing their former diffimulations, their litle
regard of his fvvete, and fatherly admoni-
tions, and their meruelous ingratitude both
tovvards him their late Superior, and the
fathers, by vvhom they had receaued no smal
benefite in their education and learning.
But God be thanked, yet al thefe are not nor
euer vvere fo manie, neither in England nor
abroad, as they vfe to count themfelues.
For vpon occafion of their accufing the fathers
fome yeares agoe, in the name of our nation,
trial vvas made amogft the English in the lovv
countries by manie feueral letters, and fub-
fcriptions to a general attestation, remaning
in record to be fene; vvhere fo manie of the
eldeft

M. .
M.

1. Io. 2.

eldeſt and chiefeſt clergie men of our nation,
and ſome chiefe of the laitie alſo, and ſo manie others of good account, teſtified the great
and charitable offices of the fathers tovvards
our contrie, that of three or foure hundred,
ſcarſe foureteene refuſed to ſubſcribe. Of
which ſome vvere oppoſites to the fathers,
and ſome neutrals. And in England ſcarſe
tenne, at that time, did ſhevv themſelues
againſt the fathers.

Againe at this day, though there be ſome
more Seminarie Prieſts latly ſeduced, by the
ouer diligence of the former ringleaders, yet
they are ſtil matched, and ouer matched in
number, vvith thoſe only that be in office,
and autoritie for the ſeruice of our countrie;
vvho for that they are officers ought and muſt
by al reaſon, preuaile againſt priuat men, if
they vvere manie more, as in dede they are
rather fevver. But if vve doe alſo compare
(as vvhy ſhal vve not?) the vvhole number
aſvvel of the ancient Catholique, as later Seminarie Prieſts, which reuerence, loue, and
like vvel both the fathers and the Archprieſt,
and al other ſuperiours in our English clergie,
they vvil be founde tvventie, or thirtie times ſo manie, as the part or particle that
oppoſeth againſt the ſame Fathers, and Superiors, and the reſt of the bodie. And if
vve extend this compariſon, to al Seminarie men deſigned for the ſame vvorke, or
yet goe forvvard to al English Catholiques,
or finally

or finally obferue the iudgments of al Catholiques in the world, the further we procede, the more oddes we finde . nature and reafon moning al men of confideration, as wel to like and Ioue fo holie, and fo perfect an Order of Religious men, and to alowe and approue what fo euer fuch a vvhole Order alloweth and approueth: as alfo to prefer the ordinances and procedings of lawful Superiors, before the difliking of others, that complaine or fpeake il therof. And thus much may fuffice for declaration, that this controuerfie rifen amongft English Catholiques, is not in matter of faith, nor betwen the Seminarie Priefts and the Iefuites, as is vniuftly faid, but about the Subordination lately reftored in our clergie; and the fathers of the Societie labouring in the fame worke . and fo is betwen the bodie of English Catholiques, that is al the heads with moft of the members, agreing wholy with the fathers; and a fmal partie of oppofits difliking the fame Subordination, and the fathers of the Societie.

To returne therfore whence I am digreffed, I moft hartely wish, and in our L. I. Ch. I inftantlie befech al our difcontented brethren, to liue and dye in peace , and perfect vnion, fo much as in vs lieth, with al the world, but more efpecially with al Catholiques , and moft of al with our Superiors, brethren, and felow foldiars . as this our bleffed brother M. Wharton now a martyr, moft gladly and louingly acknowleged his appointed Superiour, the R. R. Archprieft;

R. Archprieſt; and moſt ſincerely alwayes agreed with the reuerend fathers of the Societie of Iefus. And yet was he as ancient, as graue, and as learned a Graduate of the Vniuerſitie of Oxford, as whoſoeuer of the diſcontented moſt vrgeth theſe reſpects.

For he was felovv and companion in Trinitie College vvith the ſame M. George Blackwel novv Archprieſt, vvith M. Thomas Ford and M. Edward Burden both martyrs, and with M. William Sutton, after of the Societie: neither did he diſdaine that his equals, yea diuerſe otherwiſe his inferios, in degre. yeares, and lerning, were put in office, himſelfe remaining in his priuat ſtate. As yvere ſundrie of the tvvelue Aſſiſtants. Whom he alſo obeyed, and for his humiltie feruent charitie, and other great vertues, is now exalted to a glorious croune of martyrdome. Which together vvith his Prieſthode and holie profeſſion, the ſame F. Sutton (by way of probable conieƈture) congratulated vvith him long before, in a letter dated at Muſſipont the 17. of Nouember. 1584. which yet remaineth in the English College in Dovvay; by the ſame prouidence of God (as I may interpret) by which it was vvritten. The copie wherof I haue here adioined as it is in latin, ſuppoſing manie vvil deſire to reade it. Surely it is à letter vvorthie of a Ieſuit to a Seminarie Prieſt. The Superſcription only is in English, and is thus.

F   TO M.

TO M. CHRISTOPHER WHARTON
IN THE ENGLISH COLLEGE
AT RHEMES.

M Agnum mihi attulerunt solatium (opti-
me Christophore) tuæ literæ, quibus
intellexi te non solum deserta Anglicana nostra
Ægypto, à qua iam pridem pedem subtraxisti,
Ecclesiæ matris obsequentissimum esse filium, ac
iam illius fœlicissimi Collegij alumnum; verum
etiam ad sacros Ordines, hoc est (vt nunc rem
interpretor) ad ipsa martyrij auspicia aspirasse.
Fælicem ego illum esse prædico, qui nunc in An-
glia existens, sacro Reconciliationis fædere, se
Deo, ac S. matri Ecclesiæ astringit; Fælicio-
rem verò qui maiori perfectionis desiderio inar-
descens, ad fontem illum (quem in hoc Martyrum
Seminario Deus mihi aperuisse visus est) accur-
rit, vt maiori posteà cum fiducia animiq; for-
titudine certamen pro fide ineat. Fælicissimum
denique qui sacratissimis consecrandi Dominici
Corporis mysterijs initiatus, suum iam quasi
sanguinem, pro eiusdem pientissimi Domini hono-
re, eiusque corpore mystico consecrasse videtur.
Hos tu siue fælicitatis, siue perfectionis gradus
partim attigisse videris, partim præsentis ani-
mi præparatione conscendere conaris. Quamuis
enim

*enim non omnibus martyrij corona,etiam cum hoc
cupiant, conceditur ; ingentis tamen meriti est illa
gloriosa sanctæ fidei confessio, quam tu tuiq; con-
fortes quotidie facitis, hoc præsertim tam infælici
nostræ infælicissimæ Angliæ statu ac tempore.Vbi
tanta Sanctorum Mysteriorum conculcatio ; tan-
tus diuini honoris contemptus ; tamque horrenda
rerum sacrarum, ac personarum prophanatio &
despectus ; vt iam vere fidelis sit seruus, ac dile-
ctus Domini Saluatoris, eiusq; immaculatæ spon-
sæ Ecclesiæ Filius, qui se contra istas ruinas vt
murum opponere, qui Sancta,Sancta,inclamare ac
vere Sancta eaq; augustissima Mysteria,cælestiaq;
sanctitatum iura,ab atrocissimis hisce contumelijs
vindicare contendit - Et hic quidem est tuus sta-
tus, hæc conditio, hic ordo sacer. Nunquam mihi
tam coniunctus fuisti, quanquã & domestica,illius
Collegij in quo olim vnà viximus, & peculiari ami
citia, olim charissimus , quam nunc es sub vexillo
Crucis, huiusque sanctæ militiæ communione.*

*At enim quid nos miseri vermiculi humi
repentes, quibus tanta munia, tamque excelsa
concredita sunt? Nunquid tam eminentis digni-
tatis altissima mysteria, vel semel à longe aspicere,
nedum attrectare, nedum consecrare digni su-
mus ? Nunquid cælestis Ianuæ claues gestare, ac
animabus prætioso cælestis Agni sanguine redem-*

ptis, Paradisi

ptis, *Paradisi aditum reserare digni? Verè qui
in tremendis hisce officijs versantur, identidem se
animúmque totum ac spiritum recolligere habent,
oculósque interiores ab exteriori rerum strepitu,
visibilíque specie subtractos in diuiniora defigere,
ibi se coram infinita & superbenedicta Dei Ma-
iestate prosternere, ac paululum animo reuoluere,
quanta cum eius dignatione, fauore, & gratia, iam
coram illa immensa Diuinitate, quam tremunt
Angeli, eiusque Throno, ac mensa regali, verse-
tur is, qui suo demerito, propter illius summo ho-
nori irrogatam iniuriam, iam diu vt hostis &
extorris in tenebras exteriores amandandus fue-
rat, nihílq́; adhuc egit, quod ad tantas tamq́;
inueteratas contractas maculas eluendas satis [-
set. Tum in profundissimam quandam humilita-
tem coram Deo suo descendere, imò in abyssum ali-
quā suæ miseriæ, abiectionis, indignitatis & nihilei
tatis se abscondere, ac sacratissimis Christi vulne-
ribus lauandum se humillime prebere, petere suspi-
cijs ac gemitibus puritatem cordis, diuinam sa-
pientiam, gratias ac virtutes, vt in domo Dei
sui coram sanctissimo eius Throno, coram oculis
tantæ Maiestatis, & splendoris, inspectante illo
beatissimo ac lucidissimo sanctorum choro, in su-
scepto munere dignè, vel saltem non indignè, &
sine offensa versari queat. Sed quid ego hæc,
                                                    aliaue*

*aliaue tibi propino, qui iam ad fontem sedes,
vnde vberrimè diuinæ disciplinæ fluenta iam
diu in multos redundarunt ? Hoc mihi concedet
spero tua humanitas, vt dum te pro veteri nostra
amicitia affari, adeoq; salutare libuit, interim me-
ipsum his verbis cõmonerem. Quæso mi reueren-
de ac dilecte domine Christophore, vt in tuis san-
ctis sacrificijs mei memoriam facere velis, meq; re-
liquarum tuarum deuotionum participem efficias.
Saluta precor meo nomine D. Edouardũ Burdenũ
& si quis sit alius Collegij S. Trinitatis: Item D.
Edmundum Leukenorum, & Arthurum Strat-
fordum, aliosq; nostros familiares & in Christo di-
lectos. Vale. Mussiponti. 17. Nouemb.
1584.*

Vestri semper amantissimus

GVILIELMVS SVTTONVS.

Else vvhere this Epistle may be translated into English. For novv after this long
digression, I make hast to recite briefly,
the other Martyrs of this holie yeare.

In Iu-

IN Iulie folovving it nappened, that search being made in the Countie and Citie of Lincolne, for certaine malefactors, that had committed a robberie; there vvere found in a common Inne, at the signe of the Sarazens head, tvvo strangers close in their chamber (vvho vvere in dede Priests, their names M. Thomas Sprot, and M. Thomas Hunt) vvhom the searchers vehemently suspecting to be the men they sought for, arrested them vpon suspicion of felonie, examined them straightly and seuerally, vvhat vvere their names, vvhere they vvere borne, vvhat condition or trade of life they vvere of, vvhence they came, vvhither they vvent, and what busines they had there, vvhom they knevv in the Citie or therabout: so pressing them, that to clere themselues of the false suspition of robberie, they confessed, that they vvere Catholiques, fled thither in hope to liue there more quietly, as strangers for a time, then they could do where they vvere more knovvne. The same officers searching their males, found therin holie Oyle, and tvvo Breuiaries, which gaue suspition that they vvere Priests. Vvhervpó they vvere brought to the Maior, and by him examined vpon these foure Articles. First, vvhether they had bene at the Church vvithin these tenne, or tvvelue veares? 2. If the Pope should inuade the Realme, vvhether they vvould take part with him, or vvith the Queene?
3. VVhe-

3. Whether they did take the Quene to be Supreme gouernesse of the Church of England? 4. Whether they vvere Priests, or no?

To these Interrogatories they ansvvered briefly, and conformably ech to other, vvith litle difference of vvordes, to this effect.

To the first, that they vvere brought vp from their infancie, in the Catholique faith, and vvere neuer at the Protestants Church. To the second, that when such a case shal happen, which is not likelie, they wil ansvver it. To the third, that the Pope is Supreme head of the Catholiq; Church, through-out the vvorld. To the fourth they ansvvered as before, that they vvere Catholiques: and further they thought themselues not bound to ansvvere. For as al Christians are bound to be Catholiques: so al are bound to confesse the same Catholique faith. But no man being bound to be a Priest, neither is he bound to confesse, vvhether he be a Priest or no. Neuer thelesse vpon this last Article, they vvere presently araigned before Iudge Glanduil, vvho contrarie to the vsual custome, vvould needs handle this matter before al others, in the general sessions, which chanced to be there the same vveke. An Indictement therfore vvas framed, and publiquely read, charging them that they vvere Seminarie Priests; and therfore traitors; possessed vvith malice against their Quene, and Countrie; vvith other horrible, odious,

and

and wicked termes, moſt falſe and iniurious.
And then hauing no other proofe, nor vvit-
neſſe to produce, the ſame Iudge proteſted
to the Iurie, that he vvas aſſured that they
were Prieſts;and therfore with manie sharpe
words admonished them ſo to find it. The
poore Iurie making much difficultie to auerre
ſo much, vvithout either confeſſion of the
parties, or anie lavvful vvitneſſes againſt
them, yet for verie feare, vpon the Iudge his
conſcience, againſt their owne conſciences,
brought in for their verdict,that the ſaid priſoners were guiltie. By and by M. Glanduil
gaue ſentence of death againſt them, that
they should returne firſt to the priſon whence they
came, thence be drawne on a hurdle to the place of
execution, there be hanged til they were halfe dead,
then be diſmembred, vnbowled, quartered,and their
heads and quarters diſpoſed of, at the tle Queens
pleaſure. Which they ioyfully heard,thanked
God, and pardoned their perſecutors. But
before, and partly alſo after this ſentence,
they had diſputation vvith certaine abſurde
preachers, that auouched diuerſe ſtrange
doctrines, too abominable to be here recited. Which neuertheleſſe the glourious
Martyrs clerly confuting,ſo confounded the
ſame heretiques, and edified the people,
that the Magiſtrats commanded the Mini-
ſters to hold their peace. And in ſteed of
their babling, proſecuted their ovvne farre
                                    ſtronger

ftronger arguments, of fetters, halters,
and butchers kniues. Al which the victo-
rious Martyrs anfwering vvith true chriftian
courage, receiued their triumphant crou-
nes, and put al their perfecutors to that
non plus, which our bleffed Sauiour fpeaketh
of : *when they haue killed the bodie, they can do* Luc. 12.
no more.

And not manie dayes after M. Gláduil their
Iudge, receiued alfo his owne Iudgement,
and due pay for his workes. For riding
abroad for his pleafure, nere to his owne
houfe with one man, fodainly in the plaine
filde, he fel from his horfe to the grounde,
the horfe not ftumbling at al, but running a-
vvay a greate pace, the feruant ftept quickly
to his matter, and affaying to help him vp,
foúd him dead, wherat being much aftonished,
he pofted fo faft as he could to the next villa-
ge, cryin; that his matter was dead. The people
in haft running to the place found it fo. And
not knowing who elfe could be charged
thervvith, they prefently apprehended the
fame fervingman, vpon fufpition that he
had murthered his mafter. But vewing
the corps, they faw euidently, that a fpirit and no man had donne this act. For
they found part of his braines ftraingely
comming forth, both at his nofe and mouth,
not hauing anie other hurt in his head, but
towards the right fide behind a great dimple

F 5   or hole

or hole, vvherin a child might haue put his
fiſt; neither his skinne, nor his hat broken
at al, nor a heare of his head vvanting to anıe
mans iudgement. They found likevviſe his
right shoulder ſore ſcorched, like burnd
leather, as blacke as pitch; and from thence
along vpon his arme a great gash, as it had
bene made vvith a knife, but not deepe; and
in the calfe of his legge on the ſame ſide, they
found an other hole, about an inch broad,
and three inches deepe, and (which is moſt
ſtrange) not ſo much as a threde of his hoſe,
nor of his other aparel could bo found to be
broken. In the meane while, the horſe
that ranne avvay, with much ado vvas taken, but could by no meanes be brought nere
to the place, vvhere his maſter fel dovvne.

A Gaine the ſame moneth of Iulij, an
other vertous learned Prieſt, called M.
N. Palaſer, by like crueltie was iudged and
put to death at Durham; only for that he was
a Seminarie Prieſt, and returned to his countrie, contrarie to the ſtatute made in the 27.
yeare of the Quenes raigne. And other three
Gentlemen and a gentlewoman vvere alſo
condemned to dye, by the ſame ſtatute, for
conuerſing vvith the ſame Prieſt, and not
bewraying him to the Magiſtrat. Tvvo of the
Gentlemē, called M. Iohn Norton, and M.N.
Talbot receiued their reward, and glorious
croune vvith their goſtlie father. Miſtreſſe
Norton

Norton (the condemned gentlewoman) being supposed to be vvithchild was reprived. The third Gentleman, contenting of frailtie, to goe to their Church, yet liueth. as the others might haue donne, if they had also yelded therunto.

Ikewise at Lancaster vvithin the same moneth, other tvvo Seminarie Priests, M. Robert Nutter, and M. Edvvard Thvving vvere condemned and put to death, for their Priesthood. The elder of them M. Nutter, vvas one of those Priests and prisoners, which being brought by their kepers from their seueral prisons, to the tovvre wharfe, in the yeare of our Lord, 1585. and there commanded to enter into a shippe, readie prouided to carie them into banishment, declared publikly to the commissioners, that they did not accept of that banishment, as of anie grace or mercie at al, for they had not committed anie fault, neither againſt their Quene nor countrie, as this pretended mercie falſly preſuppoſed; and therfore in expreſſe termes requeſted rather to be tried, and to anſvvere their accuſers at Weſtminſter, and at Tiburne, then to be thus caried againſt their vvills, out of their natiue Countrie, from their freinds, and neighboures vvhom they vvere to ſerue, according to their Prieſtlie functions. Affirming moreouer, that though perforce they vvere caried avvay, yet they vvould aſſuredly returne

to the

to the fame worke, fo foone as God, and
their fpiritual Superiors, would permit them
fo to doe . As this bleffed Martyr for his
part , and diuerfe others haue wel and moft
happely performed .   M. Thwing was no
leffe refolued in this glorious quarel , as wel
appeared both by his life and death , and
particularly by his godlie letters , to his brother , fifter, and others, which may be published in a larger relation . Only here for
a tafte of his fwete and zealous good fpirit,
I shal recite part of two letters written by
him in prifon , vnto me that write ihis.

In the former of which, he congratulateth
with his freinds , his owne imprifonment,
‘‘in thefe words : My felfe am now prifoner
‘‘for Chrift, in Lancafter Caftle, expecting
‘‘nothing but execution , at the next Affifes.
‘‘I defire you to commend me to the deuout
‘‘praiers of my freinds with you , that by their
‘‘help , I may confummat my courfe to Gods
‘‘glorie, and the good of my countrie . I pray
‘‘God profper you , and al yours, for euer.
‘‘From my prifon and paradife . This laft of
‘‘Maij. 1600. *Al yours in Chrift.*   E. Th.

His other letter written but few daies before
his martyrdom with like confolation of his
expected good end , he concludeth thus :
‘‘This day the Iudges come to Lancafter,
‘‘where I am in expectation of a happie death,
‘‘if it fo pleafe God almightie. I pray you com-
‘‘mend me moft derely to myn vncle , and my
                                              brother.

brother. I pray God bleſſe them both. and „
to al your good Prieſts and ſcholars, vvhoſe „
good endeuors God alvvayes proſper ; to „
his owne more glorie. *Ego autem iam delibor,* „
& tēpus reſolutionis meæ inſtat. before this come „
vnto you, I ſhal, if God make me vvorthie, „
conclude an vnhappie life, with a moſt hap- „
pie death. *Omnia poſſum in eo qui me confortat.* „
From Lancaſter Caſtle, the 21. of Iulij, this „
holie yeare 1600.

AI yours in Chriſt.

EDVVARD THVVEING.

SIX OTHER MARTYRS

A Gaine this laſt ſpring (before the ſame
yeare vvas ended, by our Engliſh account) it hath pleaſed God, to glorifie ſix
more Martyrs in our countrie. VVhoſe names I haue alſo thought neceſſarie to adde
hereunto, hoping herafter to make more
ample relation of them and the reſt. The
firſt of theſe vvas M. Iohn Pibush. VVho
being condemned about ſix yeares before,
only for that he vvas a Seminarie Prieſt; and
al that time moſt cruelly vſed, at laſt receiued his happie crovvne, at London the
eleuenth of Februarie. And the 27. of the
ſame

fame monech, M. Roger Filcock, and M. Marck Barckvvorth, alfo Seminarie Priefts, in the fame place, and for the fame caufe, and maiftris Line a vvidovv gentlewoman, for receiuing **prifts** in her houfe, receiued the like revvard in erernal glorie.

About the fame time alfo, other tvvo Seminarie Priefts, M. Thurftan Hunt, and M. Robert Midleton, being taken in Lancashire, and from thence fent to London, vvere prefently returned thither againe, and fo condemned and executed at Lancafter meerly for their Priefthood.

Thus we haue fixtene glorious and confpicous Martyrs (befides thofe that are ftarued in prifons, and by other afflictions, for the fame faith) vvithin the fpace of twelue moneths, that is, in this one holie yeare, for euerie hundreth yeres fince Chrift one. A moft happie Iubiley to them; a fingular confolation to al Catholiques; and a happie example alfo of Gods mercie, tovvards al of other Religions, that vvil confider their ovvne eftates, vvherin they liue; and the true caufe, for which al thefe, and fome hundreths more thefe late yeares, haue beftovved their liues. For fo they fhal clerly fee, that they vvere al accufed and condemned, for the old, true Holie, Catholique, and Apoftolique faith; as offenders againft certaine nevv Statutes made of late (the like neuer heard of before in a Chriftian Countrie,

trie, nor as yet approued for good, elsvvhere
in the vvorld) and moſt ſpecially vrged to
go to the Proteſtants Churches. Which
alone would haue ſaued their temporal
liues longer.

For the ſame cauſe alſo manie other an-
cienr, and moſt conſtant Catholique priſoners in the Citie of Yorke, by the commandement of the L. Burley, Preſident of the
North partes, and his aſſiſtants, haue bene
this yeare violently, and often dravvne and
haled, by meere force to heretical Sermons.
And aſtervvards, becauſe they reproued the
prechers for diuerſe blaſphemies, and other
falſe and abſurde doctrines, haue bene ſhut
vp in ſtreicter priſons, laden with irons,
and pinched vvith famine; neither did they
forbeare, nor feare, to reprehend blaſphemies, vvhen they vvere brought to the ſame
place againe. But certaine of them being
learned, openly reproued the blaſphemous
prechers, and aftervvards before the ſame
Preſident, and others, clerly confuted their
errors. Others of leſſe learning, yet alſo of
great zeale, ſtopped their ovvne eares, in
ſight of the perſecutors. who therfore appointed to ech of them, two men to hold
downe their hands, al the ſeimon time. and
yet would they not for al that, harken
to the ſermons, but partly by ſtrugling and
chiding with their tormenters, partly by
whiſpering and talking among themſelues,
they ma-

they made fuch a blacke *Sanctus*, that neither one nor other could much marke, vvhat the preacher faid. So vnpoffible it is, either for Catholiques to be inreft, or for perfecuters to haue their vvole vvilles, vvhere the furie of herefie rageth. And much leffe is it poffible to extinguish the Catholique faith by force and violence. for the more it is fovved with teares, and watered vvith blond, the more it increafeth and profpereth, As we fee not only in the primitiue Church, but alfo novv in England, where through Gods fpecial grace, and by the prayers and bloud of fo manie Martyrs, there be farre more Catholiques at this day, then were fourtie yeares agoe.

DEO GRATIAS.

Yours al and euer: T. W.
a Seminarie Prieft.

A Chayne of Twelve Links
1617

A

CHAYNE OF

TWELVE LINKS.

TO WIT XII CATHO

LICK CONDITIONS CON

cerning certaine graces & Indulgences,
of Christes Catholick Church.

With an explication of the matter of
Indulgences, of the Stations at Rome,
& how to gaine the Pardons belonging
to the same: of the Iubilies, & other pardons, instituted and ordained by the said
Church, for the benefite of all Catholick people: with the Reasons &
groundes she hath for the
same.

Translated out of Italian into English
By I. W.

Whereunto are annexed, the Indulgences graunted vnto the Society of
the Rosary of our Blessed Lady,
together with those that are
geuen to holy Graynes, Crosses, &
Medales, of the English pardon,
& the Pardon of Boromeus.

1617.

THE TRANSLATOR
TO THE CATHO-
lick and Christian Reader.

TWo or three reasons moued me
(dear Catholick Reader) to spēd
a few houres in translating this
litle Treatise of Indulgences, out of Italian, into our vulgare tongue. The
which, although it may seeme to some,
to be a thing of noe greate importance,
yet he that shall attentiuely peruse the
same, and with diligence consider the
pointes that are handled, shall, I doubt
not, either reape some commoditie therby, or at least remaine so satisfied of the
matter it self, that it shall not repent him
of his labour therin.

The first & principall reason that moued me hereunto, was, the present occasion of this holy Iubilie, considering
what a wonderful treasure is imparted
vnto vs herein for the good of our soules.

For most certaine it is, that a mã may
be then, in such disposition, through
the grace of God, and his owne good endeuour, that he may make him selfe, as

A 2

pure & cleane as the infant that is newly baptized, or as cleare from sinne, as the Angels in heauen.

The second reason that moued me was, for that many Catholickes of our owne nation being wholly ignorant of the latin tongue, or not so sufficiently instructed in this doctrine as they ought: may many times for want of knowledg, deceaue them selues, or otherwise be deceaued in gayning the benefite of the same. And for as much as there be many thousandes of people, which haply shall neuer liue to see the like time againe: my hearty wish and desire was, that none should be depriued of so great a treasure, which all that wil, may so assuredly enioy. The particulers whereof, each one shal best be informed in by his ghostly father.

The third reason was, because so many in these our daies, who, in this matter, do professe them selues open enemies to the Catholick, Romane, and Apostolick Church, from whence, as from the onely Fountaine, thes indulgences doe flow: doe scoffe and iest at such diuine & spitual

tual helpes, diſtributed by Chriſtes holy Spouſe, for the good of her children,
as though they were mere deceiptes and
toies, onely inuented to beguile the ſimple ſorte of people : wheareas indeede
they haue bene practiſed and remained in
vſe in al Catholick Countries in Chriſtē-
dome, for the ſpace of more then a thouſand yeares together, being confirmed
by Scriptures, Fathers, Doctors, Councels, general, & prouincial, from time to
time, as true, wholſome, and ſounde
doctrine.

An other reaſon that induced me hereunto, may be, that whereas Pope Gregory the 13. of bleſſed memory, ſeeing
the deſolation of our Countrie, graunted certaine Indulgēces to Graines, Croſ
ſes, and Medales, thereby to animate,
not onely the remnante of Catholicks
which were left in England, but alſo to
ſtir vp the Catholick people in other Coū
tries, to pray for the reduction of the ſaid
Iland, and reunion thereof with the ſea
Apoſtolick, from whence we firſt receaued our faith. And for that the ſame Indulgences haue euer ſince continued, and
haue

haue bene now lately cōfirmed (by word
of mouth) by him that sitteth in S. Peters Chaire, Paulus the fifth, this verie
yeare 1605, the 30. of May : For this
cause, I say, it seemed to me conuenient,
to translate this litle sequent discourse of
Indulgences, partly to accompany those
which are graunted to the Society of the
Rosary, as also those of the afore named
Graines, Crosses, and Medales of the En
glish Pardon : and partly also to shew
the fruite, vtility, vse, and maner of proceding therein, which I doubt not, but
wil redound to the profit of some, contentment of many, and hurt or hindrance
of none. And so in our Sauiour Iesus, I
bid thee farewel. This 20 of October.
1605.   I. W.

The

THE AVGMENTER,
to the deuout Catholick, and Chriſtian
Reader.

I Seeing this litle Treatiſe of Indulgences (Chriſtian Reader) ſo neceſſary for our Countrie, in readineſſe
to be printed anew, and withal the Stations (mentioned in the firſt Paragraph
of the ſame) in an other litle Booke ;
I thought good to ioine and place them
both together, that the deuout Engliſh
Catholick in one litle volume and breefe
Summary, might haue al thinges neceſſary touching that ſubiect. I haue alſo
added ſomthing, for the better knowledg how to gaine the Indulgences belonging to the ſaid Stations.

Secondly, leſte pe haps ſome new and
infirme Catholike, might deſire to ſee the
power in gods Church to graunt Indulgences, & alſo the groundes, antiquity,
profes, and practiſe thereof : & leſt alſo this Treatiſe might fale into the hādes
of ſome vnlearned heritike, who might
ſuppoſe the Catholiks to haue no authority for the ſame : I haue adioyned ſome
reaſons & groundes thereof, which were

wanting in the former edition, being firſt
ſet forth in a Catholike Country, where
ſuch profes were thought needeleſſe.

Thirdly I haue added a Commendation & Praier, for the better gayning of al
ſortes of Indulgences & other graces at
Gods hande, and to effect that the Catholike and deuout Reader, may haue,
if not an actual intention, yet at the leaſt
a virtual to the gayning thereof. Fare
well.

Your ſaruant in
all hum.lity. B I.

OB

OF the Auth rity & power left in Chrifts Church for to gene Indulgences.

IN Sainct Mathews Gofpel, our Sauiour faid to S. Peter, *What thing foeuer thou loofeft in earth, it fhal be loofed in heauen*. (ca. 6.) This promife is moft large and general: it extendeth vnto al bondes whatfoeuer may hinder men from the obteyning of life euerlafting. Therefore in thefe wordes, is founded this power in gods Church, not onely to abfolue from finnes, in the Sacrament of Penance, but alfo from Cenfures whatfoeue:: & l.kewife to difpence in Lawes, in Vowes, in oathes, &c. fo that there be a reafonable caufe to vfe this authority. When it is faid, *Whatfoeuer thou loofeft &c.* al bonde is included, becaufe there is no exception. Wherefore as S. Peter being the fupreame Paftour, in Chrift his place, may abfolue finners, rightly difpofed in the Sacrament of Penance, applying Chrifts merits vnto them: fo may he likewife, out of the Sacramét, abfolue the fame finners from the temporal punifhment, applying to them the fufteringes

A 5

feringes & satisfactions of Christ, and of
his Sainctes. (Bel . de Indul . lib . 1 . c .
3 . Tollet . lib . 6 . Instruc. ca 22 . Cost.
Encherid . ca . 12 .

The reason wherefore the sinne it self
& mortal guilt thereof & eternal punishment is forgeuen in the Sacrament, & the
temporal punishment and satisfaction,
forthe of the Sacrament, is this, that although the power to absolue be general,
neuerthelesse thinges must be ffected &
performed, correspondent and sutable
to their nature . Mortal offences are not
forgeuen & remitted, without the infusion of grace : infusion of grace, is not
geuen by the ministery of man, but in a
Sacrament : but the guilt of paine or te-
poral satisfaction remayning, after the
fault. & sinne it self be remitted, requireth not any new infusion of grace, to
the loosing and remitting thereof, for it
presupposeth the state of grace obtained
before . This Bellarmine in the place recited .

A seconde place to proue this power to graunt Indulgences, is taken out of
S. Mathew ca. 18 . spoken to the Ap-
postles.

poftles in g neral. The wordes be thefe.
*Whatſoeuer you ſhal binde vpon earth, ſhal be
bound alſo in heauen: and whatſoeuer you
ſhal looſe vpon earth, ſhal be looſed alſo in
heauen.* Thefe wordes are general, and
there is no reafon why they fhoulde ex‑
tend more to the finne it felf, then to the
paine & punifhment thereof, feing that
the paine due to finne, is as remiffible, as
the finne it felf : & as to the one are ap‑
plyed Chrifts merits, fo to the other his
fatisfactiôs : and feing our Sauiour Chrift
forgaue both to the man ficke of the pal‑
ſey , & to the woman taken in adultery .
(Mat . 9 . Io . 4. Bel . loc . cit . & Co‑
fter . ibid .

The 3 . place is taken out of the 20 .
of S . Iohn, where our Sauiour faid to his
Apoftles, *Whoſe ſinnes you forgeue, they are
forgeuen* . Sinnes are not perfectly & to‑
tally forgeuen, except the temporal pu‑
nifhment and fatisfaction belonging ther
to, be alfo remitted & taken away .
Tollet . ibid .

This power is alfo proued by the con‑
tinual practife of the Church of Chrift ,
& what the Church haith had alwaies in

A 6　　　　prac

Practise, must come from God; though the ground thereof should not be knowe.

It is manifest that euen in the Apostles time, this practise of Indulgences was in vse, as appeareth by S. Paule, in the second to the Corinthians ca. 2. wheare he saith to that people. *Whom you haue pardoned, I also pardon, for that which I haue pardoned, in the person of Christ & for you, I haue done it, that we be not circumuented of Satan*. To the better vnderstanding hereof. The Corinthians requested S. Paule that the incestious person, (who now in great contrition & sorow of minde, was in doing of his penance, & for this fault & crime excommunicated by S. Paule) might be released & pardoned touching the rest of his satisfaction that remained vndone, lest that the greatnesse of his tormentes, might driue him to dispaire (for he was deliuered to Sathan.) S. Paule consented to their intreaty, & commaunded them in his name to pardon this haynous offender for the rest of his penance that was not performed.

In this fact, there is nothing wanting
to

to a perfect Indulgence or pardon. Here
is authority in the graunter of this pardon, for S. Paule affirmeth him felf, to do
that which he did, in the perſo of Chriſt.
Secondly there was ſufficient cauſe of the
graunt hereof, to wit, leſt the offender
ſhould be ouerwhelmed with ſorow : &
this graunt was at the requeſt of the Corinthians. Thirdly the receauer of this
Indulgence, was in the ſtate of grace, as
may be ſeene by his great contrition and
hearty ſorow for his fault committed.

Nomore is now required in geuing of
Indulgences, but authority in the graunter, piety in the cauſe, & ſtate of grace
in the receauer. Al theſe three were here
preſent : and alſo this was after the fault
was remitted. S. Tho. & Theodor.
vpon this place. Bell. lib 1. cap 3. de
Indulg. Toll. lib. 6. Inſtruc. cap. 22.

After the Apoſtles time, the vſe of Indulgences were preſently practiſed, as
may be ſeene by Tertulian, lib. 1. ad
Martyres, cap. 1. By S. Ciprian, lib.
3. Epiſt. 15. & in ſerm vlt. de lapſis.

Neither do there want general Councels & Prouincial, for the graunting of

A 7 Indul

Indulgences, as in the first Councell of
Nicene, Can. 11. Ancyra Ca. 5. La-
odic. Can. 2. & others cited by Bellar.
supra, and likewise Cotterus & Tollet in
the places aboue named: and also of the
general Councels of Claramontane, of
Laterane, of Lions, of Vienns, and of
Constance, & the Conncel of Trent, as
may be seene in Bellarmine li. 1. de In-
dulgen. cap. 3. with 40. authorities
more, at the least. I wil alledg onely the
Councel of Trent at large in this pointe,
by which may be seene the practise of
the Church. In the 25. Session of this
Councel, is this decreed & declared.

Seeing the power to geue Indulgences, is by Christ graunted & geuen to the
Church, and also that the said Church in
most auncient times, haith vsed this power geuen her from aboue : this holy Si-
node doth teach and commaund the vse
thereof, and to be most wholesome to
the people, and to be approued by the
authority of holy Councels, and the vse
st I ro be obserued in the Church of Christ.
And those who either affirme Indulgences to be vnprofitable, or deny power in
the

the Church to geue them : with her curſe
& moſt greauous cenſure, ſhe condem-
neth . Thus the Coun.el . Here is a full
proofe for Indulgences, both from whó
the power cometh, to wit, from Chriſt ,
and that the power is geuen by God , to
his Church : that the practiſe is moſt auncient, both commaunded and commended, and the oppugners condemned for
heritikes .

What is contracted by ſinne, and that ordina-
r.ly, there remayneth a temporal pu-
niſhment & ſatisfaction, after
the ſinne it ſelf be remit-
ted .

EVery ſinner by ſinne, incurres two
euils, to wit, the fault, or guilt of
ſinne it ſelf : and the paine or puniſhment due to the ſame , although not
alike in mortal and venial ſinne . In mortal ſinne, the offender incurreth a mortal fault and guilt , which conſiſteth in
this, that he looſeth the frendſhip of god,
and purchaſeth his diſ leaſure : and he
alſo incurreth an euer'aſting paine or pu-

A 8 niſhment

nishment due to the same sinne, so that
after his corporal death, he is obliged to
eternal torments. In venial sin, though
the sinner loose not the grace & fauor of
almighty God, yet neuerthelesse he con-
tracteth a venial fault, wherby gods loue
is abated, and also a temporal punishment, which by penance and satisfactió,
is to be paid, either in this life, or in purgatory. This mortal crime, and the e-
ternal punishment thereunto belonging,
is to be forgeuen by the Sacrament of penance, either in act, or at the least in desire. This venial offence, and the punishment thereto due, either in the Sácramēt,
or by taking of holy water, ot by other
actes of deuotion, or by Indulgences, is
remitted, as Tollet declareth, l:.6. I ı-
struct ca 24. But one thing is to be noted, that neither in morta' sinne, neither
in venial, the temporal paine or satisfactió is necessarily forgeuen with the fault
it self, as the protestants would haue it.
The fault of Adam, and the eternal paine
we e forgeuen him: yet neuertheleffe for
his temporal satisfaction to gods iustice,
he was expelled Paradise, subiect to the
                                    miseries

miferies of this life, and alfo to death it
felf in the ende (gen. 2 .) and this not
onely to him felf, but to al his pofterity,
as S. Paule affirmeth. Ro. 5.

Infants newly baptized, are purged frō
original finne, yet notwithftanding they
are not free from the paine due therunto,
for many in their infancy endure much
paine, and alfo dye in the ftate of inno-
cency.

Dauid, after that three-foulde finne
was forgeuen him (the Adultery, the
death of Vrias, and the loffe of the battel,) yet notwithftanding, for his temporal punifhment, and fatisfaction to gods
iuftice, that child begotten in adultery
dyed. And left any fhould fuppofe or im-
pute that death for a future caueat to Dauid for the time to come : in the fame
place is declared manifeftly, the childes
death, to be the punifhmente of the fault
forgeuen. The wordes are thefe.

*Becaufe thou haft caufed the name of God to
be blafphemed : the child that is borne to
thee, fhal dye.* 2. Reg. 12. Againe, although the finne of Dauid, in numbring
of his people, was remitted : yet after

this, for temporal satisfaction of that fault, he was demaunded whether he would choose battel, famine, or pestilence. 2. Reg. 24. & Bellar. li. 1. de Indul. ca. 3. & li. 4. pæn. ca. 2. & sequentibus.

By which is declared, that ordinarily there remaineth a temporal punishment, after the sinne it self be forgeuen, which is a special grounde for Indulgences, & denyed by the heritikes of our time, as Bellarmine haith declared in his fourth & 2. booke of penance, and the ensuing chapters.

Of the valour & condition of every good worke done in the state of grace, and what part thereof is required to Indulgences.

EVery good action of iust men, done in the state of grace, haith a dooble valour, to wit, merite, & Satisfaction. In Tobie (cap. 4) almes deede is said to deliuer from al sinne, & from death. And neuerthelesse in Sainct Mathew 25. it is said. *Come ye blessed of*

my

my *Father, receaue the kingdome prepared for you, for I was an hungred, and you gaue me to eate &c.* In the first, there is Satisfaction for sinne : in the latter place, merit. Like may be said of Fasting. In the last Chapter of Ionas, the Niniuites are mentioned, to haue apeased Gods wrath by Fasting, and so satisfactory.

In the 6. of S. Mathew, our Sauiour promiseth reward for Fasting where he saith. *And thy Father which seeth* (thee fast) *in secret, wil repay thee.* And so meritorious. The like may be said of prayer, and other actions done in the state of grace. As good workes are laborious & painful, they are satisfactory : & as they are good and performed in charity, they are meritorious, These workes hauing a dooble valour, must haue a dooble reward. Bellar. lib. 1. ca. 3. Tol. lib. 6. ca. 22.

Againe, euery good worke, as it is meritorious, is applyed to the doer thereof, and can not be seperated from him : but not as it is satisfactory. That man is said to merit, that worketh wel : but none, sauing Christ him self, can merit for an

B 2   other

other, none but Chrift, can communicate their merit to an other. For though
a man pray, faft, or geue almes deedes ne
uer fo many for others : no fhare or part
of thofe good workes, is communicable
to them, but onely to the doer thereof
him felf. Of this kinde fpake S, Paule,
when he faid, that euery one fhould receaue his owne proper rewarde. 1. cor.
3. And the pfalmift alfo when he affirmed, that God fhould rewarde euery one
according to their workes. pf. 61.

Neuertheleffe as good workes are im-
petratory and fatisfactory, : they may
be imparted and communicated vnto o-
thers. In this fenfe Dauid affirmed him
felf to be partaker of al thofe that feared
God. pf. 118. As for example. The
good workes of one man in temporal affaires, can not merit or deferue, that an
other man, fhal be a fit and iuft gouernor
in the common wealth : nomore can the
good workes in fpiritual affaires, merit
that an other may haue his finnes forgeuen him. Wel may one impetrate & obtaine at Gods hand, that an other man
may haue contrition for his finnes and a-
mendement

mendement of life (for this is ordinary to
the Sainctes of god)but the contrite mã,
must merite now, by his owne workes,
grace, and remiſſion of ſinns. By others
praiers, he had that good motion : but
by his owne merit and deſerts, he muſt
be ſaued. And like as in a temporal matter, one man may ſatisfy for an other, or
pay the debtes of an other : ſo in ſpiritual affaires, one may truly ſatisfy for an o-
ther, or pay the temporal puniſhment
due to an other. And as in temporales,
with one & the ſelf ſame money, a mã cã
not pay a dooble debt : ſo in, with on e,
& the ſelf ſame act, or good worke, one
can not ſatisfie both for him ſelf, & for
an other.

Bel. lib. 1. ca. 2. Tol. li. 6. Inſtr.
ca. 21. Coſt. Ench. ca. 12. And in the
third condition of this treatiſe.

By this may be ſeene, that they which
are within the vnity of Gods Church,
may ſatisfy one for an other : And alſo
from whence Indulgences are deriued,
to wit, from the merits of our Sauioure
Chriſt, and his Sainctes, as they are ſatisfactory for ſinne, as in the ſecoud con-

B 3   dition

dition of this booke is manifest.

Yet notwithstanding, these satisfactions do not equally procede frō our blessed Sauiour and his Sainctes, as heritikes
abfurdly fay that Catholikes affirme.
For we peremptorily both say and teach,
that our blessed Sauiour, is our absolute
Redemer, Propitiator, & onely Sauiour,
& to his merits alone, we afcribe the remission of Original finne, actual & mortal finne, and the eternal paine and satif-
faction thereunto belouging: al this, I
fay, we afcribe to him felt alone, and to
none other. Yea we alfo attribute vnto him more then this, to wit, that so
powerful are the merits of his facred paffion, that by the vertue thereof, he can
delegate and communicate this power &
remission of finnes, and temporal fatisfaction, vnto others. And we alfo confeffe, the fatisfactions of the Sainctes, to
be of no force or valour at al, if they were
not ioyned with his: and that they take
their force from him, & that our Sauiours fatisfactions, are infinite, in them
felues, neuer to be exhaufted. And that
the adioyning of the fatisfactions of the
                              Sainctes

Sainctes vnto Chriftes, are fuperaboun-
dant and not neceffary, and onely they
extend to temporal fatisfaction, and no
further. But euen as Chrift haith communicated attributes proper by nature to
him felf, & to others by priuiledg, and
grace, as remiffion of finne, the name of
Rock, light of the world, and fuch like,
and alfo his very name of God : fo for
the honour of his Sainctes, Chrift wil
haue their fatisfactions to be adioyned
with his, afwel in reguard it might be
manifefted of what accompt they are of
in his fight, as alfo to declare fró whence
their power came, to wit, from his fatisfactions : And that as Chrift is glorified in his Sainctes, fo he fuffereth in
his Sainctes, (as it is plaine in the acts of
the Apoftles, by his owne wordes faying,
Saule, Saule, why perfecuteft thou me. Act.
9.) he fatisfyeth in his Sainctes and by
his Sainctes, and in this fenfe, S. Paule
faid, ad Col. 1. that he fulfilled in his
owne flefh, thofe thinges, which were
wanting to Chrifts paffion. Bel. li. 1.
Indul. ca. 3. & 4. & Coft. Ench. c.
22.

B 4   Thus

Thus you see, first, that there is a pow-er, and authority in Chriſte his Church, to geue and graunt Indulgences. Second-ly, that after the fault and crime be re-mitted, there remayneth a temporal ſa-tisfaction to be performed. Thirdly, that onely that part of good workes which is ſatisfactory, is applyed to Indulgences. And laſtly, that one may ſatiſfy for an o-ther.   Now to the Conditions.

THE 1. CONDITION.

What an Indulgence is .

AN Indulgence, as it is ordinarily taken in the catholike Church
is a remission or forgeuenesse of
sinnes, either in part or in whole : yet
not of the mortal crime or guilt it self of
sinne(which is remitted otherwise in the
Sacrament of Penance) but of the paine,
(not eternal, but temporal) due vnto mā
for his sinnes, after they be forgeuen by
Sacramental confession.

S. Tho . 4 . Sent . d . 10 . art . 5 . Quodl . 8
Io . Vign . de Indul . ver . 19 .
Bel . de Indul . ca · 1 .

The 2. condition.

From whence Indulgences are deriued .

INdulgences doe spring and growe,
from the infinite merit, and supera-
boundant satisfaction, of the most
pretious bloud of our Lord and Sauiour
Iesus, one onely drop whereof, had bene
sufficient for the ful redemption of al the

world

world. Also from the singuler merit of the most Blessed Virgin his Mother, and of other holy Sainctes, and Martirs. For which respect Indulgences are said to be, A treasure gathered together, and layde vp in the holy catholik Church, flowing from the aforesaid merits.

Franc . de Maior . 4 . sent . d. 19 .

Sot . 4 . Sent . d. 21 . q . 1 . &c.

Bel . Indul . ca . 2 .

Armil . de Indul . parag . 8 .

Clem . 6 . Extrau . Unigen . tit . de pœnit . & remis.

The 3 . condition.

The effect of Indulgences.

INdulgences worke the same effecte wholly and entyrely, which the penance due for the sinne (after the same is Sacramentally forgeuen) when it should haue bene fulfilled by the penitent , would haue done. Wherefore the contrite penitent getting the said Indulgences, satisfyeth for his sinnes, in the remission of the temporal punishmente due thereunto, as if he had satisfyed by

doing

doing his penance, the debt being payed
which he owed, with the aforesaid treasure of the catholike Church, deriued f ō
the infinite merits of our Sauiour Chrift,
& alfo frō the merits of his holy Sainēts.

Caiet . quodl . tom . ı .
Bel . cap . 7 . de . Indul .
Armil . Indul . paragr . 6 .

The 4 . condition.

Of the diſtributour of Indulgences.

Two fortes of diſtributoures there
be of the treafure of Indulgences, to wit, the vnlimited, & the
limited. The vnlimited diſtributour or
geuer, is cheifly and onely the Pope, S.
Peters lawful Succeſſor, and Chriſtes
Vicar heare on earth. The limited diſtributoures, are the Popes Legates, who
by ſpecial, or general commiſſion from
him, may graunt Indulgences in their
Legacies : Archbiſhops, and Metropoli-
tanes, in their prouinces : Biſhops and
Prelates, in their dioces : as alfo Religious men, and feculer Preiſtes, according to the authority graunted them, by

his

his special commission or priuiledg.

S . Tho . 4 . sen . d . 20 . art . 9 . qnodl . 1 .
S . Anton . p . p . 1 . tit . 10 . parag . 3 . de
Indul .
Sot . 4 . sent . d . 21 . q . 1 . art . 4 . ad 1 .
Bel . ca . 11 . de Indul .

The 5 : condition .

Of the operation of Indulgences .

INdulgēces do operate & worke in the vertue of the foresaid merites and satisfactions, two sundry waies . The first is, by the authority and power of him that graunteth them . And secondly by the deuotion and charity of him or her that gayneth them .

The 6 . condition .

Of the extension of Indulgences .

NOte that Indulgences do extend aswel to the high Forum, or tribunal of our Sauiour Chrift , as to the internal Forum or Court of the holy Church . But not to the external iudicial court , concerning the punishmentes

which

which the offenders of the law do deserue
for their offences : that is to say, no mã
by Indulgences can be deliuered from
the punishmentes which belong to the
external contentious court, either ecclesiastical, or secular; nor yet also from a-
ny natural paines or punishmentes.

Bel. ca. 7. de Indul.

Felin. de Indul.

S. Tho. 4. sent. dist. 20. q. 1. art. 5.

The 7. condition.

Of the precepts of Indulgences.

TO obtaine this special treasure of
Indulgences, or any part therof, there is required a fit disposition in him that shal receaue the same,
that is to say, that he be, not onely in the
state of grace, but also that he performe
truly and sincerely, al and euery precept
which he that geueth the said Indulgence
shal appoint, or commaund, or so much
thereof as shal be necessary, according to
the intention of the geuer, who cõmonly geueth choice of two, three, or more
thinges to be done, according as euery
mans

mans estate, ability, opportunity, & o-
ther circumstances require : without the
accomplishing whereof, the said Indulgences can not be obtained .

Sot . 4 . sent . dist . 21 . q . 2 . art . 3 .
Bel . ca . 13 . de Indul .

The 8 condition .

Of the application of Indulgences .

Indulgences can not be applyed to
any one that is in mortal sinne,
but onely to such as are contrite,
and confessed of al their mortal sinnes :
or at least-wise, haue an intention and
purpose to do the same, at due and conuenient time, according as the wordes of
the Bul wherein the said Indulgences are
published, shal import, and not otherwise .

S . Tho . 4 . sent . d . 20 . art . 5 . quodl . 1
Sum . confes . l . 3 . tit . 24 . q . 186 .
Hugol . Tab . 2 . cap . 9 . para . 1 num . 5 .
Bel . cap . 9 . & 10 . de Indul .
Tabiena Indul . parag . 3 .

Tn 9 . condition .

Of

THose onely do Indulgences a -
uaile and profit, who obtaine
and get them, and not others : so
as we can not get Indulgences for an o-
ther, except the Bul wherby they be published, do expresly specify the same,
which is very seldome, and not without
extraordinary cause.

*S. Anton.p.p.tit. 10.ca.3. de.In-
dulg. parag. 1.*
Bel.ca.9.de Indul.

The 10. condition.

Of Indulgences for the dead.

CErtaine it is among al Catholiks,
that Indulgences profit the dead,
(I mean that departed this life in
the faith of the catholike Church) for as
the suffrages of the liuing do profit the
dead by way of impetration : so do they
profit them by way of satisfaction, which
is, by applying the merits and satisfactions of Christ and his Sainctes vnto
them by Indulgences : for that they being

ing vnited by Charity to the holy church
before their departure, merited and de-
serued so much by that vnion, that the
Suffrages of the said Church, might be
applyed vnto them now deceased.

Sot . 4 . sent . dist . 1 2 . q . 2 . art . 3 .
Bel . cap . 14 . de Indul .

The 11. condition.

Of the cause of Indulgences.

Indulgences ought not to be, nor are
not graunted, but for mere spiritual
causes, or at the least wise for temporal causes annexed vnto spiritual :
and in this case, without iust cause, the
pope him self can not dispense, for that
he is not Lord or maister of this spiritual treasure of the Church, but the distri-
buter onely, which distribution, he can
not make, without a iust and lawful spiritual cause as is aforesaid.

S . Tho . 4 . sent . dist 2 0 . q . 1 . art . vlt .
Io . Vig . de sac . ord. ver . 2 2 .
Bel . ca . 1 2 . de Indul .
Tab . Indul . parag . 8 .

The

Of the vtility and fruite of Indulgences.

THe vtility and fruit that is reaped by Indulgences, is of no light rekoning, or smale accompt : for besides the merit that is gotten by deuout receauing them, not onely increase of grace in this world is thereunto annexed, but also a greater degree of glory in the world to come.

Bel .ca . 10 . de Indul .
& com . Theol . op .

A FVRTHER DECLARA-
tion concerning the matter of Indulgences,
together with a breife explication of the
Stations, Iubilies, and other pardons,
worthy to be considered & knowne
of such as are desireous to ob-
taine the fruit thereof.

What a Station is, and who was the
first instituter and author thereof.

Paragr. 1.

IT is to be vnderstoode, that Stations are none other thinges, then diuers perpetual graces and Indulgences, graunted by the popes of Rome (who are the onely true disposers and distributers of that treasure) to certaine Churches within and without the City of Rome.

They are called Stations, of the etymology of the latin word *Statio*, asmuch to say, as a Port, Hauen, or Roade, wher the shippes or vessels of the Sea, may remaine secure from the tempestuous dangers thereof. Whereupon Indulgences, **vnto**

vnto the which we haue recourse for the auoyding of paines & punishmentes due for our sinnes, and obtayning mercy of our B. Sauiour, who is our onely and secure refuge, are ordinarily called Stations

They may in like manner be called Stations, because the said Indulgences be ratified and perpetually established in the aforesaid particuler and famous Churches of Rome.

S. Gregory the great, our Apostle of England, was the first that ordained and appointed them in certaine Churches of the said City, aswel in the Aduent and Lent, as in other times of the yeare, the which do continue to this present day, as in the Roman Missal and elf-where is to be seene.

Paul . de indul . l . 2 . ca . 1 .
Io . Eck . de Indul .
Io . Vig . de Indul .
S . Anton . p . p . de Indul . parag . 8 .
Petr . Sot . de Indul .
Alphon . de Cast . de Indul .
Concil Later .
Concil . Vien .

Concil

Concil . Trid .ſeſ. 25 . decr .de .Indul .

*Of the diſpoſition and intention which is re-
quiſite, for the gayning of pardons &
Indulgences.*

Paragr . 2 .

For obtayning the pardons and Indulgences which are graunted at
the Stations, it is to be vnderſtood
that he which wil get the ſame, muſt haue
a diſpoſitió to fulfil that which is required in the Bul of the graunt of the ſaid
Indulgence, which commonly is publi-
ſhed certaine daies before : and that he
pray for ſuch thinges as are ſpecified in
the ſaid Bul, or at leaſt wiſe direct his intention in praier to the intention of the
geuer of thoſe Indulgences : and thereby ſhal he truly receaue and reape that
ſpiritual treaſure , which the diſtributer
hath appointed to be beſtowed on ſuch
as ſhal performe the ſame .

What is a Iubily.

The

The 3. Paragraph.

THe Iubily which now the Catholike Church folemnizeth, is none other thing then a general and ful abfolution and remiffion of al the punifhmentes due for finne (after the guilt of the fame be facramentally forge-uen) for the which we are to make fatiffaction, either in this life or in purgato-ry. For which general remiffion and increafe of Grace, it is great reafon that euery one make feaft & Iubily feeing that no man can receaue greater ioy in this life, then the forgeueneffe of his finnes, and that of a feruant to the deuil which he was before, is now hereby become the child of god, and of being debter of fuch punifhments, is by this made free & difcharged of them al.

Of the name, Antiquity, & Celebra-tion of the Iubily.

Paragraph. 4.

THe name of Iubily is deriued from the hebrew word Iobel, which fignifieth the yeare of re-

miſſion. And it is one of the moſt auncient traditions in the catholike Church for
that it was figured in the Iubily of the old
Teſtament, which was accuſtomed to be
celebrated among the Iewes, from 50.
yeares to 50. In which yeare of Iubily,
al debtors were forgeuen : al landes &
poſſeſſions ſould, were reſtored vnto the
former owners : al ſeruants and ſlaues,
were deliuered out of boundage &c.

The Iubily of the Iewes, was but a
tipe or figure of this amongſt vs Chriſtians, by which, through the merits of
Chriſt, men obtaine perfect remiſſion of
their ſinnes, freedome from the ſeruitude
of the deuil, the fruit of al good workes,
and the poſſeſſion of heauen. Wherfore
the ſaid Iubily haith not onely al the ſaid
priuiledges that other plenary Indulgences haue, but the popes alſo are wont at
this time, to graunt authority to approued preiſts, to abſolue from al reſerued
excommunications, & enormous crimes
whatſoeuer (being truly penitent, and
contrite) to the end that the faithful may
be aptly diſpoſed to receaue ſo great a be
neſite.

And

And although the custom of the church was wont to celebrate the Iubily from a 100 . yeare to a 100 . to auoid suspition for simbolizing therein with the Iewish sinagoge , and especially for the mistery contained in the *Scripture* of the hūdreth fruit, as pope Bonifacius declareth, Anno 1294 . Yet forasmuch as the life of man is short, & vncertaine to attaine vnto that number of yeares, Clement the 6 . ordained, that it should be celebrated from 50 . to 50 .

And againe, that al Christians might enioy the fruit hereof, Paulus the 2 . appointed it from 25 . yeare to 25 . as now it is obserued . Notwithstanding, in vrgent necessities of the catholike Church, out of the aforesaid designed times (as for example in time of warres, plagues, or other calamities) the popes are wont to open the same treasure , to thende that al faithful christians wel disposed, may be made partakers of so great a benesite .

S. Anton . p . p . tit . 10 . ca . 5 . para . 7 .
Verat . . de Indul .
Paul . de Indul ca . 1 . li . 1 .
Bel . ca . 1 . de Indul . & Iubil .

What

*What is ment by a Quarantene, & remission
of a third or fourth part of sinne.*

Paragraph 5.

Ftentimes this Clause is founde
in the Bul or promulgation of
Indulgences, *Concedimus tot annos, & totidem quadragenos &c.*
We graunt so many yeares of Indulgence
and so many quarantenes &c. which many vnderstand not. For explication wher
of, it is to be vnderstood, that a quarantene, is as much as 40 daies onely of Indulgence, & not of monethes or yeares,
that is to say, a remission of the punishments for sinnes, which shoulde haue
bene otherwise done for 40 daies. As
for example, when it is said, there are
graunted ten yeares of Indulgence, & as
many quarantenes, it is asmuch to say
as ten yeares, and ten times 40. daies.

Moreouer when in any Bul it is said,
*Concedimus remissionem tertiæ, vel quartæ
partis peccatorum &c.* We graunt remission of the third or fourth parte of
sinnes &c: it is to be vnderstoode of the
                                        remis

fion of the punifhmentes or paines due to the third o. fourth part of our finnes, which ought otherwife to haue beene done either in this life, or in the next in purgatory.

Sot . 4 . fent . diſt . 21 . q . 2 . art .1 .

How the great numbers of yeares of Indul-gences are to be vnderſtoode.

Paragraph 6.

WHen there fhal be founde in any Bul, or graunt of Indul-gences, any great number of yeares, as for example, in doing fuch or fuch thinges, you fhal gaine ten or twen-ty thoufand yeares, or fome grea'er num-ber of Indulgences : it is to be noted, that thefe yeares are vnderſtoode accor-ding to the number of the yeares of this life, proportionably to the penance or punifhments enioyned for finnes by the facred canons. And although the world fhould not laft fo longe, yet notwith-ſtanding intenfiuely the paine in purgato ry may be fo fharpe & extreme in one hour, yea in a minute, that it may be e-

C 5   qual

qual to the extension of many yeares.
As for example, in the last day the soules
of them that shal arise, and were but lately deceased, shal suffer as much paine
intensiuely in so short a time, as extensiue
ly they should haue had to suffer in ten,
or twenty thousande yeares, if both the
world and purgatory should haue so long
endured.

S. Anton . p . p . tit . 10 . para . 3 .
Tabiena verb . Indul . para . 14 .

Of the act it self which is required for the
gaining of Indulgences.

Paragraph 7.

WHen it is at any time expressly
set downe, in the graunt of
Indulgences without limita-
tion, that he which shal gaine the said
Indulgences, shal actually do such, and
such thinges : then in that case, those who
are sick and impotent, although their wil
be neuer so good to performe that which
is prescribed, yet shal they not gaine the
said Indulgences, because the wil onely
sufficeth not for obtaining the same, but
the

the effect withal is required. But if it
be specified, that in steed of the former
workes, such as be impotent, shal do som
other deedes of piety, then in doing the
same, they shal gaine the said Indulgences aswel and as amply as shal the other.

But if it be not specified, the although
his good wil shal not help him to gaine
the Indulgence, yet neuerthelesse it shal
help him both to the increase of grace &
merit in this life, and also of glory in the
life to come.

Armil . indul . para . 5 .
Tabien . indul . para . 16 . & 18 .
S . Anton . p . p . tit . 10 . ca . 7 . de indul.
parag . 2 .
Sot . 4 . sent . dist 21 . q . 2 . art . 3 .
Sum . confes . ls . 3 . tit . 34 . q . 187 .
Siluest . indul . para . 19 .

Whether he that cometh far of, obtaine grea-
ter indulgences, or he that is at home .

Paragraph 8.

One that cometh from a far country to any place, where the said
Indul

Indulgences are, to gaine the same, shal not obtaine any more or greater, then he that dwelleth neare at hande: because Indulgences are not measured according to the paynes or trauel that is taken, but accordīg to the wil of him that graūteth them. Yet neuerthelesse he that taketh such paines and labour to obtaine the pardons, shal merit more, & receiue more grace therein, if withal he be in like and equal degree of grace and charity with the other nearer home. For otherwise one that is at home, hauing greater charity, may merit much more, then an other far of with lesse charity, although in the external worke he take the greater paines and labour, for so much as the merit is measured principally, according to the greatnesse of the charity.

S . Tho . 4 . sent . dist 31 . art . vlt . quodl .
1.

S . Bonau . ibid.
Vig . de sac . ord . vers . 22 .
Tab . indul . parag . 2 .

What almes are required to be geuen, for the gayning of indulgences .

       Parag

Paragraph. 9.

Hen any deterininate and set Almes are specified in the Bul to be distributed for gaining of the Indulgence, as for example, a groate, six pence, or more, or less : then it behoueth for the gayning thereof, to geue the almes as it is appointed,

But if the Bul do indeterminately say that for to gaine such Indulgence, almes shal be geuen, and no somme specified : then he that geueth neuer so lite (geuing it in charity by way of almes) doth obtaine the pardon.

Note also that the said almes, may be bestowed vpon what Church, poore body, or other pious vse, or necessity, any man wil choose, when it is not specified to whom the same is to be geuen.

But it is good for euery man, to geue according to his ability ; the riche man, the gift of a rich man ; the poore man, the gift of a poore man ; and the Scripture saith, that he that haith much, shal geue much, and he that haith litle, shall geue litle.

S. Tho. 4. sent. dist. 21. art. vlt. quodl.

1.
S . Bonau . ibid .
Sil . indulg . para .21

Whether a pardon may be gayned more then
once at one tyme .

Paragraph. 10

IF the wordes of the Bul do prescribe
Indulgences to endure for a day, two,
eight, or any other number, and that
he which wil gaine the same, must doe it
within the space of the prefixed time,
without specifying how often : then can
the said pardon be gotten but once onely, although a mã performe al the thinges
prescribed oftner . But when the words
toties, quoties, (how oft soeuer) shal be
found therein : then so often as a man
shal do those thinges commanded by the
Bul, so often shal he obtaine the foresaid
Indulgences .

Pet . Sot . de indul . l . 3 .
Sot . 4 . sent . dist . 21 . q . 1 .
Silu . indul . parag . 19 . 21 . & 22 .

What preparation a man ought to make for
the

Paragraph. 11.

HE that purpofeth to gaine a Iubilie or Indulgence, ought prefently to refolue to purge his foule
of al vncleaneffe, I meane of al mortal
finne, and to procure that he may be in
gods grace and fauour : and fincerely and
deuoutly to performe, the ordinances &
pious workes which are impofed · And
although, after diliget preparation made
for his confeffion, he fhould forgeat a
mortal finne, yet is he abfolued thereof,
and obtaineth grace by that Sacrament,
to gayne the faid Iubily or Indulgence :
becaufe finnes forgotten, are not refer-
ued, when fuffici nt diligence is vfed ther
in, yet if after he remember the faid finne,
he is bound to confeffe the fame.

And note that when any Iubily or Indulgence is graunted, and that fuch and
fuch thinges are to be done for the obtaining thereof, as to faft three certaine
daies, to vifit fome holy places, to pray
for the Pope, and for the conuerfion of
infidels and heritikes, to geue almes, to
confeffe

confeſſe, communicate, and the like : it
ſhal be good, firſt to make his confeſſiõ
that therby being in the fauour of god,
he do the ſaid faſtings, almes, & other
good workes in ſtate of grace, and then
ſhal God as vnto his friend, much the ſo-
ner graunt him the pardon which he de-
ſireth. But eſpecially at the leaſt, that
he haue true and hearty contrition for
his ſinnes when he beginneth the aforeſaid works of piety : and that in any
caſe, we preſume not vpon the wordes
of the Indulgence, more then they import and ſignify.

S. Anton . p .p . tit · 10 . ca . 30 .
Pet . palud . 4 . ſent .
Tab . indul . para . 23 .

Whether a man being in deadly ſinne, be ca-
pable of Indulgences or no .

Paragraph · 12 .

There is great difference to ſay,
that one haith committed mortal ſinne, & that one is in mortal ſinne. For he that hauing ſinned mortally

tally, and doth repent him thereof, with
contrition, & ful purpose to confesse the
same, at conuenient time appointed by
the Church : it can not be said that he is
in mortal sinne. But he that hauing sin-
ned mortally, and doth not repent him,
but rather goeth forward therein : he is
said to be in mortal sinne. Whereupon
the first is capable of Indulgences, but
not the second.

And although the second being in deadly sinne, doing those thinges which are
appointed by the Bul for gayning of Indulgences, obtaineth them not : yet neuerthelesse our Lord of his infinite loue
and charity, may geue him in recompēce
of this and of other good workes, some
temporal blessing, and also a disposition
to receaue grace gratificant, that is to
say, grace that may make him grateful.

Elis . de Indul . art . 8 .

Tab . de Indul . para . 30 .

Whether the Pope can geue any man a par-
don for deadly sinne, without Sacra-
mental Confession .

Paragraph . 13 .

IT is anſweared, he can not .

For note that we attribute farre more to the power of the meaneſt Preiſt that euer was in the Sacrament of Confeſſion, then we do to any Pope or Patriarch in the world , or to al the Buls, Pardons, or Indulgences whatſoeuer out of the ſame . The reaſon is, for that the effecte of the remiſſion of ſinnes , procedeth from Chriſt more aboundantly , in the grace of the Sacraments which be miniſtred by the Preiſt by vertue of his preiſthood, then it doth by the higheſt iuriſdiction of any man out of the Sacraments . Wherefore it is a notorious ſlander to ſay as many do, that for money you may haue a pardon for ſinne without any penance or confeſſion at al : for the Sacrament of penance haith euer bene of ſuch neceſſity ſince Chriſtes inſtitution thereof for the taking away of mortall ſinne, that no man could euer worke the ſame abſolutly, without the vſe thereof except our Sauiour Chriſt him ſelf.

S . Tho . in multis locis .

Et com

Of penance impofed for finnes, and the times
appointed for the fame.

Paragraph. 14.

THe penance that ought to be
done for finnes, afwel for the offence it felf, as for the quantity
thereof, is, *de iure diuino*, to wit, of Diuine law or ordinance, which the holy
Scripture witnesseth when it faith, *Iux-*
ta menfuram delicti, erit & plagarum mo-
dus. According to the quantity of the
offence, fhal the maner of punifhment be:
notwithftanding that the impofing therof, and the time wherein the faid penance
is to be done, is, *de iure pofitiuo*, of pofi-
tiue law, that is to fay, it appertaineth to
the holy Church, aud Canons thereof :
who in auncient times, vfed to impofe
more feuere and rigorous penance for
mortal finnes, then now a daies is obferued, to wit, for euery mortal finne feauen yeares penance.

And note that penance is to be geuen
greater or leffer, agreable to the enor-
mity of the finne committed. For ac-

D 2　　　　cording

cording to Diuines, the manner of im-
poſing ſuch penances, of ſeauen yeares,
for mortal ſinnes, the Church tooke from
the vſe which is found in the holy Scripture where it is mētioned, that our Lord
God in the puniſhing of ſinnes, commonly did vſe the aforeſaid number of ſeauen.

As when he deliuered the children of
Iſrael for 7 yeares into the handes of the
Madianites. And made Nabugodono-
zor to eate graſſe for 7 . yeares . Elizeus
likewiſe commaunded Naaman to be
waſhed 7. times in the flood of Iordan .
And the ſiſter of Moiſes ſtoode 7. daies
ſeperated from the company and ſocie-
ty of others, and the like .

S . Tho . 4 . ſent . diſt . 17 .
Sot . 4 . ſent . diſt . 21 . q . 2 . art . 1 .
Cap . hoc ipſum 33 . q . 2 .
Et Cap . menſuram de panitent . diſt . 1 .
q . 1 . art . 3 .

Of the profit that ariſeth by ſatisfaction for
ſinnes in this life.

Paragraph . 15.

First

Irſt the penitent is to vnderſtand , that ſatisfaction for ſinnes, muſt needes be done either in this life , or in the next : which being ſo , it ſhal greatly auaile him to ſatisfie for the ſame in doing the penance that is enioyned him , during the time whileſt yet he liueth.

For one that in this life is in the fauour and grace of god, and performirg the werkes of ſatisfaction : ſhal beſides the ſaid ſatisfaction, merit alſo , which is not ſo with thoſe in the other life in purgatory, for then they are in ſtate onely to ſatisfie, and not to merit, for as much as merit belongeth to them which are labonrers , and not to thoſe that can labour no longer, and are come to their iourneis ende : of whom the Scripture ſaith . *Amodò iam dicit ſpiritus, vt requieſcant a laboribus ſuis* . From henceforth now ſaith the ſpirit, they ſhal reſt from their laboures . Neither ſhal theſe penalties ceaſe, vntil the ſoule be wholly purged from al vncleanceſſe .

S . Tho . quodl . 2 . art . vlt .
Eliſ . de indul . art . 4 .

D 3 *Armilla*

Armilla de indul . para . 8 .

Pet . Sot . li . 1 .

Viguer . de Thesaur . Eccl. vers . 20 ,

Whether penance imposed by the Confessor, may be left vndone to gaine Indulgences .

Paragraph . 16 .

Hen the penance imposed by the Confessor, is either lesse or as much as is the Indulgence that is graunted : in this case the penitent, if he be truly contrite, gaining such Indulgences, is not bound vnder paine of deadly sinne, to performe the aforesaid penance.

But because no man is certaine of his being in the grace of God or of his good disposition when he receaueth the Indulgences : therefore euery one ought to do his penance imposed, notwithstanding the gaining of the said Indulgences. And although he were certaine of his wel disposing, yet may he not conueniently leaue the same vndone ; for in accomplishing that, it auaileth him not onely to satisfaction, but also to merit .

Besides

Besides, the holy Church geueth the said
Iudulgences, as spurres to prick vs forward in wel doing, and therefore a man
ought not to deceaue him self in being
vnwilling to performe his penance, for
Charity can not be idle : And many
times such as do neg'ect these satisfactory Exercises, do grow so coulde, that
soone after they also loose Charity.

S . Tho . 4 . sent . dist . 20 . art . 4 .
Silu . indul . parag . 13 .
Tab . iudul . parag . 13 .
Sum . confes . li . 3 . tit . 34 . q . 18 . &
190.

How the number of Indu'gences, de pænitentiis iniunctis, *are to be vnderstoode.*

Paragraph 17.

IF in any Bul or other Graunt, there
be mention made of any number of
yeares of Indulgences *de pænitentiis
miunctis,* to wit of inioyned penances :
it is to be vnderstoode, not onely of
such penance as is inioyned by the Confessor, and not performed by the peni‑
tent, but also of such as the Confessor

haith omitted to inioyne, & such as are taxed by the Canons of the Church, or otherwise determined by Gods diuine iustice.

For which cause cõmonly the Bul spea-keth in the plural number, to wit, *De pænitentiis iniurctis*, of inioyned penan-ces, and not, *De pænitentia iniuncta*, of an inioyned penance. Thereby to sig-nify, that in those wordes, the former 3. conditions are comprehended, that is to say, the penance inioyned by the Confessor, that which is assigned by the Canons, and the penance which is or-deined by God him selfe.

S. Tho. 4. sent. dist. 20. q. 1. art. 3. quodl. 2.
Elis. de indul. li. 2. ca. 5.
Vig. d. valore indul. parag. 21.
Sot. 4. sent. dist. 21. q. 4. art. 5.
Armil. indul. parag. 16.

Whether the Pope can graunt Indulgences to the dead.

Paragraph. 18.

Certaine

CErtaine it is amongst Catholick Doctors, that the Popes holinesse may graunt Indulgences, aswel to the dead, as to the liuing, and in so doing, he may absolue them from their paine. But they are geuen one way to the dead, and an other way to the liuing.

For vnto the liuing Indulgence is graunted by way of absolution, as being immediatly subiect to the Pope : but vnto the dead it is geuen by way of Suffrage : in so much as the Pope dispensing the spiritual treasures of the Church, for the debt of punishments which are due for sinnes, satisfieth our Lord therewith, in such wise as he accepteth the same.

And this may be declared by a familiar example, to wit, if the Pope of his good fauour and charity, would deliuer al those that are imprisoned in the City of Rome for debtes, paying for them so much as euery one oweth to his creditors : he might with al iust reason, and wirthout any further adoe, lawfully discharge out of prison, those which are his owne subiects hauing absolute iurisdiction ouer them. But if he would deli-

D 5 uer

uer others imprisoned for the like debt, (for example) that are subiect to an other absolute prince of Italy : iuridically he could not do it. But by disbursing the money, and paying their said debts, he might intreate the prince in their behalfe, to take the money, and release the debtors out of prison : and in that case it may be said, that the Pope by way of inrreaty and praier, deliuered the prisoners, although it were in the Princes power to accept the same or noe. Euen so it falleth out in this dispensation of the treasure of Indulgences, which is as it were money geuen vs by the Pope, to satisfy the debts we owe vnto God for our sinnes (and must be paid before we can be released) and bestowed vpon vs that are liuing, and immediatly subiect to his holines, and thereby are iuridically absolued thereof. But for the dead, seeing he payeth for them also : he is to intreate for them by way of Suffrage, trusting in the mercy and goodnesse of God, who is much more ready to graunt, then we are to demaund the same.

   S. Tho. 4. sens. dist. 22.

Sot. ibidem q . 2 . art . 3 .
Vig . de sae . ord . verf . 14 .

Of the infinite valew of Indulgences.
Paragraph. 19.

FOr three caufes efpecially are Indulgences faid to be of infinite valew . The firft is , in refpect of our
Lord and Sauiour him felf : and this is called the merit and fatisfaction of Chrift,
in that he did not onely merit, but alfo
fatisfy for al finnes. The fecond is in refpect of Chriftes holy Sainctes : and this
is the paines, laboures, fufferings, & o-
ther penalties which they indured in this
world , being of much more valew, then
their finnes required fatisfaction. The
third is in refpect of the Church : & in
this are comprehended al pious & charitable workes, both fpiritual and temporal, which haue bene wrought by her
meanes, the valew whereof remaineth
at her difpofition, to diftribute vpon iuft
caufes , to fuch as haue neede thereof.

Wherefore al this treafure and fpiritu
al dowrie , wherewith Chrifte his holy
Spoufe is fo infinitely enriched, remaineth

neth to be lent freely vnto sinners, wherby to satisfy and pay the ransome and
debtes which they owe for their sinnes &
offences.

S. Anton. p. p. tit 10. *para.* 1. *de ind.*

*That he which gayneth a plenary Indulgence
as he ought, if presently he dye, he
goeth to heauen.*

Paragraph. 20.

A man, hauing done so much as is
commaunded for the gayning of
a plenary Indulgence, if at that
instant (being truly contrite for al his
sinnes) he should chance to dye, and hauing, to his power, performed al that
which a good christian was bound to do:
he may be assured to go to eternal glory,
without passing through the fire of purgatory. But when his Confessor in that
point of death, haith not graunted him
a plenary Indulgence, or when after such
a graunt and gayne thereof, he haith
committed a venial sinne or a mortal, of
which he is confessed, but haith not done
satisfaction for the same: he can not assure him self from being exempted from
some

fome punifhment. And therefore it is good and meritorious to helpe the foule of the departed, by way of praier and fuffrage prefently afrer his departure out of this life, which God graunt we may all doe to his honour and glory.   Amen.

S . Anton .p . p . tit . 10 .de indul . ca . 3 .
Sum . confef . l . 3 . tit . 34 . q . 182 .
Hoftien . 6 .
Sil . parag . 33 . Indul . &c .

OF THE STATIONS
AT ROME.

There haith bene at Rome, a continual holy custome of the people, for these thousande yeares at the least, at diuers times solemnly to visit certaine principal Churches, therein to offer vp their deuotions for them selues, and the whole Church of God.

These solemne meetings, are commoly called Stations : and by diuers Popes haue bene graunted to those Churches, either specially vpon the Station daies, or generally al the yeare, verie large Indulgences.

I wil here note the dayes and places of the said Stations. The Indulgences in euery of these Churches, are neuer lesse then of ten thousande yeares. And because often times there is a plenary Indulgence, and the deliuery of a soule out of purgatory : I will heare set downe, when either of these so great graces may be obtained : which wil also be profitable for those which by halowed graynes wil gayne the Stations.

The

The rymes of the Stations .

THe firſt Sonday in Aduent , at
S . Maria Maior.
    The 2 . Sonday, at S . Croſſe,
in Ieruſalem , a plenary .
The third Sonday, at S . Peter.
    Wedneſday in the Imber weeke, at S .
Maria Maior .
    Friday in the Imber weeke, at SS . A-
poſtoli, a plenary .
    Saturday, at S . Peter.
The fourth Sonday, at SS . Ap . a plenary .
    Chriſtmaſſe eue , at S . Maria Maior .
In the night folowing, at the Chapel of
    the Cribbe in the ſame Church, a ple-
nary .
    Chriſtmaſſe day in the morning, at S .
Anaſtaſia, a plenary .
    At the thirde Maſſe on Chriſtmaſſe
day, at S . Maria Maior .
    On S. Stephens day, at S . Stephens,
a plenary .
    S . Iohns day, at S . Maria Maior.
                            Innocents

Innocents day, at S. Paules, a plenary.

New yeares day, at S. *Maria* trans Tiberim, a plenary.

Twelfth day, at S. Peter, a plenary.

The Sonday of Septuagessima, at S. Laurence *extra muros*, a soule out of purgatory.

The Sonday of Sexagessima, at Sainct Paule.

The Sonday of Quinquagessima, at S. Peter.

Ash Wednesday, at S. Sabina, a plenary.

Thursday, at S. George.
Fryday, at SS. Iohn and Paule.

Saturday, at S. Triphon, a plenary. The first Sonday in Lent, at S. Iohn Lateran, a plenary, & infinite Indulgences.

Monday, at S. Peter in vinculis, a plenary.

Tewsday, at S. Anastasia, a plenary, and a soule out of purgatory.

Wednesday, at S. Maria Maior.
Thursday, at S. Laurence in Pal: perna, a plenary.

Fryday, at SS. Apost. a plenary.
                              Saturday

Saturday, at S . Peter, a plenary .

The second Sonday in Lent, at S . Maria in Nauicella .

Monday, at S . Clement .

Tewsday. at S . Balbina .

Wednesday, at S . Cecily .

Thursday, at S . Maria *trans Tiberim.*

Friday, at S . Vitalis .

Saturday, at S . Peter and Mercelline : plenary .

The 3 . Sonday in Lent, at Sainct Laurence *extra muros* : a soule out of purgatory .

Monday, at S . Marke .

Tewsday, at S . Potentiana .

Wednesday, at S . Sixtus .

Thursday, at SS . Cosma and Damianus .

Friday, at S . Laurence in Lucina .

Saturday, at S . Susan : a plenary .

The fourth Sonday in Lent, at S . Crosse : a plenary, & a soule out of purgatory .

Monday, at SS . quatuor Coronati .

Tewsday, at S . Laurence in Damaso .

Wednesday, at S . Paule .

Thursday, at S . Siluester .

Friday, at S . Eusebius .

E 1   Saturday

Saturday, at S. Nicholas in Carcere, 2 plenary.

The fifth Sonday in Lent, at S. Peter.

Monday, at S. Chrilogone.

Tewsday, at S. Ciriacus.

Wednesday, at S. Marcellus.

Thursday, at S. Apolinaris.

Friday, at S. Stephens, a soule out of purgatory.

Saturday, at S. Iohn, *ante portam latinam*, a soule out of purgatory.

Palme Sonday, at S. Iohn Lateran, a plenary twice.

Monday, at S. Praxedes, a plenary.

Tewsday, at S. Prisca, a plenary.

Wednesday, at S. Maria Maior, a plenary.

Thursday, at S. Iohn Lateran, a plenary twice.

Friday, at S. Crosse, a plenary and many other Indulgences.

Saturday, at S. Iohn Lateran, a plenary.

Easter day, at S. Maria Maior, a plenary.

Monday, at S. Peter, a plenary.

Tewsday, at S. Paule, a plenary.

Wednesday

Wednesday, at S. Laurence, *extra muros*, a soule out of purgatory.

Thursday, at SS. Apostoli, a plenary
Friday, at S. Maria rotunda.

Saturday, at S. Iohn Lateran, a plenary twice.

Low Sonday, at S. Pancratius, a plenary twice.

On S. Marks day, at S. Peter.
Monday in Rogation weeke, at S. Maria Maior.

Tewsday, at S. Iohn Lateran.
Wednesday, at S. Peter.

Ascention day, at S. Peter.
Whitson eue, at S. Iohn Lateran, a plenary.

Whitsonday, at S. Peter, infinite Indulgences, and a Plenary.

Monday, at S. Peter in vinculis, a plenary.

Tewsday, at S. Anastasia.
Wednesday, at S. Maria Maior

Thursday, at S. Laurence *extra muros*, a soule out of purgatory.

Friday, at ss. Apostoli, a plenary.
Saturday, at S. Peter, a soule out of purgatory,

E 2   Wednesday

Wednesday of the Imber weeke in September, at S. *Maria* Maior.

Friday of the same weeke, at ss. Apostoli, a plenary.

Saturday folowing, at s. Peter.

The Stations and their daies, and also the Indulgences thereunto belonging, being knowne : it remaineth likewise to know how these pardons may be gayned, for a precious salue is to smale purpose, except the ingredience, force, and vse thereof be made manifest.

How the Indulgences belonging to the Stations, may be gayned.

The meanes how to obtaine these pardons are diuers, as the people and societies to whom they are graunted are diuers.

When they are graunted to any society, sodality, or confraternity ; for the gayning thereof nomore is required, but vpon the Station dayes to do that which there is appointed, (alwaies prouided,

that

that the doer be in ftate of grace) As for
example . The benefite of thefe Stations
are graunted to the foceity of the Rofary . To any of this body, to gaine thefe
pardons, neither Medal nor Graine is required, but onely on the Station daies,
to vifit fyue Altars (in other Countries)
and at euery one to fay fiue pater noft.
and fiue Aues : and in our owne Country, at one Altar to fay fiue pater nofters
and fiue Aues , fiue times ouer .

The maner how to gaine the Indulgences of
the ftations graunted to our Englifh
Pardon, & to Boromeus Pardon .

More generally are thefe Indulgēces geuē to our coūtry mē by
our Englifh pardon (as in the
fixt graunt thereof may be feene) wher
in to them, for reciting of the Corone
or Rofary, of the feauen pfalmes, or the
Lytanies, for the conuerfion of heritikes
vpon any of the ftation daies in Rome :
are graunted the Indulgences of the ftations, as fully as if they had bene that
day at the ftations perfonally prefent.
Neuertheleffe to the gayning hereof, is

required a Graine, Medal, or Crosse of
our English pardon graunted by Gregory the 13. and now confirmed by Paule
the fifth.

Againe, the benefite of the Stations is
graunted to al those who haue any of
the Corones, Rosaries, Crosses, Medals,
or pictures, hallowed at the instance of
the Duke of Ferare by Paule the fifth, as
appeareth in the 9. graunt thereof: so
that they present them selues before som
Altar or Oratory, & say one pater nost.
and one Aue, in the honour of the blessed Trinity, and shal pray for the extirpation of herisie, and the exaltation of
the Catholik Church, concord and peace
of christian Princes, and the Popes holines. And also in saying one Deprofundis for the departed, they shal gaine the
Indulgence of that station day, either for
them selues, or for the departed, as fully, as if they had visited that Church
wheare the Station is that day.

Furthermore the same Indulgences of
the Station are graunted to those, who
haue any of the Medals, or other halowed thinges of S. Charles Boromeus his
                                    pardon

pardon, in as ful and ample maner as before; so that vpon the said Station daies they say fiue pater nosters, and fiue Aues, before any of the Medals or Images, hauing his Indulgence, in the remembrãce of the precious bloud of our Sauiour Iesu Christ shed for vs in his passion; and this aswel for the departed, as for the liuing. And lastly who shal say one miserere, or one Creede, or *Te deum*, in reuerence of the precious bloud of our Sauiour, or kisse the ground seauen times: shal gaine the Indulgences as fully, as if they had personally performed the stations in Rome that day, as may appeare in the said Indulgence in the number 11. & 12. Thus much touching the Indulgences of the stations.

why

Why so many are desireous to be admitted
into societies , notwithstanding the large
Indulgences graunted to our Country .

Although the Indulgences in Societies , are not so large as els-
wheare : neuerthelesse other benefites and spiritual helps , are by them
obtained, and not ordinary in pardons.
For those who are admitted to any society, are in particular and more eminent
maner, partakers both in life and death,
of al the suffrages, sacrifices, Masses,
praiers, vigils, fastes, disciplines, studies,
recollections, almes deedes, mortifica-
tions, obediences, intercessions, impe-
trations, and al the trauels, paines , laboures , and al other meritorious good
actes , which haue , are , and shal be exercised, and performed, by that order &
society .

This extraordinary and particular participation, is to be estemed as a matter
of great accompt : aud the thinges to be
done, for the gayning of these benefites,
verie smale, and not to be performed vnder

der any bonde of sinne, and if for a time neglected, not any new admittance required, but onely to returne againe to their former Exercise, as is to be seene in the Indulgences of the Rosary, fol. 25.

㊉㊉㊉㊉㊉㊉㊉㊉㊉㊉㊉㊉㊉㊉㊉㊉㊉㊉㊉㊉㊉㊉㊉㊉㊉㊉ ㊉㊉㊉㊉

A CATALOGVE OF

the Indulgences and pardons, graunted vnto those that be of the Socie ty of the Rosary of our B. Lady, with a note of the Institution and vse thereof.

Translated out of the Original copy printed at Rome. Anno. 1605.

THe Rosary or Psalter of the B. Virgin Mary, that is to say, siftene pater nosters, and a hundreth and siftie aues; was instituted and
    E 5   ordained

ordained by the Patriarch S . Dominick
(to extinguish the heresye of the Albi-
genses) instructed by the B . Virgin Mary , and inuented by her assignment, after the maner of the psalter of Dauid ,
the which containeth 150. psalmes , as
the Rosary containeth 15 . Pater nosters
and 150. Aues, for the honour of the
Mother of God .

There be 15 Misteries of our Sauiour
Iesus Christ, and the B . Virgin, presented bearein . For the contemplatiō wherof, at euery one in particular, one pater
noster, and 10. Aues, must be recited, as
shal be declared .

The first fiue Misteries, which are called ioyful, do represent the fiue ioyes of
the B . Virgin . The first, when she was
saluted by the Angel Gabriel ; For the
which ioy, there is appointed one Pater
noster, and ten Aues . The second, when
the B . Virgin wente to visit S . Eliza-
beth ; For the which is appointed one
Pater noster and ten Aues . The third ,
when the B . Virgin Mary was deliuered
of our Sahioure Iesus Christ ; For the
which also is appointed one Pater noster
and

and ten Aues. The fourth ioy was when she presented our Sauiour Iesus in the Temple; For the which is ordained one Pater noster and ten Aues. The fifth ioy was, when the B. Virgin *Mary* did finde her Sonne Iesus in the Temple, in the middest of the Doctors, disputing with them, for the which also is ordained one Pater noster & ten Aues.

The other fiue Misteries are named dolorous, & do containe fiue great greifes or sorowes. The first sorow was, when our Sauiour Iesus Christ, being in his agony, did pray in the garden, & therewith swet drops of bloud and water. The seconde greif was, when he was cruelly whipped at a piller. The third, when he was crowned with thornes. The 4. when he bearing his Crosse to the mount of Caluary, & met his Mother. The 5. when he being crucifyed betwixt two theeues, yelded vp his soule into his Fathers handes: For euery one of which Misteries, are to be said, one Pater noster & ten Aues, as abouesaid.

The last fiue Misteries which are called glorious, do containe fiue glorious

actes

actes. The first, when our Sauiour did rise from death to lyfe. The second when he ascended into heauen. The third whē he sent the holy Ghost vpon his Disciples. The fourth, when the B. Virgin Mary was assumpted into heauen both body and soule. In the fifth is considered the glory of al Sainctes, and how the B. Virgin was crowned by her deare Son and exalted aboue al the queares of Angels : and for euery one of these Misteries are appointed one Pater noster and ten Aues. And after this accompt, the whol Rosary doth containe 15. Pater nosters, & 150 Aues : The which wholie, euery one that is admitted and ascribed into the society of the Rosary, ought to recite once euery weeke.

But yet it is graunted (for to auoide tediousnes) to deuide it into three equal partes ; so that in one day may be said 5. Pater nosters, and 50 Aues, in consideration of the first fiue Misteries : in an other day, the fiue next ; and lastly, in a third, the fiue last, and so performe the whole Rosary euery weeke. And if by negligence or forgetfulnesse, it be forgot :
                                              there

there is noe sinne committed thereby, although the rewarde, or merit, which by the reciting thereof, might haue bene obtained, be lost. But yet in an other weeke, after it be recited, the rewarde may be gayned againe.

If any one be sicke, or for any other lawful cause, can not him self personally recite this Rosary, (so he be ascribed into this Society) he may procure an other to say it for him in his name, and it wil profit him asmuch in the participating of the spiritual rewarde thereof, as if he had recited it himself.

Moreouer it is to be vnderstoode, that this Rosary may be said of any man, for those that are deceased, whose names are enrolled in the booke of this Societye, who are truly partakers of those spiritual giftes, which those that remaine yet aliue do enioy. Lastly it is also graunted, that this Rosary may be said, fitting, standing, walking, or kneling, in any place whatsoeuer.

Indulgences graunted by diuers Popes and
Prelates of the holy Church vnto
this Society.

Pope

Ope Vrbanus the fourth did grant
vnto al those that recite with deuotion, the Aue Maria : thirtie
daies of Indulgence : & as many vnto
those that do cal vpon the name of Iesus.

Iohn the 22. did after confirme & do-
ble the aboue named Indulgences of Vrbanus 4.

Alexander Bishop of Forolinium (a
Citie in Italy called Forly, where *Titus
Liuius* was borne) & Apostolical Legate
a latere, into Germany : did graunt to al
& euery one that recite the Rosary, a
hundreth & twenty daies of Indulgence.

Againe he graunted fourtie daies of Indulgence to euery one that is present in
the Church where this Society is founded whilest that the Anthem or *Salue Regina* after Complin, is song vpon Satur-
dayes and holy daies.

Also he graunted 100 daies of Indulgence vnto euery one so oft as they shal
say fiue Pater nosters & 50 Aues, in the
feast of the Annuntiation, Visitation, Af-
sumption, Natiuity, and Purification of
the B. Virgin Mary, as it appeareth by
Letters dated at Colen which begin, *Et
si gloriosus*

fi gloriofus &c. Anno. 1476.

The moſt reuerend Lord Mathius Guardus, Patriarch of Venice, graunted 120 daies of Indulgence to al thoſe that ſhal ſay the foreſaid Rofary.

Sixtus 4. in his Breue which beginneth *O ues Dominica gregis* Anno 1478. graúted as is aforeſaid, in three feaſtes of the B. Virgin Mary, the Annuntiation, Natiuity, and Aſſumption : ſeauen yeares, & as many quarantenes of enioyned penances.

Alſo in an other Breue, which beginneth, *Ea qua ex fidelium.* Anno 1479. he confirmed & approued this Pſalter or Rofary, and this methode or forme of praying, & graunted for euery Rofary, fiue yeares of Indulgences, & as many quarantenes.

Innocentius 8. graunted vnto the true penitent, & confeſſed brethren reciting the Rofary, 100 yeares, & as many quarantenes, & to thoſe that in the end of the Aue Maria, do name Ieſus, fiue yeares & as many quarantenes, as it appeareth by his Breue *Splendor paternæ* dated at Rome, Anno 1488.

Alexander

Alexander 6 . at Rome Anno 1494. in his Breue which beginneth *Illius qui perfecta Charitas est* , did not onely confirme , but alfo dooble, al the Indulgences graunted by his predeceffors together with many other priuiledges graunted in the faid Breue .

Iulius 2 . at Rome, An . 1503. in his Breue , *Ineffabilia Virginis Mariæ*, did confirme al that was graunted by his Predeceffors .

Leo 10 . at Rome An . 1520 . in his Breue that beginneth *Pastoris æterri*. doth number & confirme the aboue named Indulgences of Alexander the Bifhop of *Forolinium*, & the two Breues of Sixtus 4 . And he faith, that Innocentius 8 . An . 1483 . the third day of October did graunt by word of mouth , to al the abouefaid , that fhal fay the holy Rofary within a weeke, a plenary Indulgēce once in their life . & once at the hour of death . Alfo he addeth , that Raymundus Cardinal of S. *Mariæ noue* . when he was Legate in Germany, did graunt for euery Rofary, 100 daies of Indulgence . And alfo that diuers & many Bifhops

fhops, haue graunted 40. daies of Indulgence for euery Rofary. And he doth approue & confirme al the abouefaid moft
amply. And moreouer he graunteth to
the aboue named brethren being truly
penitent, and confeffed, or haue a full
purpofe to be confeffed, faying three
times the Rofary in one weeke, for euery time, ten yeares, & ten quarantenes
of the enioyned penances.

Adrianus 6. doth graunt, that he
which lying at the point of death, and
fhal hould in his hand a halowed wax
candle of the fociety of the Rofary, and
depart out of this life, fhal obtaine a plenary indulgence of al his finnes, if fo be
that before his death, he haue recyted
once the pfalter or Rofary.

Alfo he that reciteth in the Chapel
of the Rofary, (or in that part of the
Church where an Altar of the Rofary is)
the third part of the Rofary, for euery
day in which he doth this, he fhal obtaine 50. yeares of Indulgence, by the
graunt of the aboue named Adrian 6.
as it appeareth in his Breue which beginneth *Illius qui Dominicum gregem &c*. do-

ted

ted at Rome in the yeare of the Incarnation of Chriſt 1523, the Calends of A-
pril, in the 1. yeare of his popedome.

Clemens the 7. did extend the aboue
named Indulgence vnto al the brethren,
that ſhal recite with deuotion, the ſame
third part of the Roſary in any oratory,
or Church ſituated in what place ſoeuer.

And he graunted alſo many other priuiledges vnto the ſame brethren, as it appeareth in his Breue which beginneth,
Ineffabilia glorioſæ Virginis Mariæ : dated at Bononia in Italy, An. 1529. the
7. yeare of his reigne, the tenth of the
Calendes of April.

The ſame Clement the 7. at Rome,
the 8. day of May, the 11. yeare of his
reigne, in his Breue which beginneth,
Et ſi temporalium cura, doth rehearſe the
aboue named Indulgences of Sixtus 4. &
Leo 10. and he confirmeth them. And
he addeth, that Leo did inſtitute and
graunt vnto the aforeſaid brethren wher
ſoeuer they ſhal be, viſiting fiue altars,
of any Church whatſoeuer, or one or 2.
altars fiue times,, if there be not fiue, al
the Indulgences of the Stations of the
City

City of Rome, if they recite at euery altar, or euery visitation, fine Pater nost,
& as many Aues. This he doth ratify &
confirme: and moreouer he doth graunt
for euery Rosary, two yeares of Indulgence.

Paulus 3. at Rome, An. 1534. in
his Breue which beginneth *Rationi con-
gruit*. doth relate the Indulgences of Sixtus 4. and of Leo 10. together with the
whole Breue aforesaid of Clement the 7.
and doth confirme the same in most ample manner. And in the yeare 1527.
he haith graunted vnto others that shal
say, or cause to be said, (or to them that
heare) a masse of the holy Rosary, the
same Indulgences graunted any way vnto the brethren of the society of the Rosary. Dated in Rome, at S. Markes, 31.
of August, in the yeare aboue said.

Iulius 3. haith confirmed & graunted, by a breue put forth the 24. of August, 1551. al the priuiledges and Indulgences graunted any way to the brethren of the society of the Rosary: the
Breue beginneth in this wise. *Sincere de-
uotionis &c.*

Paulus

Paulus 4. in his Breue that beginneth *Ea Apostolicæ sedis &c*. dated at Rome, the 9. of March 1561. did confirme al the abouesaid priuiledges.

Pius 4. did graunt a plenary Indulgéce to endure for euer, in euery Feaft of our B. Lady, to al faithful Chriftian people being contrite & confeffed, or hauing a purpofe to be confeffed in due time, if they vifit in the feftiual daies of the B. Virgin, the Altar or Chapel of the fame Rofary, in the Church of *S. Maria fupra Mineruam* in the City of Rome. Alfo he haith graunted the Indulgence to the pro ceffion in the fame fociety, by a Breue which beginneth *Dum præclaram*, dated at Rome the day before the Calends of May, the fecond yeare of his reigne.

Pius 5. confirmed al and euery one of the forefaid Graunts, Indulgences, re-miffions, relaxations, Immunities, priui-ledges, & other graces graúted by al o ther Popes, Legates *de latere*, of the fea Apoftolick, & others hauing the fame authority : & alfo he renewed them in the fame maner of force that they were firft graunted in.

Alfo

Also he graunted vnto the same confraternities, or societies & the brethren
thereof, that the brethren deputed for
this purpose, may freely and lawfully
exact & take, al oblations, bequests,
giftes, & such like offered any way, either by willes, legacies, or any other last
Testaments, of what sort, quantity, or
quality soeuer it be, & that they may be-
stow it in pious workes of the said society, without the licence of any person,
yea though it be the ordinary or Bishop
of the place. And that euery one may
be the more ready and prompt to enter
into this society, he haith also graunted
a plenary Indulgence or remission & for-
geuenes of al sinnes, to al those, & euery one thereof, that are receaued into the
society by the aforesaid deputies, at the
first time they be receaued being confessed and communicated, in the Church or
chapel, or at the altar of the said society,
& do recite at the least, the third part of
the Rosary, praying for the peace & trā-
quility of the holy Romane Church.

And vnto those also that at the point
of death, are confessed & do communi-

F 3   cate

cate, a plenary Indulgence.

Also he graunted a plenary Indulgence vnto him that saith the Rosary, being confessed and communicated on the day of the Annuntiation of the B . Virgin.

Also 40 . daies to those that say the Rosary euery day : and also seauen daies so often as they cal vpon, or name, the holy names of Iesus, & Maria.

Also he graunted ten yeares, & as many quarantenes of Indulgence, to those that do communicate, & say one part of the Rosary, in the daies of the Resurrection of our *Sauiour*, & of the Annuntiation & Assumption of the B . Virgin.

Also he graunted the said Indulgences to al brethren that recite at the least the third part of the Rosary on al the rest of the festiuities of our Sauiour Iesus Christ, & the glorious Virgin, comprehended amongst the other misteries of the Rosary.

Also he graunted them to al faithful christians, though they be not of the said society, as also to the brethren if they be present with deuotion at the procession of the said Rosary, the which is on the first day in euery moneth at Euensong.

Also

Alfo he graunted feauen yeares and as many quadragens of enioyned penance, to al the brethren that recite euery weeke the whole Rofary. And he further decreed, that as wel the brethren, as alfo the aboue named; fhal not be molefted in any wife by any man.

Al thofe forefaid thinges are to be fene in three Breues which he graunted together, with many other priuiledges & graces contained therein. *Iniunctum nobis*. 4. of Iuly. 1566. *Inter defiderabilia* 28. of Iune. 1569. *Confueuerunt*. 17. of September. 1569.

The moft reuerend Maifter General of the whole order of Dominicans, did receaue by his Letters dated at Rome, the 3 of March, 1573. al the brethren of the fame fociety, vnto the participation of al the forefaid fpiritual benefites.

Gregory the 13. (hauing intelligéce how that the fame day the Turkifh nauy was miraculoufly taken by the fleete of Pius 5. the Pope, Philip the King of Spaine, & the Venetians, the brethren of this Rofary in a proceffion, did pray vnto the B. Virgin, for the obtayning of

F 4 that

that victory) of his owne accorde, for the perpetual memory of the thing, did commaund, that on the firſt Sonday of October, the feaſt of this victory, vnder the title of the holy Roſary, ſhould be celebrated with his office, as it appeareth by his Breue which beginneth.

Monet apoſtolus &c. An. 1573. as alſo in the proper Churches and Chapels of this holy confraternity (which can not be inſtituted but in the conuents of the Dominicans, or with licence of the general thereof) In which day. al Chriſtians of both ſexe, aſwel brethren, as other, that being truly penitent & confeſſed, viſiting the Church of the bleſſed Virgin Mary of Minerua in Rome, ſhal obtaine a plenary Indulgence & remiſſion of al their ſinnes, as it appeareth by his Breue which beginneth *Exp. vobis*. at the requeſt of Alexandrinus, Protector of the Society of the holy Roſary. Dated at Rome, the firſt day of October, An. 1577

Alſo Gregory the 13. did graunt a ple nary Indulgence vnto thoſe that are preſent at the proceſſion, and viſit the Chapel

pel of the Rosary, the 1. Sonday of euery Moneth, hauing before communica-ted, as by his Breue *Omnibus & singulis*, dated at Rome, the 24. of October, 1577. it appeareth.

The Reuerend Procurator general of the Dominicans, by his Letters dated the 13. of October 1578. did receaue all the brethren of the said society, vnto the participation of al the spiritual benefites of the whole order.

The same Gregory the 13. did graunt 100. daies Indulgence, to al the brethrē that were exercised in any pious worke : & also a plenary Indulgēce to those that on the 3. Sonday of April, & the firſt Sonday of October, do visit the said Cha-pel of the Rosary, as appeareth by his Breue *Cum sicut*, dated at Rome, the 3. of Ianuary, 1579.

Also the same Gregory did graunt a plenary Indulgence, vnto al the brethren of the Rosary, within the Prouince of Rome, that on the 1. Sonday of euery Moneth, do confesse & communicate in the said prouincial churches. The same he graunteth vnto the sick that can not

F 5   come

come vnto the Church, so that being cō-
municated, they recite deuoutly the seauen psalmes, or the Rosary, or Corone,
before some holy Image or picture, *Ad
augendam deuotionem vestram*. Dated at
Rome the 29 of August. 1579.

The same Indulgence he graunted for
10 yeares to those that visit the Chapel
of the Rosary in the Church of the blessed Virgin Mary in Minerua, on the day
of the Translation of the holy Image,
which was the 6. of December, 1579.
so that they be confessed & communicated. *Cum sicut accepimus*. Dated at Rome
the 6. of Nouember, 1579.

The same Gregory the thirtenth, in
his Breue which beginneth. *Pastoris æ-
terni, qui non vult mortem &c.* amongst
those wordes he saith in this wise· *Omnibus & singulis vtriusq̃ sexus confratribus
&c.* To al & euery one of both sortes of
brethren, of the society of the Rosary,
remayning in any place, being truly penitent, confessed, & communicated, that
visit the Chapel of the Rosary, on those
daies. when the Feasts of the misteries
of the Rosary are celebrated : & also are
present

present at the procession which is accustomed to be made the first Sonday of euery Moneth at Euensong : we do graunt & geue by Apostolical authority, with the tenour of these presents, a plenary Indulgence of al their sinnes : & also al & euery Indulgence & remission of sinnes graunted to any confraternities of the same Rosary, either in particuler or general, or hereafter to be geuen : & thereby we do communicate & declare, that they are comunicated vnto al other confraternities of the same Rosary wheresoeuer they be . Dated at Rome , the 8 · of May . 1581 .

Also he graunted the same Indulgence as aboue, to the confessed, & communicated, which either by reason of sicknes, or hindred by some other lawful impediment, can not be present at the procession, so that they recite the Rosary . *Ad futuram rei memoriam cupientes* . Dated at Rome, the 24. of September 1583 .

Sixtus the 5 . confirmed al the aboue named Indulgences, and withal graunted the same Indulgences that are graunted vnto those that be present at the procession

ſeſſion which is on the firſt Sonday of e-
uery Month, vnto trauelers, mariners, &
ſeruants, if they recite the whole Roſary,
& vnto the ſick & ſuch as be otherwiſe
lawfully hindered, if they recite the third
part of the Roſary, together with a purpoſe to confeſſe their ſinnes, & communicate at accuſtomed times, as alſo vnto
thoſe that viſit the Chapel of the Roſary, on thoſe daies when the Feaſtes of the
miſteries thereof are celebrated, as it appeareth in his Breue dated the 30 of Ianuary, 1586. which beginneth, *Dum ineffabilia.*

Whether Indulgences may be obtayned , except the gayners thereof, directly and expreſly performe the thinges commaunded , and for the intention and ende commaũded : And whether an actual intention be required iueuery Indulgence for gayning thereof.

INdulgences are of two ſortes at the leaſt . One ſorte bindeth and commaundeth, not onely the action of the gayners, but alſo their intention .

As where the geuer of the Indulgence ſaith, whoſoeuer ſhal recite the Corone, Roſary, 7 pſalmes, or Lytanies &c . for the exaltation of the Church, or for the Popes holineſſe, extirpation of hereſy , or conuerſion of our Country, &c . ſhal gaine ſuch Indulgences. In theſe and others of like nature, both the performáce of the thing commaunded, and alſo the intention & end of the gainer, is neceſſarily required, as is ſaid before in the 7 . Condition of this Treatiſe, and alſo in the 7 . paragraph .

In an other ſort of Indulgences, only the

ly the performance of the thing commaū-
ded, is necessary for the gayning thereof,
but not the intention of the doer, to do
it for this or that end, as is to be seene
in the pardons graunted to the reciters
of the office or praiers contayned in the
new reformed Breuiaries, or Primars:
wherin Indulgences are geuen to al those
who say the office of our B . Lady, the
office of the dead, 7 . psalmes, or Lytanies, or other praiers therin contained ,
& their intention not any way bound to
this or that end , as there is to be seene ;
& also in the first pardon of Boromeus.

And againe, it is manifest by our English pardons & others, wherein the intention of the doer is not any way bound
for this or that end, as in the fourth number of our English Indulgence is manifest where it is said . Whosoeuer saih or
heareth Masse deuoutly, maketh or heareth a sermon, examineth their conscience, reconcileth the contentious, induceth to good life, or reduceth from vice,
with many other such like : gaine all the
Indulgences belonging to the Churches
of our B . Lady of Loretto, & of S . Mary Ma

ry Maior, & S . Iohn Lateran, & many
other, as appeareth in oui Englifh pardon, number 4 . 5 . 7 . 10 . 12 . 14 . and
in Boromeus 2 . 3 . 4 . 7 . 16 . 19 . &
the like in Ferars pardon, & elfwhere .
Wherein is manifeft that al thofe, who
haue a graine, Medale, Croffe, Image,
or picture of fuch pardons vpon them, &
they in the ftate of grace : their intention in faying fuch praiers , or performing
fuch actions, is no way bound either by
promife, vow, penance, or any other ex-
clufiue intention or application : but by
thefe their ordinary deuotions, good &
meritorious actions, they gaine the a-
forefaid pardons .

Neuerthelefe, for the more fatisfaction in this kind , and the better to gaine
both fortes of Indulgences , & alfo to
make our actions & deuotions more acceptable in the fight of God, more meritorious to our felues, & the more fatif-
factory both to our felues & others ; it
is behoueful, that euery morning before
our other deuotions, or fomtimes in the
weke, or at the leaft fome times, to make
this commendation or praier following,
or fome

or some such like virtual intention and
commendation of our praiers & actions .

A Commendation & Praier for the obtay-
ning of Indulgences, & to make our deuoti-
ons & other actions , more acceptable in
Gods sight, more meritorious to our
selues, and more beneficial vnto
others .

IN these my deuotions & other mine
actions, (good Lord) I commende,
remember, & pray, for the exaltati -
on of the catholick Church, the propa -
gation of the catholick Faith, the extir -
pation of heresy, & for al the necessities
of Gods Church . For the protection &
direction of the Popes holines, and the
whole christian world . For the concord
& vnion of the clergy, and al christian
Princes, with al other people . For the
preseruation of the iust , & iustification of
sinners . For the conuersion of England
Scotlande, & Irelande . For the conuersion of Iewes, Turkes, & Pagans, & al
that be out of the church of Christ . For
mercy & grace to al sortes of people, as
shal seeme good , o Lorde, to thy diuine
                                    Maiestie

Maieftie. I commend vnto thee (mofte
merciful God) my Father, mother, brethren, & fifters, (*here may be placed, huf-
bande, wife, children, or whom we woulde*)
kinsfolkes, frendes, & acquaintāce. For
al my ghoftly fathers. (*if a Priefte, ghoftly children.*) For al my benefactors quick
& dead. For al thofe who haue commended them felues vnto my praiers.
For al thofe whom in vnity, Charity, pro
mife, or other bonde, I ftande charged
to pray for if I did remember them. For
al foules departed this life in the ftate of
grace, & efpecially thofe which I am any
way bound to pray for. For the gayning of al Indulgences whatfoeuer, that
my praiers, deuotions, & other actions
extend vnto both for liuing & dead. Finally for al thofe whom I haue any way
offēded, greued, or wronged, in goodes,
in fame, in deede, word, or thought.
For eafe & releafe to al captiues, & for
al catholick prifoners, that it may pleafe
thee, good Lord, either to graunt them
liberty without faile in faith, or Charity; or patience, (to thine honour & glory, their owne foules health, & edifica-

tion

tion of others) to endure whatſoeuer it
ſhal pleaſe thy diuine Maieſty to impoſe
vpon them. For conſtancy to al perſecuted for the catholick faith, & releaſe of
their troubles when thy wil is. For al
others that are in troubles either of body
or minde. For whomſoeuer, or whatſo -
euer els thy wiſdome knoweth neceſſary,
& my fralty can not aſke. Amen.

The peace of our Lord Ieſu Chriſt ,
the vertue of his B. paſſion, the ſigne
of the holy Croſſe, the intireneſſe of the
humility of the bleſſed Virgin Mary, the
bleſſing of al Sainctes, the keping of al
Angels, & the ſuffrages of al the elect &
choſen of God; be with me, & betwene
me & mine enemies, now, & in the hour
of my death. Amen.

IN

INDVLGENCES

GRAVNTED VNTO HOLY GRAI-
nes, by Pope GREGORY the 13. of
blessed memory, at the request of the
English Seminary, & of late confirmed by Paulus Quintus.

They that haue any of these graines in what place soeuer they be,
gaine al the Indulgences graun-
ted vnto the Society of the blessed Trinitie in Rome, if they do fulfill that which
is there commaunded. But those onely
do obtaine the Indulgences folowing,
that haue deuoted them selues to the re-
stoaring of the catholick faith in England, or labour any way for that cause,
or pray for England.

2. Whosoeuer hauing one of these halowed graines, & being contrite, with a
ful purpose, at the least, to confesse and
communicate so sone as he can commo-
diously : shal recite the Corone or Rosary of our B. Lady ; or shal reade the
Passion of our *Sauiour*; or the 7. psalmes

G　2　　　　　　　　or the

or the Lytanies, praying for the Popes holines, or for the ſtate of the catholicke Church, or for the propagation of the catholick faith, or for the conuerſion of the Kingdomes of England, Ireland, & Scotland, or of heritikes : ſhal gaine for ſo often as he doth this, a plenary In-dulgence.

3. Whoſoeuer, being confeſſed, ſhal communicate in the feaſt of the B. Tri-nity, Whitſonday, & al the feaſts of our Sauiour, & the B. Virgin, & of al the A-poſtles, of S. Thomas the Archbiſhop of Canturbury, of S. Edmund, of Sainct Gregory the firſt Apoſtle of England, or in the feaſt of the Patrones of the Dio-ceſe or place, or in the feaſt of a *Sainct* of whom there is any notable Relique, Church, or Chapel in that place, or on e-uery Sonday throughout the yeare : ſhal obtaine a plenary Indulgence for him ſelf or for ſome faithful ſoule departed, if he offer the ſame vp for him by way of ſuf-frage.

4. So often as one ſhal confeſſe his ſinnes to an approued confeſſor, or be contrite with a purpoſe to confeſſe, and
ſhal

ſhal heare Maſſe with deuotion, or a ſer-
mon, or ſhal examine his conſcience, or
ſhal teach or heare al the chriſtian doctrine, or part therof, or ſhal endeuour to
reconcile the fallen out, or ſhal labour
to induce any one vnto piety & workes
of charity, either by connſel, or by his
own example, or ſhal ſtriue to withdraw
either him ſelf or any other, from the
prophane communion of heritikes, per-
ſwading them to imbrace the Catholick
religion : ſhal obtaine al the Indulgences of our Ladies Church of Lauretto,
of S. Mary Maior, & of S. Iohn Lateran at Rome.

5. He that hauing one of theſe graines
& ſhal deuoutly faſt according to the
cuſtome of the church, the Eue of al the
Feaſtes of our B. Lady : ſhal gaine 100.
yeres of Indulgence : but if he faſt them
in bread & drink onely, he ſhal obtaine
a thouſand yeares.

6. He that reciteth a Corone or Roſary, or the 7. pſalmes, or Lytanies, for
the conuerſion of heritikes, in Aduent,
Lent, or other daies, when the Stations
be at Rome : ſhal gaine the ſame Indul-

G 3 gence

gence of the Stations, as if he had perfonally visited the said Churches.

7 . Also he that induceth any one to the
detestation of his euil life past, or of some
enormous crime, (especially of heresy,
schisme, or blasphemy) shal obtaine a
1000 yeares Indulgence.

8 . He that shal say 7 . pater nosters,
& 7 . Aues, or shal say a Corone, or Ro
sary, or the 7 . psalmes, or Lytanies,
with deuotion before almighty God, or
before some Altar, or Image, for the
conuersion of England, Ireland, & Scotland : shal obtaine al those Indulgences
which they doe that visit the seauen Churches of Rome.

9 . If any Preist, hauing one of these
graines about him, shal say Masse for the
dead twice in a weeke, or the Masse that
doth occur for the day, offering it vp for
any soule in purgatory : shal deliuer the
soule from paines by way of suffrage, &
those that are not Preistes, if being cō-
fessed & communicated, they recite the
7 . psalmes together with the Rosary, or
Corone of our B. Lady, or if they can
not read, do recite a Corone or Rosary
twice

twice : ſhal obtaine the ſame once euery Moneth.

10. He that in the point of death, ſhal recite the Corone or Roſary, or the 7. pſalmes, or Lytanies, or if he can not recite them, ſhal ſay IESVS, at the leaſte in his heart if he can not ſpeake, or being confeſſed or contrite, with a purpoſe to confeſſe : ſhal obtaine a plenary Indulgence.

11. He that being confeſſed or contrite, is accuſtomed to celebrate *Maſſe*, or to heare *Maſſe*, or cauſe Maſſe to be ſaid, praying for the Pope, or for the propagation of the faith, or of the Catholick Church, or for the conuerſion of heritikes, or Infidels : ſhal obtaine a plenary Indulgence once euery Moneth.

12. He that ſhal ſay, *Deus propitius eſto mihi peccatori*, or ſhal ſprincle him ſelf with holy water, or ſhal reuerence any Image of Chriſt, of the holy Croſſe, or of any Sainct, or ſhal ſalute our B. Lady in the morning, Noone, or night, or ſhal geue thankes to God for the benefites that he haith receaued : ſhal gaine ten yeares Indulgence.

G 4 What

13. Whatſoeuer is graunted in theſe Indulgences to thoſe that recite the Coroncs or Roſaries, or 7. pſalmes : is alſo vnderſtoode , to be graunted vnto thoſe that inſtead thereof, ſhal pray mẽ çally for the ſpace of an houre ,or of half an houre ; or for the ſpace of a *Miſerere*, ſhal diſcipline themſelues , or ſhal weɾe haire-cloath for a day, or a night .

14. He that ſhal in great ɖaunger of his life, or apprehenſion for the Catho - like Faith, or being apprehended, ſhal expect the torture, rack, or ſtripes, or any kinde of ſcorne ; or by longe impriſonment, ſhal fal into a Feuer, or any o ther diſeaſe : ſo often as he thinketh him ſelf to ſtand in neede, ſo often by ſay ing of oue Pater noſter and an Aue , he ſhal obtaine a ful remiſſion of al his ſinnes . Alſo in the very ſuffering of ſuch moleſtations, if he offer them vp deuoutly vnto God for the reſtoaring of the Catholike Faith into thoſe Coun - tries, or ſhal pray vnto God for them that inflict the ſame vpon him, he ſhal obtaine he aforeſaid pardon .

15. When it ſhal happen that any of theſe

thefe Graines be broken or lofte : then
may he which had the fame take an other
graine not hallowed in ftead thereof once
twice, & oftner, & it fhal haue the fame
Indulgences.

And moreouer in thofe Countries,
where it fhal be treafon, or any other
-great paine be laid vpon fuch as carry a-
ny fuch thing : it fhal be lawful for them
which had any fuch graine or graines,
to choofe vnto them felues, or others in
place thereof, any Iewel or coral, one,
or more, or any kind of ftone, or beade,
or a litle croffe, or the Image of any Sańct
of any matter, or els a deathes head of
bone, mettal, or wood, fo often as he
fhal haue neede.

Other Indulgences graunted onely to
Crucifixes & Medales, besides
the aforesaid, & also vnto
Crosses .

HE that hauing a hallowed Cru-
cifix or Medal, & behoulding
or kissing the same deuoutly :
doth gaine an hundreth daies of Indulgence.

He that shal say or cause Masse to be
said, euery Friday, on an Altar where a-
ny such Crncifix or Medal is : shal deliuer
a soule out of purgatory . And the same
also may he doe on al soules day, & euery day of the octaues thereof folowing .

Thirdly it shal also be lawful, to chose
in stead of these Crucifixes & Medales,
any other thing, as is aboue said of the
Graines .

THE INDVLGENCE
OF S. CHARLES
BOROMEVS.

AL that being contrite, & hauing
at leaſt ful purpoſe to confeſſe &
communicate, ſo ſoone as poſ-
ſibly they may, ſhal ſay the office of our
B. Lady, or one paire of Beades, or a Roſary, or reade the Paſſion of our Sauiour
Ieſu Chriſt, or ſhal ſay the 7. penitenti-
al pſalmes, or Lytanies, although it be
with obligation, praying for his holines,
or for the Catholike Church, or for the
propagation of the catholike Faith, or
for the conuerſion of England, Scotland,
& Ireland: for euery time gayneth a plenary Indulgence.

2. So ofté as any being cófeſſed, or hauing a purpoſe to confeſſe, ſhal heare
Maſſe, or a Sermon, or examine his có-
ſcience, or ſhal teach the Chriſtian doctrine, or ſome part thereof, or procure á
atonement betwene ſuch as are at diſſention, or ſhal cauſe any one either by counſel

sel or example, to exercise some act of
piety or charity, or shal édeuour to draw
either him self or other from the company of heritikes, counseling them to imbrace the catholike faith : shal obtaine
al the Indulgences of our B . Lady of Loretto .

3 . Whosoeuer shal procure any one to
detest his wicked life past, or some enormous sinne, as principally of heresye
shisme, or blasphemy : shal obtaine ten
yeares of Indulgence .

4 . Fasting according to the custome
of the Church, the eues of our B . Lady :
gaineth twenty yeares, & fasting with
bread and water, 100 yeares of Indulgence .

5 . Whosoeuer shal say 7 . Pater nosters & 7 . Aues, or his Beades, or the
Rosary, or 7 . psalmes, or Lytanies deuoutly, before any Altar, or Image, for
the conuersion of England , Scotland ,
& Ireland, shal obtaine those Indulgences, as they which visit the 7 . Churches
of Rome ,

6 . When any Catholike shal be in pe-
ril to be taken, or loose his life for the
catholike

catholike faith, or being taken, fhal be
racked or fuffer any torture, or blow, or
fhame, or by longe imprifonment falleth
ficke : for euery time that he fhal finde
conuenient, faying a Pater nofter & A-
ue, obtaineth a plenary Indulgence, the
which he alfo fhal obtayne, that in fuffering the faid aduerfities, fhal offer them
vnto God for reconciliation of thofe that
do torment him, or fhal pray our B. Sauiour for them.

7. Euery time that any fhal doe reuerence to the Croffe or Images, or geue
thankes vnto God for the benefites receaued, or in the beginning of any good
worke, or time of temptation, fhall
thrice make the figne of the Croffe, and
fay thrice, *Deus in adiutorium meum in-
tende*, or fhal doe fome other good work
of piety or charity : for euery time fhal
obtaine ten yeares of Indulgence.

8. Euery time that any fhal confeffe &
communicate, or fay Maffe, afwel of deuotion as obligation, & fhal pray for
the exaltation of the catholike Church,
& extirpation of herefy : fhal gayne a
plenary Indulgence, & praying for the
foules

foules in purgatory, fhal deliuer for e-
uery time one foule from purgatory in
maner of fuffrages, according to his intention.

9. Whofoeuer fhal caufe 3. Maffes to
be faid either in one or diuers daies:
fhal deliuer twelue times in a yeare, for
euery time a foule from purgatory, by
maner of fuffrages, according to his intention.

10. He that fhal pray for his holines,
& for the exaltation of the Church, on
the holy Thurfday, or Eafter, or Afcen-
tion day, being confeffed & communicating: fhal gaine thofe Indulgences that
his holines is wont to geue thofe dayes
at his benedictions, as if him felf were
there prefent.

11. At the daies of the Stations in
Rome, at what foeuer time of the yeare
it be, faying before the faid Images, or
Medales, 5. Pater nofters, & 5. Aues,
in remembrance of the precious bloud of
our Sauiour Iefus Chrift fhed for vs in his
paffion: fhal gaine the fame Indulgences afwel for the liuing as the dead.

12. Saying a Miferere, or one Crede,
                                or Te

or *Te Deum &c .* in reuerence of the precious bloud of our Sauiour Iesus Christ shed for vs, or kissing 7 . tymes the ground : shal obtaine the Indulgences, as if he should personally make the Stations in Rome that day .

13 . Those that being contrite, hearing Masse, shal pray for his holines, the catholike Princes, & for the peace of those Estates : gaineth those Indulgences that they do, which visit al the Churches , in & out of the City of Rome .

14 He that praieth for the coseruation, & augmentation of the Religious : shal be partaker of al their Sacrifices, praiers, disciplines , Fastes, & other good works done by them, as if he were one of them .

15 . Whosoeuer (hauing one of these said hallowed thinges) shal pray before the Sepulchre where reposeth S . Charles Boromeus his blessed Body, or shal here Masse, or pray in any Church dedicated to the said holy Sainct , or before any Altar or Image of that S . gayneth the same Indulgences as if he should personally visit the body of S . Iames in Galitia.

He that

16. He that on the Feaſt of S. Charles, being the 4. of Nouember, confeſſed & communicated, doth ſay 5. Pater noſters, & 5. Aues, in the honour of our Sauiour Ieſus Chriſt: gaineth a plenary Indulgence & remiſſion of al his ſinnes.

17. His holines alſo graunteth, that any one ſhal ſatisfye for al the defects, committed without aduertence in ſaying the diuine Office, or that of our B. Lady, or in hearing or ſaying Maſſe, or any other praier or ſpiritual worke, : in ſaying a Pater noſter & an Aue, or the Pſalme *Laudate dominum omnes gentes*, or *Deprofundis*, or kiſſing any of theſe hallowed thinges, or ſaying thrice Ieſus, & once *Salue Regina*.

18. Any one being hindered by any euil diſpoſition, or any lawful cauſe, from hering of Maſſe, or being a Preiſt, from ſaying Maſſe, or can not ſay his Office or other obligatory praiers : ſaying 5. Pater noſters & 5. Aues, in reuerence of the precious bloud of our Sauiour : gaineth thoſe Indulgences as if he had fulfilled the thinges aboue mentioned.

19 He that in the point of death, ſaying

ing

ing once Iesus in heart, if he be not a-
ble to say it by word of mouth, being
at least contrite, if he be not able to confesse & communicate: obtaineth a plenary Indulgence, in forme of Iubily, hauing about him, or kissing one of these
hallowed thinges.

Al these said Indulgences in al thinges
may be applyed to the soules in purgatory, in praying for them: & to obtaine
them, it is sufficient to haue some of these
hallowed thinges of his owne, or borow
ed, or when they are broken or lost, he
that had them, may take in place of them
any other thing, although not hallowed,
for once or diuers times, which shal haue
the same Indulgence.

In Countries where it is forbidden vnder paine of death, or other great punishment, to haue any of these hallowed
thinges about him: it is graunted vnto
al those that haue any of these said hallowed thinges, to take in place of them, a-
ny other such corral, litle Crosse, or I-
mage of some Sainct, of whatsoeuer matter, or of a death head of bone, mettal,
or wood, euery time it shal neede.

H   These

These Indulgences are graunted with condition, that these Images be kept secretly in houses : & that both Images & Medales, be but of our Sauiour, our B. Lady, or some Sainct.

FINIS.

ROBERT PERSONS
A Little Treatise
1620

A LITTLE

TREATISE CONCERNING
TRIAL OF SPIRITS:

TAKEN FOR THE MOST
part out of the Works of the *R.F.*
ROBERT PARSONS,
of the Societie of
IESVS.

WHEREVNTO IS ADDED
a Comparison of a true Roman Ca-
tholike with a Protestant, wher-
by may bee discouered the
difference of their
Spirits.

With an Appendix taken out of **a**
later Writer.

My dearest beleeue not euery Spirit, but
prooue the Spirits if they be of God, because
many false Prophets are gone out into the
world. 1.Ioh.4.1.

✠
IHS

Permissu Superiorum, 1620.

A LITTLE
TREATISE CONCERNING
TRIALL OF SPIRITS.

WRITTEN FIRST BY THE
R. F. ROBERT PARSONS,
P. of the Societie of Iesus,
against Master
CHARKE.

NEWLY SET FORTH, WITH AN
Appendix taken out of a later
Writer.

☩
I H S

1. IOHN 4. 1.

*My dearest beleeue not euery Spirit, but
proue the Spirits if they be of God because
many false Prophets are gone out into the
world.*

———————————————

Permissu Superiorum.
1620.

AN ANSVVERE
TO MASTER Charke his Preface, touching discerning of Spirits.

After *Charke*, besides the matter in question betweene him and his Aduersarie, maketh a Preface to the Reader, touching the vtilitie, necessitie, and way of trying spirits: alledging the words of Saint *Iohn*, whereby we are willed not to beleeue euery spirit, but to Trie the spirits whether they bee of God. Which (hee saith) hee and his fellowes offer to doe; and wee refuse. But that this is clearely false, and a formall speech onely, without truth or substance: our deeds do testifie; which are alwaies (with indifferent men) as good as words. Our bookes are extant, whereby we haue called to triall all Sectaries of our time, as they rose vp, and shewed new spirits; as *Luther*, *Corolostad*,

1. Iohn 4.

A 2   *Swinglius,*

Swinglius, Munster, Stankarus, and *Caluin,* whom our Aduersaries follow, as one of the laſt. And now in England, if wee had not been willing, or rather deſirous of this Triall of ſpirits : we would neuer haue laboured ſo much to obtaine the ſame of our aduerſaries, in free Printing, Preaching, or Diſputation : and much leſſe would wee haue aduentured our liues in comming and offering the ſame to them at home, with ſo vnequall conditions on our ſide, as we haue done, and doe daily, for the triall of truth. And if all theſe our offers and endeauours, ioyned with ſo many petitions and ſupplications for triall, haue obtained vs nothing hitherto, but offence, accuſations, extreame rackings, and cruell death: mee thinke M.*Charke* had little cauſe to make this Preface of our refuſing triall, and their offering the ſame; except it were onely for lacke of other matter, and to keepe the cuſtome of ſaying ſomewhat in the beginning.

But perhaps M.*Charke* will ſay, that although we offer triall, yet not ſuch, nor by ſuch meanes, as in his opinion is lawfull, ſure, and conuenient. When wee come

(marginal note: Which part more deſire the triall of Spirits.)

come to the combate : then remaineth it
to be examined, which part doth alledge
beſt meanes : which ſhall bee the argument of this my anſwere to this Preface.
And I will endeauour to ſhew, that all Who doe
the meanes of triall which M. *Charke* offer beſt
and his fellowes will ſeeme to allow in meanes
word, (for they offer none in deed) are of triall.
neither ſure, poſſible, nor euident : but
onely meere ſhifts to auoid all triall: and
that we (on the contrary part,) doe not
onely allow, but alſo offer, all the beſt
and ſureſt wayes of triall that euer were
vſed in Gods Church, for diſcerning an
hereticall ſpirit from a Catholike.

The onely meanes of triall which M. Onely
Charke will ſeeme to allow, is the Scrip- Scripture
ture : whereto onely he would haue all
triall referred : and that which cannot be
tried therehence by him, muſt ſtand vn-
tried. And then, as if we refuſed all triall of Scripture, he vſeth his pleaſure in
ſpeech againſt vs. But this is a ſhift common to all ſuch as M. *Charke* is. And the *Lib.2.de*
cauſe thereof I will declare immediately. *nu. & con-*
Saint *Auguſtine* doth teſtifie it of the He- *cap.c.31.*
retikes of his time. And all the Sectaries *& lib.3.*
of our dayes doe make it plaine by expe- *cont.Don.*
A 3   rience, *cap.15.*

rience, referring themselues in words
each one to the holy Scripture onely, for
maintenance of their errors, and denying
all other means of triall, wherby the true
meaning of Scripture may be knowne.

Three causes of appealing only to Scripture. The causes of this shift in all new teachers are principally three. The first, to get credit with the people by naming of Scripture, and to seeme to honour it more then their aduersaries doe, by referring the whole triall of matters vnto it. The second is, by excluding Councels, Fathers, and Ancestors of the Church, (who from time to time haue declared the true sense of Scripture vnto vs,) to reserue vnto themselues libertie and authority, to make what meaning of Scripture they please, and thereby to giue colour to euery fansie they list to reach. The third cause is, that by chalenging of only Scripture, they may deliuer themselues from all ordinances or doctrines left vnto vs by the first pillers of Christ his Church, though not expresly set downe in Scripture: and thereby assume authoritie of allowing or not allowing, of controuling or permitting, whatsoeuer liketh or serueth their turnes for the time. So

Martin

Martin Luther, after hee had denied all testimony of man, besides himselfe, hee beginneth thus about the number of Sacraments: *Principio neganda mihi sunt septem Sacramenta, & tantum tria pro tempore ponenda.* First of all I must deny seuen Sacraments, and appoint three for the time. Marry this time lasted not long : for in the same place he saith, that if he would speak according to the vse of only Scripture, hee hath but one Sacrament for vs ; that is, Baptisme. But yet the confession of *Auspurge*, which pretendeth to follow *Luther* in all things, doth allow three, by onely Scripture. Marrie *Melancthon* (which professeth onely Scripture more then the rest, and would seeme to know *Luthers* meaning best of all men, for that he liued with him) holdeth foure by only Scripture : and *Iohn Caluin* holdeth two.

Againe, by onely Scripture, *Iohn Caluin* found the title, of *Head of the Church*, in King *Henry*, to be Antichristian, which now, our followers of *Caluin* in England, doe finde by onely Scripture to be most Christian. Marrie yet the Magdeburgians by onely Scripture doe condemne

De captiu. Babilon. in initio.

Cap. de Sacram.

In editio ult. loc. com.

In Institut.

Com. in Amos.

Vid Engb. Eck. & Luth. cont. latom. de incendia-riis.

A 4

demne the same still. In like sort, by only Scripture the Protestants defended a great while against Catholikes, that no Heretikes might bee burned, or put to death, whereof large bookes were written on both parts. But now our Protestants in England, hauing burned some themselues, haue found (as they write) that it is euident by Scripture that they may be burned. *Luther* by onely Scripture, found that his followers, and the Sacramentaries could not both be saued together; and therefore hee condemned the one for arrant Heretikes. Doctor *Fulke* findeth by the same Scripture, that both parts are good Catholikes, and neither of them Heretikes. Finally, how many things doth M. *Whitgift* defend against *T. Cartwright* , to bee lawfull by Scripture ? as Bishops, Deanes, Archdeacons, Officials, Holy-dayes, and an hundred more, which in Geneua are holden to be flat contrary to the same Scripture? So that this appellation to onely Scripture bringeth good ease in many matters. For by this a man maketh himselfe Iudge and Censurer, not onely of all Fathers, Doctors, Councels, Histories, Examples,

Presi-

D. *Fulke*
against
Brif. Mot.
pag. 98.
*Artic.*28.
ont. Leu.
*tom.*2.
Wittenb.
*fol.*503.
Against
*Brill.*Mot.
pag. 82.
In his
Defence
of the
Answere
to the
Admoni-
tion.

Prefidents, Cuftomes, Vfages, Prefcrip-
tions, and the like : but alfo of the books
of Scripture, and fenfe it felfe, referuing
all interpretation vnto himfelfe. But Catholikes, albeit they giue the foueraignty
to Scripture in all things : yet binding
themfelues to other things befide, for the
better vnderftanding of the meaning of
Scripture, (as to Councels, ancient Fathers, tradition of the Apoftles, and Primatiue Church, with the like) are reftrai-
ned from this libertie of chopping and
changing, affirming and denying, allowing and mifliking at their pleafures. For
albeit they hauing wits as other men
haue, might draw fome probable appa-
rance of Scriptures to their owne deuices, as euery Heretike hitherto hath done:
yet, the ancient interpretation of holy
Fathers, and receiued confent of the
Church not allowing the fame, it would
preuaile nothing. Marry the felfe-wil- The ad-
led Heretike, that reiecteth all things but uantage
Scripture, and therein alloweth nothing that Hæ
but his owne expofition, may runne and retikes
range, and deuife opinions at his plea- haue by
fure : for he is fure neuer to be conuicted Scripture
thereof, allowing no man to be judge of
                                    his

his interpretation, but onely himſelfe, or
ſome of his owne opinion. This we ſee
fulfilled in all Heretikes, and Sectaries
that now liue: whom it is vnpoſſible ſo
to conuince by onely Scriptures, but they
will alwayes haue ſome probable ſhew,
whereby to defend themſelues and their
owne imaginations. M. *Charke* therefore
chanting ſo much vpon this point of only
Scriptures, treadeth the path of his forefathers, and pleadeth for a priuiledge of
eaſe: which whether we will allow him
or no, hee entreth vpon it, of his owne
authoritie, and draweth Scripture to euerie deuice of his owne braine, ſo violently, as a man may take compaſſion to ſee
it. I ſhall haue many examples hereafter
in this Anſwere; but yet one, which is
the chiefe ground of this his Preface, I
cannot omit.

1. *Iohn* 4.   After he had proued out of Saint *Iohn*,
that we muſt trie Spirits, and not beleeue
euery new Spirit: (which is true:) hee
will needs alledge out of the ſame Apoſtle, a full and plaine rule (as he tearmeth
it) whereby to diſcerne and trie his and

1. *Iohn* 4. our Spirits. The rule is this: *Euery ſpirit*
which acknowledgeth Ieſus Chriſt to haue
come

come in fleſh, is of God : and euery ſpirit which diſſolueth Ieſus, is not of God, but of Antichriſt. Heere now may bee ſeene what difference there is in expoſition of the Scriptures. For the ancient Fathers interpreted this place, (as of it ſelfe it is moſt euident) to bee giuen as a rule a-gainſt the Iewes, which denied Chriſt to haue taken fleſh : Alſo againſt *Ebion* and *Cherinthus*,Heretikes,now gone into the world, as fore-runners of Antichriſt,and diſſoluing Ieſus:that is,denying his God-head ; and conſequently,denying the Son of God to haue come in fleſh. *Martin Luther* interpreteth this place to be vn-derſtood of M. *Charke* and his fellowes: ſaying, *That ſpirit is not of God, but of Antichriſt, which diſſolueth Chriſts fleſh in the Sacrament.*But to vs Catholikes how can it be by any deuice wreſted,who nei-ther deny Chriſt to haue come in fleſh, nor yet do diſſolue the name of Ieſus,by any doctrine of ours ? But yet, marke how M. *Charke* interpreteth this place; and confeſſe,that he hath a ſingular grace in abuſing Scripture.

Whatſoeuer ſpirit (ſaith he) *ſhall confeſſe Chriſt to haue come in fleſh as a Prophet, a-* lone

Diuerſity of inter-pretati-ons.

Tom.7. Wittemb. Fol.414.

M. Charks grace in interpre-ting Scripture

lone to teach (*as Papists doe not, teaching traditions besides the written Word:*) *also, as a King alone to rule* (*as Papists doe not, defending the Popes authoritie:*) *also, as a Priest, alone to sanctifie* (*as Papists doe not, vpholding the Masse:*) *this spirit is of God, and the other of Antichrist.* Is it maruell if these men build what they list vpon Scripture, when they can found so many absurdities vpon one sentence thereof ? I would heere aske first, whether Master *Charke* thinketh that we exclude Christ, when we allow Prophets to teach vnder him, Kings to raigne vnder him, Priests to sanctifie vnder him, or no ? If he thinke we exclude Christ ; hee is to fond to reason against sensible men, knowing not what they hold. But if he thinke we allow Prophets, Kings and Priests, vnder Christ onely, and in his name : how can he call this the spirit of Antichrist ? Doe not the Scriptures allow Prophets and teachers vnder Christ in the Church ? *Ephes*.4. *Act.* 5 ? Also Kings and Rulers, (though Puritans would haue none) 1.*Pet*.2. *Act.* 2 ? Also may not Priests sanctifie by the Word of God, 2.*Tim*.4? How then are these things accounted
Anti-

Antichriſtian ? Do not Proteſtants teach the ſame ? What deepe Myſteries of Puritaniſme are theſe, *Chriſt is a Prophet alone, a King alone, a Prieſt alone* ?

Againe, I aske, What doe the traditions of Chriſt and his Apoſtles (for of thoſe onely we talke, when we compare them with Scripture) impeach the teaching of Chriſt and his Apoſtles ? What doth the ſpirituall authoritie of the Pope vnder Chriſt, diminiſh the Kingly power and authority of Chriſt ? How doth the Prieſt-hood of men, as from Chriſt, or the Sacrifice of the Altar inſtituted by Chriſt, diſgrace Chriſts Prieſthood, or his ſufficient Sacrifice once for all offered on the Croſſe ? There is noted in the Margent, the Epiſtle to the Hebrewes, where it is ſaid: that, that Sacrifice on the Croſſe was once offred for euer for our redemption. Which we both grant and teach in that manner as then it was done : but yet that impeacheth nothing this daily Sacrifice of ours, which muſt bee in the Church vntill the end of the world, (as *Daniel* prophecied,) and that in euery place amongſt the Gentiles : (that is, in all the world) as *Malachie* foretold, being

called

Their myſteries are the ouerthrow of all Gouernors : as Maſter Whitgiſt proueth againſt M. Cartw. touching the Maſſe

Heb.7. & 9.

Dan.12.

Malac.1.

In declar.
Ancib.11.
Aug.l.20.
com.f.iust.
cap.21.
Naz. orat.
1.in lul.
Hom.17.
called by Saint *Ciril* and other Fathers,
incruentum Sacrificium: the vnbloudie Sa-
crifice : which being one and the selfe-
same, with that which was offered once
vpon the Crosse, is appointed by Christ
to be offered daily in remembrance and
thankesgiuing for that bloudy Sacrifice,
as Saint *Chrysostome* doth prooue at large
vpon the Epistle to the Hebrews:whom,
and other his like, if M. *Charke* and his
fellowes would not disdaine to reade
and beleeue : they would be ashamed to
cauill, and blaspheme Gods mysteries as
they doe. But for a large and ful answere
of this common obiection of theirs, out
of the Epistle to the Hebrewes, touching
Christ once bloudily offered for all: I referre the Reader, amongst many other, to
certaine particular, ancient, and learned
Fathers, of the Primitiue Church, who
doe handle this obiection, and answere

In cap.8.
Epist.ad
Hebr.
it of purpose. The one is *Theodoret*, Bishop of Cyrus, who handleth this question : *Why Christians doe now vse to sacri-*
fice in the new Testament, seeing the olde
Law with all Sacrifices were abolished , *by*
the one Sacrifice of Christ ? The other is

Epist. 23.
ad Bonif.
S. *Augustine*, who proposeth this doubt:
How

How we sacrifice Chrift enery day vpon the Altar, feeing he is faid to be facrifised once for all vpon the Croffe? And then hee an-fwereth it, both fully and largely, in that fenfe as I haue faid before: So that this objection was a common thing in the Primitiue Church, and commonly an-fwered by euery Writer, which M. *Chark* and his fellowes doe make fo much adoe about now, crying out that we deny the vertue of Chrifts Paffion, the effects of his offices, and the like. See the fame an-fwered alfo by *Eufebius, lib.* 1. *Demonft. Enang. cap.6. & 10.* And by *Theophilaƈt. in cap.5. ad Hebr.*

And fo, hauing anfwered now the fubftance of all that which M. *Charke* hath in his Preface, I might heere make an end, but that I haue promifed to fhew how we offer him and his fellowes moft reafonable meanes of triall, and that they indeed admit none at all. For what is it to name Scripture in words, when all the controuerfie is about fenfe therof, wher-in they admit no judge but themfelues? If we bring Scripture neuer fo plaine, yet will they fhift it off, with fome imperti-nent interpretation: And what remedie

The Ad-uerfarie admit-teth no triall.

or

or further triall haue we then? I will giue
an example or two for the instruction of
the Reader in their proceedings. The
most of the ancient Fathers wrote books
in praise of Virginity aboue wedlocke,&
vsed to proue it by the saying of Christ :
Mat. 19,   *There be Eunuches which haue gelded them-*
selues for the kingdome of heauen, he that
can take it , let him take it. Also by the
1. Cor. 7. words of Saint *Paul* : *He that ioyneth his*
virgin in mariage doth well, and hee that
ioyneth her not, doth better. Which words
Lib. de vo- being alledged against *Martin Luther,*
tis Monast. who preferred mariage (yea though it
in initio. were of a vowed Nunne) before virginitie ; he answered it thus : That Christ by
his words terrified men from virginitie
and continence , and Saint *Paul* by this
speech did disswade them from the same.
Now what could bee replied in this case
trow you?

    Another example may be touching
Of S. Iohn Saint *Iohn Baptist:*of whom the Scripture
Baptist. saith, first, concerning his place of liuing,
Luke 1, that *he was in the wildernesse vntill the day*
& 3. *of his appearing to Israel.* Secondly, tou-
Matth. 3. ching his apparell : I O H N *was apparel-*
led with the haires of Camels. Thirdly, tou-
ching

ching his diet : *his meate was locusts and wilde hony.* Of which three things, the old Fathers of the Primatiue Church did gather a great and singular austeritie of S. *Iohns* life, and doe affirme withall, that Eremites and Monkes, and other religious people did take their paterne of strait liuing from him. For which cause Saint *Chrysostome*, doth often call S. *Iohn Baptist Monachum, & principem vita monastica* : a Monke, *and Prince of monasticall life* : which Protestants being not able to abide, doe rage maruellously against Saint *Chrysostome*; condemning him of rashnes and falsehood, for vsing those tearmes, wherfore they fall to interpret the alledged words of Scripture farre otherewise, saying : That by the desert wherein he liued vntill he began to Preach, is vnderstood nothing else, *a but his priuate life at home in his fathers owne house.* And for his apparell (say they) of Camels haire, it was not strange apparell, but vsuall to Mountaine men, b that is, *vndulata* (saith another :) *Water-chamlet, harsome and decent, albeit somewhat plentiful in that countrie.* And lastly, touching his diet of Locusts and wilde hony : it was no hard fare,

Cent.5.c.6 pag.711.

a *Sarcer. in c.1. Lu. & mag. Cent 1.l.1. cap.20.* b *Marloras.in c.3. Matth. Cytraus in c.3. Math.* COSMI-OS. EVPO-RISTOS. *Ma.Cen.1. l.1 c.4.et 6*

B (say

(say they) for the Locusts were Creuises,
cast away by the fishers of Iordan, as vncleane by the Law, but eaten of *Iohn*, by
the libertie of the Gospel. And the wilde
hony was no vnpleasant thing, as the Fathers do imagine : but it was (say *Cossiue*
& *Strigelius*)that pleasant Manna which
Apothecaries vse to keepe in their shops :
So that, according to these men, all that
austerity of life, which the Scriptures so
particularly doe recount, and all antiquitie doth wonder at, in Saint *Iohn Baptist*,
commeth but to this; that he was brought
vp priuately in his Fathers house, clad in
Chamblet, and fedde with Creuisses and
sweet Manna. What great hardnesse was
this ?

   A third example may bee about the
controuersie of Reall presence in the Sacrament ; for which wee bring plaine
words of Scripture out of foure diuers
places of the new Testament, where the
same words are repeated without exposition or alteration : to wit, *Hoc est corpus
meum, This is my body* : which words did
seeme so plaine and cleare for the Reall
presence of Christ in the Sacrament, to al
antiquitie, as no man without great offence

*In cap. 1.
Matth.
In cap. 1.
Marc..*

*Math. 26.
Marc. 14.
Luc. 22.
1. Cor. 11.*

fence might doubt thereof, as the words
of [a] S. *Ambrose* are, and as the same [b] *Cy-*
ril in another place proueth at large, to
aske onely, *quomodo,* how it may be, is the
part of an vnbeleeuing Iew : seeing God
was able (as he saith) as well to doe this,
as to turne the rod of *Moyses* into a Serpent. To which purpose also, holy *Epi-*
phanius saith, That albeit the Host seeme
to vs of a round forme, and insensible :
yet whosoeuer beleeueth it not to be the
very true body of Christ, seeing he hath
said it is; *excidit a gratia, & salute,* such a
one is fallen from grace and saluation.
And S. *Chrysostome* saith, Wee must not
beleeue sense and reason in this matter.
Sed quoniam ille dixit, hoc est corpus meum,
credamus, etiamsi sensui absurdum esse vi-
deatur: But because Christ hath said, *This*
is my body, wee must beleeue it, although
it seeme absurd to our sense : *Hoc idem*
corpus cruentatum, lancea vulneratum, &
quod in cælum extulit. This is the very same
body, whose blood was shed, and which was
wounded with the speare, and which hee ca-
ried vp with him to heauen. All which notwithstanding, our aduersaries haue found
out a new exposition of these words, *This*

[a] *Catac.4.*
[b] *Lib.4.in*
Io.cap.13.
In Anco-
rano.

Hom.83.
in Matth.
& 60.ad
pop. An-
tioch.

Hom. 24.
in Epist.ad
Cor.

is my body, affirming, that it must be con-
strued, this is only the signe of my body.
For the which construction, as they haue
neither Scripture, nor ancient Father for
their warrant or example : so agree they
not amongst themselues of this exposition. For *Luther* in his time, numbreth vp
eight diuers and contrary expositions of
Sacramentaries vpon these words, comming from eight diuers spirits of the Di-
uell, as he affirmeth. And a learned Bishop of our time hath gathered 84. giuen
by diuers Sacramentaries vpon the same:
So that once go out of the high way, and
there is no end of erring.

In confess.
Braui. tom.
2. germ.
fol. 257.
Claud. de
Sand. r.
rep. 1. de
Euch.

And because I haue heere made mention of Doctor *Luther*, a man by Master
Charke opinion, illuminated singularly
by the holy Ghost, and compared to *Eli-*
as, by the common phrase of all Protestants: I will repeate heere what he had
reuealed to him by his holy spirit, touching this interpretation of M. *Charke*
and his fellowes.

The Let-
ter be-
ginneth
thus: *Cha-*
rissimis in
Christo a-
micis &
Christianis
Argentine

First, hee writeth thus to the Protestants, that is, to the true Christians, as he
calleth them, of Argentina : *Hoc diffiteri*
nec possum, nec volo, si Corolostadius. *&c.*
This

This can I not, nor will deny, but if Coro- This was
loſtadius, or any man elſe,could for this fiue an honeſt
yeares haue perſwaded mee, that there had man in
beene nothing in the Sacrament but bread the mean
and wine ; he ſhould haue bound me to him which la-
by a great good turne. For I haue taken boured
great care and anxietie in diſcuſſing this to per-
matter, and haue endeauoured with all my uert this
power, and ſinewes ſtretched out,to ridde my thereby to
ſelfe of the ſame. For I did well ſee, that by hurt the
this thing I might hurt the Pope more then Pope.
in any other matter. But I doe ſee my ſelfe Luthers
captiue, no way being left to eſcape. For the Latine
text of the Goſpell is too plaine and ſtrong, words are
and ſuch as cannot eaſily be ouerthrowne by ex capite
any man, and much leſſe by words and gloſes vertigino-
deuiſed by a phantaſticall head. For I my ſu conſi-
ſelfe (God forgiue me for it) am too prone to Elis.
that part, ſo farre forth as I can perceiue the Ad Iohan-
nature of my owne Adam. Haruagi-
um Tipo-
Againe, the ſame Prophet in another graphum
place, after many moſt deteſtable words *Argilinen-*
vttered againſt M. *Charke* and his part- *ſem : cuius*
ners,ſaith thus: *His ſpiritibus credat doce-* *etiam*
ve veritatem : *ſi quem perire delectat, &c.* *mextio-*
Let him beleeue that theſe ſpirits doe teach *nem, vide*
the truth, who delighteth to damne himſelfe, apud Bi-
wheras indeed they began not their doctrine, bli.th.Geſ-
neri,fol.
B 3 *but* 501.

but by manifest lyes, and now doe defend the
same onely by lyes, divulging the same by
corrupting other mens bookes, not vouchsa-
fing to heare the anguishes of our consciences,
which crie, and say, *The words of Christ are*

a Mat. 26. *cleare and manifest,* a *Eate, this is my body.*

And againe in a certaine Treatise intituled
b *Tom. 7.* b *Against the phanaticall spirits of Sacra-*
Wittemb. *mentaries* ; He saith, talking of this inter-
pag. 380. pretation of the words : *This is my bodie :*
Age ergo quando adeo sunt impudentes, &c.
Go to then seeing they are so impudent, ther-
fore I will giue them a Lutheran exhortati-
c A Lu- *on : accursed* c *be their charitie and concord*
theran *for euer and euer.* And after comming to
exhorta- the exposition of the said words, he saith
tion. thus : *Doctor* Carolostad *wresteth misera-*
O plea- *bly this pronoune* (*This:*) Swinglius *maketh*
sant *Mar-* *leane this verbe* (*Is:*) Oecolampadius *tor-*
tia. *menteth this word* (*Body:*)*other doe butcher*
the whole text; and some doe crucifie but the
halfe thereof; so manifestly doth the diuell
hold vs by the noses. And againe in the
same worke, he hath these words; *To ex-*
pound the words of Christ, as the Sacramen-
taries : do, (This is the signe of my bodie) is
as absurde an exposition, as if a man should
interprete the Scripture thus. In the be-
ginning

ginning God made heauen and earth, that
is, *the* Cuckowe *did eate vp the Titling or
hedge Sparrow, together with her bones.*
Againe, in Saint IOHN, *And the Word
was made flesh,* that is, *a crooked staffe was
made a Kyte.* This was the opinion of holy *Luther,* touching our Aduersaries interpretation, or rather euasion, and shift;
which I haue alledged somewhat more
at large against M. *Charke,* for that hee
esteemeth and defendeth the man, as a
rare instrument of the holy Ghost. Which
if it be true; then woe to Master *Charke*
and his compartners, whose spirit is so
contrarie to this mans holy illumina-
tion.

By this now it appeareth, that the controuersie is not betweene vs, which part
prouoketh to Scripture, and which doth
not: but (as alwayes it hath bin betwixt
Heretikes and Catholikes) which part
alledgeth true meaning of Scripture:
which thing, according to the couniell of
wise *Sisinius* to *Theodosius* the Emperour,
we desire to be tried by the judgement
of ancient Fathers, indifferent in this
matter, for that they liued before our
controuersies came in question. But our

Gen.1.

*Curi ucam
cum ossi-
bus.*

Iohn 1.

*Socrat.l.5.
hist.ca.10.*

B 4 Aduer-

Aduersaries will allow no exposition but
their owne: whereby it is easie to defeate
whatsoeuer is brought against them, eyther Scripture or Doctor.

Examples of shifting Scriptures and Doctors. *Psal.* 75.

For example sake, to proue that we
may lawfully make vows, and are bound
also to performe the same, being made:
we alledge the plaine words of the Prophet, *Vouete & reddite Domino.* Vow ye,
and render your vowes to God. How
will the Aduersary auoid this, think you?

Against the rock, page 153.

M. *Fulke* answereth, *This text belongeth
onely to the olde Testament.* But what may
not be wiped away from vs, that liue vnder the new Testament, by such interpretations? Againe, to proue that there is
some state of life of more perfection in
Christianity than other, wee alledge the

Matth. 19.

cleare saying of Christ; *Si vis perfectus esse, vade, vende quæ habes, & da pauperibus,
& habebis thesaurum in cælo, & veni, se-
quere me.* If thou wilt be perfect, goe, sell
all thou hast, and giue to the poore, and
thou shalt haue a treasure in heauen, and
come, follow me. What answer haue they

Against the rock, page 154.

trow you, to this? M. *Fulke* answereth;
*This was spoken onely, as a singular triall to
that yong man alone, and not to others beside
him.*

him. What a deuice is this? May not hee as well say also, that the other words immediatly going before, were onely spoken to this yong man; to wit, *Si vis ad vitam ingredi serua mandata : If thou wilt be saued, keepe the Commandements :* and so deliuer al his Gospellers from the burden thereof? What difference is there in these two speeches of Christ, seeing they are both spoken to that yong man, and both in the singular number, as infinite other things of the Gospell are to other particular persons, as to the Cananza, to the Adulteresse, to *Nichodemus,* to the Centurion, to *Zacheus,* to the blinde, deafe, and others, which notwithstanding are common to all, in thee they touch either life or doctrine.

The like absurd shifts I might repeate in an hundred other points. What can be more plaine then the words of Scripture; *videtis quoniam ex operibus iustificatur homo, & non ex fide tantum?* Doe you see how that a man is justified by workes, and not by Faith onely ? But yet it auaileth nothing. Why so? they auoid it by interpretation. Saint *Iames* (say they) *vnderstandeth of Iustification before men,* and

Iacob, 2.

D.Fulke, *and not before God.* O poore deuice: Saint
loco citato. *Iames* hath in the same place, (talking of
Faith without workes) *Nunquid poterit fi-*
des saluare eum? Can faith without works
saue him ? Doth S. *Iames* meane heere of
saluation before men, or before God ? A-
gaine, when S. *Paul* saith, *factores legis*
Rom: 2. *iustificabuntur;* the doers of the Law shall
be iustified: which is the very same thing
that S. *Iames* in other words saith, that
men shal be iustified also by works: Doth
S. *Paul* mean before men, or before God?
If you say, before men; the text is against
you, which hath expressely, *apud Deum,*
before God. The like euasion they haue
when wee alledge the words of S. *Paul:*
1.Cor.7. *qui matrimonio iungit virginem suam, bene*
facit, & qui non iungit, melius facit: Hee
that ioyneth his virgin in mariage doth
well, and he that ioyneth her not, doth
better. Whereof we inferre, that virginitie is more acceptable, and meritorious
before God, then mariage, although mariage be holy. No (say our Aduersaries)
S. *Paul* meaneth only, that he doth better
before men, and in respect of worldly
commodities, but not before God. But
this is absurd ; for they grant the former

mer part of the fentence (*He that ioyneth his virginxe doth well*) to bee vnderftood before God ; for that it is faid alfo in other words, *non peccat*, he doth not finne ; which muft needs bee vnderftood in refpect of God. How then can they deny the fecond claufe, (*and hee that ioyneth her not, doth better*) not to be vnderftood in refpect of God alfo, and in refpect of merite and reward in the life to come, efpecially whereas Chrift promifeth the fame reward to virginitie in another place, where he faith, *There be Eunuches which haue gelded themfelues for the* king-dome of heauen, he that ean take it, let him take it ? Math.19.

You may fee now by this little (and I might fhew by many mo examples) how bootleffe it is to bring Scripture, whē we agree not vpon the interpretation. What then ? fhall we bring the ancient Fathers and Doctors of the Primatiue Church for the vnderftanding of Scripture ? Shal wee interprete it as they doe ? vnder-ftand it as they vnderftand it ? No, that our Aduerfaries will not agree vnto, but onely in matters indifferent, and out of controuerfie. Wherefoeuer in matters of

How Proteftants deny all Fathers.

of conuersie betweene vs and them, the
old Fathers doe make against them (as in
all points they doe ;) there will they deny their exposition. For example : The
consent of ancient Fathers(is alledged a-
gainst M. *Fulke*) attributing superiority
to *Peter,* vpon the words of Christ, *Thou*
Math. 16. *art* Peter, *and vpon this rocke will I build*
my Church: But he auoideth it very light-
ly thus ; *It cannot be denied, but diuers of*
Against *of the ancient Fathers (otherwise godly and*
the rock, *learned) were deceiued in opinion* of Peters
page 24. *prerogatiue.* Saint. *Ambrose, Ierome, Chry-*
sostome, Cyril, and *Theodoret,* are alledged
for expounding a peece of Scripture a-
gainst M. *Fulke, Ioh.* 5. about Antichrist.
How doth he shift it ? thus ; *I answere,*
Against *they haue no ground of this exposition.* S. Ie-
the rock- *rome,* with al the Ecclesiastical Writers are
page 191. alledged for interpreting of the words of
Daniel, Chap. 7. against the Protestants :
Ibidem. M. *Fulke, I answere, that neither* Ierome,
nor any Ecclesiasticall Writer whom hee fol-
loweth, hath any direction out of the Scrip-
ture for this interpretation. S. *Austen* is al-
Psal. 14. ledged for interpreting *Dauids* words;
He hath placed his Tabernacle in the Sunne;
of the visibility of the Church. *Fulke, Au-*
gustine

gustine doth wrongfully interpret this place. Against
Saint *Ambrose, Ephraim* and *Bede,* are al- the for-
ledged for interpretation of certain Scrip- tresse,
tures. *Fulke, Gods word is so pitifully wre-* Against
sted by them, as euery man may see the holy Purg.
Ghost neuer meant any such thing. S. *Chryso-* page 262.
stome is alledged for certaine interpretations of Scripture. *Fulke, Hee alledgeth* Against
indeed Scripture, but he applieth it madly; Purg.
and yet he often applieth it to the same pur- page 232.
pose : alas good man. The consent of Fathers is alledged for interpretation of
certaine places of Scripture, of the presi-
guration of the Crosse of Christ. *Fulke,* Against
The Fathers doe rather dally in trifeling the crosse
allegories, then soundly proue that the crosse page 146.
was presigured in those places.

I might here make vp a great volume,
if I would prosecute this argument, to
shew how these new Doctors doe contemne and reject all authority, antiquity, How
wit, learning, sanctity of our forefathers, Prote-
and of all men (in effect) that euer liued stants re-
beside themselues; yea, of their owne ject the
new Doctors & Masters also, when they interpre-
come to be contrary to any new deuice, tation of
or later fansie of theirs. This is euident their
in L V T H E R, rejected by his of-spring Writers.
about LVTHER

about the Reall presence, number of Sacraments, Imakes, bookes of the Bible,
order of Seruice, and the like. Also in
CALVIN CALVINE rejected about the head of
the Church in England, and about all the
gouernment thereof in Geneua. And I
could alledge heere diuers examples,
where hee and BEZA both are rejected
by name in diuers points, both of Puritans and Protestants in England, when
they differ from them. But that this Preface would grow to be too long. Wherefore I may perhaps (if this booke come
not otherwise to bee too great) adde a
short Table or Appendix in the end, to
shew by examples, the vnconstant dea-
lings of our Aduersaries herein, and that
in very deede, when all is done and said
that may bee, and all excuses made that
The final can bee deuised; the very conclusion is
conclusi-
on of Pro- that, onely that must be taken for truth,
testants which pleaseth them last of all to agree
for triall. vpon; and their bare words must be the
proofe thereof. For those bookes onely
be Scripture in the Bible which they appoint: and in those bookes, that onely
is the true sense which they giue out: the
Fathers erred in all things where they
differ

differ from them : the new Doctors,(as
LVTHER, CALVINE, and the reft)
faw fo much onely, of the truth, as they
agree with them, and no further. This
is the faying of our Aduerfaries; this is
the faying of all the other Sectaries of
our time : this hath beene the faying of
all Heretikes from the beginning; and
this muft needes be the faying of all Heretikes for the time to come. For except
they take this way, it is vnpoffible to
ftand or encreafe againft the Church.
And by this way a man may beginne
what Herefie hee will to morrow next,
and defend it againft all the learning,
witte, and truth of Chriftendome. Adioyne now to this, that our Aduerfaries
(notwithftanding all requeft, fute, offer,
or humble petition that wee can make)
will come to no publike difputation, or
other indifferent and lawful judgement:
but doe perfecute,imprifon,torment,and
flaughter them which offer the fame: and
then let the Reader judge whether they
defire and offer juft triall or no, as Mafter
Charke affirmeth.

Now for our parts (as I haue faid) we
offer vnto them, all the beft, fureft, and
eafieft

The va-
rietie of
trial,that
Catho-
likes doe
offer.

1.
Books of
Scripture

2.
Expresse
words.

easiest meanes that possibly can be deuised, or that euer were vsed in Gods
Church for triall of truth,or discouering
of Heresie. For, as for the bookes of
Scripture, seeing we must receiue them
vpon the credit and authoritie of the ancient Church: we are content to accept
for canonicall,and allow those, and none
other, which antiquitie in Christendome
hath agreed vpon. Next, for the contents of Scripture ; if our Aduersaries wil
stand vpon expresse and plaine words
hereof, we are content to agree thereunto,and we must needs be farre superiours
therein. For what one expresse plaine
text haue they in any one point or article
against vs, which wee doe not acknowledge literally as they doe, and as the
words doe lie ? But wee haue against
them infinite, which they cannot admit
without gloses, and fond interpretations
of their owne. For example sake, wee
haue it expresly said to *Peter* (that signi-

Supre-
macie.
HEGOV-
MINOS.

fieth a rocke) *vpon this rocke will I builde
my Church,* MATTH. 16. they haue no
where the contrary in plaine Scripture.
We haue expressely (touching the Apostles) *He that is great among you, let him be
                                                    made*

made as the yonger, Luke 22. They haue
no where, there is none greater then o-
ther among you. We haue expresly, *This* Real pre-
*is my body, Mat.*26. You haue no where, sence.
this is the signe of my body. Wee haue
expresly, *The bread which I will giue you is
my flesh, Ioh.*6. They haue no where, it is
but the signe of my flesh. Wee haue ex-
presly, *A man is iustified by workes, and not* Iustifica-
*by faith only, Iac.*2. They haue no where, tion.
a man is iustified by faith alone: No,
nor that hee is iustified by faith without
workes, talking of workes that follow
faith, whereof onely our controuersie is.
we haue expressely, *Whose sinnes ye forgiue,* Absolu-
are forgiuen: whose sinnes yee retaine, they on.
*are retained, Ioh.*20. They haue no where,
that Priests cannot forgiue or retaine
sinnes in earth. We haue expressely, *The
doers of the Law shall bee iustified, Rom.*2.
They haue no where, that the Law required at Christians hands is impossible,
or, that the doing thereof iustifieth not
Christians. We haue expressely, *Vow yee,* Vowes.
*and render your vowes, Psal.*75. They haue
no where, vow yee not: or, if you haue
vowed, breake your vowes. We haue ex-
presly, *Keepe the traditions which yee haue* Traditi-
C   *learned,* ons.

learned, either *by word or epistle,* 1.*Theff.*2.
They haue no where, the Apostles left
no traditions to the Church vnwritten.
Commā- We haue expresly, *If thou wilt enter into*
dements. *life,keepe the Commandements*: and(when
he said he did that already) *Ifthou wilt be*
perfect, goe and sell all thou haft, and giue to
the poore, and follow mee. They haue no
where, that either the Commandements
cannot be kept,or that we are not bound
vnto them, or that there is no degree of
life, one perfecter then another.We haue
Workes. expresly, *Worke your owne saluation with*
*feare and trembling,Phil.*2. They haue no
where, either that a man can worke nothing towards his owne saluation, being
holpen with the grace of God; or that a
man should make it of his beleefe, that
hee shall bee saued without all doubt or
feare. We haue expresly, *Do yee the wor-*
Penance. *thy fruits of Penance, Luke* 3. They haue
no where, that faith onely is sufficient
without all satisfaction, and all other
workes of Penance on our parts. Wee
haue expresly, *That euery man shall be sa-*
ued according to his workes, Apoc. 20.
They haue no where,that men shall bee
judged only according to their faith.We
haue

haue expreſly, *That there remaineth a re-
tribution , ſtipend , and pay to euery good
worke in heauen, Marke 9. 1. Cor. 3. Apo.
22. Pſal. 118.* They haue no where, that
good workes done in Chriſt, doe merite
nothing. We haue expreſly, *It is a holy* Prayer
cogitation to pray for the dead, 2. Mac. 12. for the
They haue no where, it is ſuperſtition or dead.
vnlawfull to doe the ſame. Wee haue an
expreſſe example *of a holy man that offe-* Sacrifice
red ſacrifice for the dead, 2. Macchab. 12. for the
They haue no example of any good man dead.
that euer reprehended it. Wee haue expreſly, that the affliction, which *Daniel* Volunta-
vſed vpon his body, was acceptable in ry corpo-
the ſight of God, *Dan.* 10. They haue rall afflicti-
no where, that ſuch voluntary corporall ons.
afflictons are in vaine. We haue expreſly, that an Angel did preſent *Tobias* good Almes.
workes, and almes deeds before God,
Tob. 12. They haue no where, that Angels cannot, or doe not the ſame. Wee
reade expreſly, that *Ieremias* the Prophet Prayer of
after he was dead prayed for the people Saints.
of Iſrael, 2. *Macch.* 15. They haue no
where the contrary to this. I leaue many
things more that I might repeate. But
this is enough (for example ſake) to

proue, that albeit our Aduersaries doe
vaunt of Scripture ; yet when it commeth to expresse words, they haue no
text against vs in lieu of so many as I
heere repeated against them: nor can
they shew, that wee are driuen to deny
any one booke of the Bible, nor to glose
vpon the plaine words of any one plaine
place of Scripture, as they are enforced
to doe.

3
Neceſſa-
ry colle-
ctions vp-
on Scrip-
ture.

But now if they will not stand onely
to plaine and expresse words of Scripture, but also (as indeede they must) to
necessary collections made and inserted
of Scripture: then must we referre our
selues to the ancient Primatiue Church,
for this meaning of Gods word. For it
is lik they knew it best, for that they liued nearer to the Writers thereof (then
wee doe) who could well declare vnto
them, what was the meaning of the same.
And then our Aduersaries well know,
how the ancient Fathers do ground Purgatory, Prayer to Saints, Sacrifice of the
Altar, vse of the Crosse, and other like
points of our Religion (besides Tradition) vpon the authoritie of Scriptures, also expounded according to their meaning :

ning : albeit our Aduerſaries deny the
ſame to be well expounded.

If our Aduerſaries will yet goe fur-
ther for the triall of our Spirits: we are   **4**
well content, and wee refuſe none that Coun-
euer antiquity vſed, for the triall of a Ca- cels.
tholike and Hereticall Spirit. The olde
Heretikes, *Samoſatenus*, *Arrius*, *Mace-*
donius, *Neſtorius* and *Eutiches*, were tried
and condemned by the Councels of An-
tioche, Nice, Conſtantinople, and Chal-
cedon ; and other Heretikes by other
Councels ſince. Wee are content to referre our ſelues to al the Chriſtian Councels that euer haue bin ſince Chriſt died.
And all men know that the laſt moſt
learned, godly, and generall Councell of
Trent was gathered for that purpoſe, and
offered all ſafe-conduct to our Aduerſaries to come thither to triall ; but they
refuſed it.

Beſides this, the ancient Fathers haue   **5**
vſed diuers times, diuers other meanes Doctors
of triall. As firſt, by referring the mat- of the old
ter to the triall of olde Doctors, which Church.
liued before the Controuerſies beganne.
This meane vſed Saint *Auguſtine* againſt *Li.1. cont.*
Iulian the Pelagian, and produceth the *Iulian.c.2.*

con-

consent of Fathers, both of the East, and
of the West Church vntill his time : and
there asketh him , who he is that dareth
to oppose himselfe to the credit of these
men ; to call them blinde ; to say they
were deceiued ; whereas they were the
very lights of the Citie of God ? The
like way did *Theodosius* the Emperour
take by the counsell of *Sisinius*, and sug-
gestion of *Nectarius*, to bring the Arrians heresie to some end, as *Socrates* writeth. And *Epiphanius* saith, this is enough
to say against all Heresies : *Ecclesia Ca-*
tholica hæc non docuit: Sancti patres hæc
minime receperunt. The Catholike Church
hath not taught this , the holy Fathers
haue not admitted this. Now, how our
Aduersaries doe flie this meanes of triall,
they are not ashamed to confesse it o-
penly.

Socr.l.5.
hist.14.10.
Lib.3.con-
tra Hæres.

§ Another way is to consider which is
the Catholike or Vniuersall Church, or
great multitude of Christians , out of
which the one part first departed. This
way vsed Saint *Augustine* against diuers
Heretikes, as namely, against the Mana-
chees, when he saith, *Multa sunt quæ in Ca-*
tholica ecclesiæ gremio me iustissime teneant:
tente

6
The Ca-
tholike
Church.

Cont. ep.
fundam.
cap.4.

tenet consensio populorum atque gentium, & tenet ipsum Catholicæ nomen: There are " many things , which vpon good cause " doe hold me in the lappe of the Catho- " like Church; for the very consent of " people and nations doth hold me. And " *Vincentius Lirinensis*, liuing about the same time, writeth to the same effect a- gainst Heresies. *In ipsa Catholica Ecclesia magnopere curandum est , vt id teneamus quod vbique, quod semper, quod ab omnibus creditum, &c. Sed hoc ita demum fit, si sequamur vniuersitatem, antiquitatem, consensionem. Sequemur autem vniuersitatem hoc modo: si hanc vnam fidem veram esse fateamur , quam tota per orbem terrarum confitetur Ecclesia : Antiquitatem vero ita, si ab his nullatenus sensibus resedamus, quos, sanctos maiores ac patres nostros celebrasse manifestum est : Consensionem quoq, itidem, si in ipsa vetustate , omnium vel certe pene omnium sacerdotum & magistrorum definitiones sententiasque sectemur.* We must " greatly take heede, in the Catholike " Church, to hold that which hath been " beleeued in euery place, alwayes, and " of all Christians, &c. And this wee " shall doe, if in our beleefe wee follow "

In his booke a- gainst the pro- phane innouati- ons of all Heresies.

C 4   " vni-

"vniuersalitie, antiquitie, and consent.

Vniuer-
salitie.
"Wee shall follow vniuersalitie, if we
"confesse that onely faith to be true,
"which the Church spred ouer all the
"world doth confesse : we shall follow
Antiqui-
tie.
"antiquitie, if we depart not from that
"meaning and sense of Scripture, which
"is euident that our forefathers and an-
"cestors haue held: we shall follow con-
Consent.
"sent, if we embrace the definitions and
"opinions either of all, or of the most
"part of Priests & teachers in antiquity.
The like way doth S. *Ierome* take against
the Luciferians: and other Fathers against
other heretikes. And how quickely our
Aduersaries Spirit were tried by this way
of Antiquity, Vniuersalitie, and Consent, all men that haue vnderstanding
may judge.

7
Succes-
sion of
Popes.
Another way there is also, and much
vsed by the Fathers against Heretikes :
and, that is, to proue their Religion
by the succession of Bishops in the See of
Rome: wherin the Successor alwaies teaching the doctrine of his Predecessor, it
must needs be a strong argument to proue
the discent and continuance of one and
the same faith from the Apostles time.

This

This argument vſeth S. *Auguſtine* in the place before alledged: *Tenet ab ipſa ſede Petri Apoſtoli (cui paſcendas oues poſt reſurrectionem dominus commendauit) vſque ad praſentem epiſcopatum ſucceſſio ſacerdotum.* The ſucceſſion of Prieſts in the Church " of Rome, euen from the Chaire of *Peter* (vnto whom our Lord, after his re- " ſurrection, commended his ſheep to be " fed) vnto this Biſhoprick that now is, " doth hold me in the Catholike church. " the ſame way of triall he vſeth, and much more at large, in his hundred threeſcore and fift Epiſtle, where he reckoneth vp al the Biſhops of Rome from *Peter* vnto *Anaſtaſius* (which was Biſhop in his time) and thinketh this a good proofe againſt the Donatiſts, that none of thoſe held or fauoured their opinion. The like way of triall vſed *Optatus Meleuitanus* againſt the ſame Donatiſts, before S. *Auguſtine,* reckoning vp al the Biſhops of Rome, vntill *Siricius,* that ſate in his time. The ſame way of triall vſed holy *Irenæus,* before either of theſe men, againſt the Heretikes of his time, reckoning vp all the Biſhops of Rome, vntill E L E V T H E R I V S that held the See in his time, *adding that by this*
ſucceſſion,

Cont. ep. fundam. cap.4. Iohn 21.

Li.2. cont. Donatiſt.

Li.3. cont. hæreſ. c.3.

succession, hee did confound the pride of all
Heretikes that durst to teach otherwise then
this See had held. And after, concluding
thus, *est plenissima hac ostensio, vnam &*
eandem viuificatricem fidem esse, quæ in Ec-
clesia ab Apostolis vsque nunc sit conseruata
" *& tradita in veritate.* This is a most full
" proofe, that one and the selfe-same.
" quickening faith, hath been deliuered
" in truth, and commended from the A-
" postles vnto this day. But now this
way of triall I know our Aduersaries will
not admit.

8   Another way of triall, is to examine
Infection what part doth hold any old condemned
with old Heresie. For as an Heretike hauing once
Heresies. lost the habit of Faith giuen him in Baptisme, is easily mooued to cope with any
Heresie, new or olde, that commeth in
his way, and serueth his turne : so most
certaine it is, that the true Catholike
Church can neuer admitte or defend any
1. *Tim.* 3. Heresie; for otherwise shee could not be
the pillar of truth. And we beleeue with
holy *Athanasius* in his Creed, *That hee*
which holdeth not the Faith wholy in all
points, shall perish eternally, howsoeuer
our Aduersaries doe salue the matter in
their

their Prophets, *Berengarius, Hu$$e, Wic-liffe*, and *Luther*, whom they say to haue been holy men, and yet to haue erred in diuers points of Faith, and to haue held their errors ob$tinatly to the day of their death. But we beleeue the contrary, as I haue $aid. And therefore, who$oeuer could $hew but one confe$$ed Here$ie to be defended by our Church, there needed no more di$putation about the matter. *Marke this gentle Rea-der.*

But now for the right v$e of this way of triall, there be two conditions to bee ob$erued of his part, which will object an old here$ie to another. The fir$t is, that the partie do indeed hold that thing which he objecteth, and not a certaine likelihood of it. For that were to $lan-der, and not to object. As when our Ad-uer$aries doe object to vs the Here$ie of *Pelagius*, about Free-will, it is a meere $lander. For we hold that mans will be-ing preuented and holpen with the grace of God, may worke well: but hee held that it could doe the $ame by the power and force of nature, without the helpe of Gods grace, as Saint *Augu$tine* proueth at large in his Booke of Free-will. The like injurie they doe vs, in many other things, *Two con-ditions. Iniurious dealing of our Aduer-$aries.*

things, which they object against vs : as the heresie of those which did sacrifice to our Lady, and the like, which wee doe not. The second condition is, that the Heresie objected be indeed such as was accounted and condemned for an heresie in the Primatiue Church, and not onely that an Heretike held it. For Heretikes doe hold diuers truthes alwaies together with falsehood. And for lacke of this condition doe our Aduersaries often a-buse the simple people. As M. *Fulk* often-times saith : prayer for the dead is an he-resie , because the Mountanists (which were Heretikes) held it. But let him proue that euer this was accounted one of *Montanus* his heresies, and then hee prooueth somewhat. But that he can neuer do: for he granteth, *Augustine, Ambrose, Chrysostome, Ierome,* and others, to haue vsed prayers for the dead, who notwithstanding were great enemies to *Montanus,* and all his errors. Wherefore this is a very malitious kind of abusing people. And I heere say againe, that let him and all the Protestants in the world proue, that wee do hold indeed, but any one thing, which was accounted an heresie in the Primitiue

tiue Church, and we will grant that wee are not the Catholike Church, but that in all other things we erre besides.

But wee in charging them with here-sies doe obserue alwaies the foresaid two conditions. As for example, we charge them with the opinion of Arrius, which denied prayer for the dead. And that they hold this very same opinion, they will not deny: And that it was accounted an heresie in the Primatiue Church: we alledge for witnesses, S. *Augustine* and *Epiphanius.* How doe they auoid this? No way, but by saying that *Augustine* and *Epiphanius* were deceiued, in recor-ding that for an Heresy, which was none: for that is M. *Fulkes* answere: which is to condemne all that age: for that those ho-ly Fathers wrote downe heresies as they were taken in those daies by the Church. The like we doe about *vigilantius,* whose opinions were (among others) that Saints were not to bee prayed to, nor their re-liques to be honored. Now that the Pro-testants hold this, no man doubteth: And that this was accounted heresie in the Primatiue Church, we cite S. *Ierome* for a witnesse which wrote against him. What shift

Prote-stants do hold old heresies.

Aug.l. de heres. ad quod vult. heres. 53. Epiphan. heres. 75. Against Bristowes Motiues. pag.15.

Lib.cont. vigilan-tium.

shift is there heere ? None, but to deface
S. *Ierom,* and commend *Vigilantius,* and
to deny it to be an Heresie : for so doth
M. *Fulke,* saying further, that I E R O M E
rather raileth then reasoneth, and that V I-
G I L A N T I V S *was a good man, and his
opinion sound.* The like order we take in
a number of other old hereticall points,
which we charge them withall : as may
be seene in the Tables and books set out
of this matter. Now if our Aduersaries
could bring vs to any such confession of
Heresie, the matter were ended. But they
cannot, and therefore I know they will
neuer admit this way of triall.

*Against
the Mo-
niues.pa.
54.*

The last way of triall (whereof I will
speake at this time) is to consider the ma-
ners of olde Heretikes, and to compare
the same with ours. And heere I would
haue also the former two conditions obserued : To wit, that wee consider such
qualities onely, as were accounted hereticall in them : that is, proper to Heretikes : and to examine them truely without partiall affection in our selues. For
example, Saint *Augustine* doth note it as
an hereticall property in the Donatists to
hate the See of Rome, and to call it *Ca-*
                                  thedram

*9
The ma-
ners of
old Here-
tikes.*

*Lib 2.con.
lit.Petil.
cap.51.*

thedram pestilentia, the Chaire of pestilence. Doth this agree to Protestants, or to vs ? As also the defaming of the said See, for the euill pretended life of some particular men ? As likewise he noteth it as an hereticall tricke in them, to perswade the people that the visible Church had erred, & oppressed the true Church, banishing her fró the sight of the world. Doe not our Aduersaries say the very same? Also he noteth the same Heretikes *for hating & condemning the life of Monkes, as also for drawing Nuns out of their Cloysters, and ioyning themselues with the same in pretended wedlocke.* Finally, he noteth it as hereticall in the Arrians, to appeale from traditions to onely Scripture. Now before Saint *Augustine*, *Optatus* noted it as hereticall in the Donatists, *to breake Altars whereupon the body and bloud of Christ were kept,* as the words of *Optatus* are. And about the same time *Victor Vticensis* wrote his storie against the Vandal Heretikes : where hée setteth forth most liuely the state of our time, by the manners and behauiours of those Heretikes, in breaking Chalices: prophaning of holy Chrisme, spoiling of Church-vestiments,

Deunitate ecclesie, cap.12. Lib.3.com lit. peti. cap.4.

Lib.2.c.9. contr. epi. parm. & ep.169.ad Euseb. Lib.1.con: Maximi- num. Lib.6.can. Donat.

Victor de persecutis- ne Van- dalica.

ments, throwing the blessed Sacrament of the Altar on the ground, with other most horrible abuses to the same, not to be repeated: in prohibiting Masse to bee said by edicts and proclamation, and a hundred things moe : which are the very exercises of our aduersaries now. The *Orat. 1. &* like things in many points doth S. *Basil* *2. in Iu-* object as Sacrilegious against *Iulian* the *lianum.* Apostata and his followers: wherefore I thinke our Aduersaries will not admit this way of triall no more then the former.

But we are content to admit these, and all other whatsoeuer, for the triall of our spirits. And for proofe thereof, wee appeale still to publike disputation, or to any other indifferent way of trial that our Aduersaries dare afford vs. Neither doe The the late examples of Master *Campian* and death of M. *Sherwin* (made away by death and *M. Cam-* torments, for that they were forward in *pian* and making and maintaining this offer) any *M. Sher-* thing discourage, or terrifie vs. For as *win.* God of his mercie gaue them grace and constancie to yeeld their liues most joyfully in that cause, which dependeth not of man, but of himselfe : so hath he giuen
the

the same desire to many a one beside them; and will (I trust) giue strength of performance, when it shall please his wisdome to appoint the time.

The rest in your two Prefaces requireth no answere (M. *Charke*) being onely speech without proofe, and words without reason. And that you thinke so magnificently of your cause, and so basely of ours, I pardon it easily; for I know the disease of all Heretikes to be pride. Ask the poorest Sectary of our time, and he will vaunt the same of his cause, that you doe of yours. And *Iulian* the Pelagian vsed the same contemptuous speech against Saint *Augustine*, and his cause: but that holy man well proueth, that all Heresie is beggery (though it beare a sway in some corners for a time:) and that only the Catholike cause is honorable indeed, hauing all the pillars of Christ his Church, and the honourable of the Citie of God, to stand with it. And if he might say so then, bringing forth *Irenaus, Cyprian, Ierome, Ambrose*, and *Basil*, for his proofes: we may much more say so now, hauing the pith of almost twelue hundred years since to stand with

To the rest of the Preface.

Vide Aug. lib. 2. cont. Iul. cap. 2.

The maiestie of the Catholike cause.

D　vs:

vs : no one man of credite euer opening
his mouth against vs, vntill within thefe
threefcore yeares, a run-agate Frier began the dance; which notwithftanding
impugneth as much you as vs: you being
(according to the nature and prefident
of all former Herefies)diuided moft hate-
fully in your owne bowels. And what a
poore faction you are, I meane your partie Proteftant, together with all the rab-
blement of Sectaries now liuing, in refpect of the Maiefty of Chriftendome befides: all men do fee,but onely you; who
fitting at home in your Parfonage by the
fire, doe imagine the credit of your caufe
abroad , by the authoritie you beare in
that Parifh alone.

Wherefore,to leaue this,and to come
at length to the Cenfure it felfe : I will
put downe the very words thereof at
large, for perfpicuitie fake, and for auoiding many long and tedious repetitions
of former fpeeches , which otherwife of
neceffitie muft haue beene made, for the
vnderftanding of that, which hath been
already written: for want whereof alfo
(if it were not of purpofe) I fee your Reply to be fo obfcure and dark(M.*Charke*)

as

as had it not beene by the helpe of the
Cenfure it felfe, which I compared with
it, I could hardly haue geffed at your
meaning in many places. Which helpe,
feeing you know that many which might
reade your booke, could not haue; it feemeth you meant not to be vnderftood of
all, but to creepe away vnder the bare
name and fhadow of a Reply, without
fuffering them to know what your Ad-
uerfarie had faid againft you. But now I
hope by putting downe the Cenfure it
felfe, all things fhall be made cleare, and
as well that, as your Reply, and my Defence fhall appeare effectually. And although I meane to vfe as great breuitie, as my poore wit can reach vnto: yet truft I to omit nothing of
fubftance, which you fay : nor
to let it paffe without
due examina-
tion.

THE TABLE OF THE
CONTENTS.

A 9

The Table of the Contents.

D 3   AN

AN APPENDIX TO THE *PRECEDENT TREATISE*,
containing two Arguments; pro-
uing Proteſtants not to haue
the holy Spirit of
GOD.

THE FIRST ARGVMENT.

If Proteſtants Spirit were the true Spi-
rit of God, it would haue the proper-
ties thereof.
But it hath not.
Ergo, *It is not the true Spirit of God.*

FIRST, it is certaine that the Spirit of
God inclineth men to humilitie, modeſtie, concord, and vnitie, &c. but this
Proteſtant Spirit (as experience of all
time, ſince it came into the world teacheth) hath ordinarily wrought in men,
quite contrary effects, to wit, Pride, Immodeſtie, Diſcord, and Diſunitie, &c. I
will exemplifie in one of their principall
men, who was ſpecially inſpired, and
had

Coloſ.3.12.
Phil.2.1,2.
1.Cor.3.
10.

D 4

Qua maior superbia, &c.

had the first fruits of this their Spirit. By which example one may gesse what is to be thought of the rest, proportionably, according as they doe, more or lesse, participate of the same Spirit.

What greater pride is there, then that one man should preter his iudgement before the whole Congregation, as though hee alone had the Spirit of God?

What intollerable pride was in *Martin Luther*, the first inspired Protestant Prophet, may bee easily seene. First, in that he being but one pettie Doctor, preferred his judgement of the sense of Scripture, before a thousand *Augustines*, a thousand *Cyprians*, and against the whole streame of ancient and present Doctors of the Catholike Church. Secondly, in his impudent boasting of his owne selfe, in calling himselfe *a faithfull Prophet*, an *Apostle* an *Euangelist*, a *liuing Saint*; and saying, that he learned not his doctrine of men, but of our Lord Iesus. Thirdly, in his very manner of speeches, set down by *Zuinglius*, in a certain book, where (hauing described, as it were, a picture of *Luther* in his anger, running vp and downe, sparkling with his eyes, breathing out smoake and fire, vomiting out reuiling words) hee setteth downe

D. Ber ser. 3. deR. sur. Luth. to. 2. Ies. Germ. fol. 522. b. & 79. to. 3. fol. 341. a. tom. 4. fol. 286. a & 280. a tom. 5. fol. 398. a b. See *Vlemberge* his booke called *Graues & iuste cause in causa, 7. & 8.*

some

ſome of theſe his words; as *Swermer*, *Di-uell*, *Knaue*, *Heretike*, *Theefe*, *Seditious*, *Hypocrite*, *Trots*, *Bots*, *Plots*, *Phls*, and ſuch like.

As for the immodeſtie of this man, his owne writings will beare witneſſe; in which hee vttereth ſuch outragious and ſcurrillous reuiling words, as I am a-ſhamed to ſet downe, not onely againſt Eccleſiaſticall perſons, but euen againſt Temporall Princes, and among other a-gainſt our King *Henry* the eight. *a Ix libel-lo Latino contra Re-gem Ang-lie.*

See the Defence of the Cenſure, page 15. where among other his words theſe are related: I doe denounce (ſaith he) the ſentence of damnation: This mad buggiſh *Thomiſt*; miſerable Booke-maker; a god lately borne in England; I ſay plainly, this *Harry* lyeth manifeſt-ly, and ſheweth himſelfe a moſt light Scurrill: Of this crime doe I *Luther* accuſe this poyſoned *Thomiſt*; I talke with a lying Scurrill, couered with the Titles of a King; a *Thomiſticall* braine, a clowniſh wit; a doltiſh head; a Bugge and Hypocrite of the *Thomiſts*; moſt wicked, fooliſh, and impudent *Harry*, &c. *Lib contra Regem Ang, homi 2. Wittemb.* *Fol. 334.* *Fol. 338.* *Fol. 337.*

The

The difcord and diſunitie of Proteſtants is moſt apparant to the world; yet to exemplifie it in L v t h e r; it is knowne, that hee doth not onely differ from *Zuinglius*, *Caluine*, and other Proteſtant Doctors, but alſo from himſelfe, ſuch being the nature of the Spirit of diſſention, that it doth not ſuffer a man to agree, neither with others, nor with himſelfe.

This difcord, Proteſtants themſelues cannot deny, but to couer this skar, firſt they ſay, that theſe diſſentions are onely light Schoole-skirmiſhes; and this alſo about ſmall matters; or at leaſt not in any fundamentall point. Secondly, they ſay, the like hath beene alwayes, euen among the ancient Fathers, and are now among vs Catholikes.

To ſtoppe theſe two ſtarting holes, I can ſhew that theſe their diſſentions, are neyther ſo light in the matter, nor ſo ſleight in the manner, as they would make men beleeue. For proofe whereof, I call to witneſſe their virulent bo kes, in which they condemne one anothr of damnable errour and hereſie, in chiefe poynts and articles of Faith. And where-

as

See *Iodocus Cocc. tom.*10. *Theſaur. lib.*8.

See *Vlenberg.cauſa* 9. & 10.

See *Caluino Turciſmo, l.*3.

as they would gladly make the holy Fa- *Iodocus*
thers , and vs , partakers of the like *Coccius,*
diſſentions; they will neuer bee able to *tom.10.*
prooue, that eyther the ancient Fathers, *lib.8.*
or wee , in our Schoole-queſtions, con- *Proteſt.*
demne one another of damnable here- *Apology.*
ſie , or that in any article of Faith, there
is any varietie of beleefe among vs.
Beſides , if there ſhould happen any varietie of opinions among vs, about matters of Faith, we haue a certaine rule and
meanes to compoſe and end controuerſies; to wit, the ſentence of the chiefe Paſtor, either alone , or with a Generall
Councell; which rule and meanes, Proteſtants want.

Another propertie of the Spirit of
God, is, that it teacheth men the certaine
and infallible truth; and neuer decei- *Ioh.16.13.*
ueth any , by teaching any thing that is
falſe; being therefore , worthily called the Spirit of Truth. But the Proteſtant Spirit , ſometimes teacheth falſe.
For euery particular pure Proteſtant, hath
in him his Spirit, by which hee is taught
what to beleeue in matters of Faith;
and yet ſince one is taught, by this their
Spirit , to hold and beleeue , in matters
of

of Faith, quite contrary to other Protestants: yea sometimes, quite contrary to
their owne selues, it followeth that this
Spirit, sometimes teacheth false, in regard
contrary doctrines cannot be all true.

If my Aduersaries shall say, that this
Spirit is infallible, and teacheth alwayes
the truth, when men that haue it, reade
and follow the Scriptures, and not their
owne deuices, or phantasies. I aske first,
whether the Spirit of Protestants, doth
neuer teach infallibly true, but when the
men that haue it, reade Scriptures, and
judge, according to that they finde written in them? If so: what shall we say, of
that inward testification of the Spirit, by
which they say, they know the Scriptures
themselues to be diuine? Since it is no
where written in Scripture; that these,
and onely these bookes, which they call
Canonicall, be diuine Scripture. Secondly, if the Protestant Spirit teacheth alwayes infallibly true, when the men that
haue it, reade the Scriptures, and judge
according to that they finde written in
them: how chance *Lutherans* and *Caluinists* agree not, for example, in the Controuersie of the Reall presence? They
both

both haue the Protestant Spirit; and, by
it they both are (as they thinke) assured,
in whatsoeuer they beleeue, as matter of
Faith; and both of them do, in this Controuersie, reade the Scripture, conferre,
places, and vse all other diligence, in
their judgement requisite, to make true
judgement; and yet they hold quite contrarie one to the other, in this important
matter of Faith, only as they suppose out
of, and according to Scripture; therefore
the Protestant Spirit, euen when men
that haue it, reade and (after their manner) follow the Scriptures, teacheth con-
traries; and consequently teacheth som-
time false; since contrary doctrines cannot both be true.

Thirdly, how, or by what signes shall
one be infallibly sure, when hee followeth the Scriptures; that thereby he may
be assured, when hee is infallibly taught
by the Spirit? For to say that we are infallibly taught by the Spirit, when wee
follow the Scripture, auaileth little, to
breed certaintie of any doctrine. If there
be no meanes to assure vs, when we follow the Scripture, since the nature of our
vnderstanding is such, that it cannot bee
assured

affured of a thing, depending vpon the fulfilling of a condition; vnleffe there bee fome means, by which it may be affuredly knowne, when the condition is fulfilled. To reade, and to conferre places of Scripture, and to vfe other diligence, is not fufficient to affure one, that hee followeth the Scripture; fince diuers holding contrarie doctrines, doe all this, and yet get not this affurance.

To run to the teftimony of the Proteftant Spirit (befides that it is a circle) cannot giue abfolute affurance, fince among thofe that haue this Spirit, fome do think they haue as good affurance, by the teftimony of it, for their opinion, as others thinke they haue for theirs. And no more reafon (at leaft fometimes) can be alledged by one, why his inward teftification fhould bee held to proceed from the true Spirit of God, then may be alledged on the contrary part by others. For to fay they are affured that their inward teftification proceedeth frō the Spirit of God, becaufe it is the true Spirit, and becaufe it is conformable to Scripture; is abfurdly to beg the queftion, giuing that for a reafon, which their Aduerfarie will require

chiefely

chiefely to be proued; or giddily to run the round, prouing the testification of their Spirit to be conformable to a place of Scripture, because it is the testification of the Spirit of God: and againe, prouing it to be the testification of the Spirit of God, because it is conformable to that same place of Scripture.

The Second Argvment.

> *If the Protestants Spirit were the true Spirit of God; then doubtlesse it would agree with the Spirit which was in them, whom themselues grant to haue had the Spirit of God.*
>
> *But it doth not agree with the Spirit, which was in them, whom themselues will grant, to haue had the Spirit of God.*
>
> Ergo, *It is not the true Spirit of God.*

FIRST, they will grant (I hope) that the Spirit of God was in the Apostles, and in their Successours, the ancient Fathers of the first fiue hundred, or sixe hundred yeares. But the Protestant Spi-

rit

rit is not like the Spirit of the Apostles, or ancient Fathers ; neither in matters beleeued, nor in the maner which they vsed, both firft to breed, and after to continue, certainty, & vnity of beliefe among Chriftians. As concerning matters beleeued, I might alledge fo many differences, as there are feuerall Controuerfies betwixt Proteftants & vs. But becaufe this would be too tedious, I refer the Reader to that which is fhewed by *Iodocus Coccius*, who in two great Volumes , fetteth downe points of Controuerfies, betwixt Proteftants and vs, and for euery point, as they are holden by vs , and denyed by proteftants, he firft fetteth downe fentences of Scripture , then the Greeke and Latine Fathers, citing at large their words, and the place, where they pronounce for vs, againft Proteftants.

Hebr.5. 4. As for the maner vfed by the Apoftles, and their Succeffors ; firft to breed, and after to continue in Chriftians, certainty, and vnity of beliefe; one fpecial obferuation was, that no man (ordinarily) fhould take vpon him the office of preaching, who was not lawfully called, appointed, and fent to preach to the people, that doctrine

Rom. 10. 15.

ctrine which he had formerly learned of
the Apoſtles, or their Succeſſours, the appointed Doctors and Paſtors of Gods
Church : yea this they ſo carefully obſer-
ued, that S. *Paul* himſelfe (although extra-
ordinarily taught, and appointed as a veſ-
ſell of election) thought it neceſſary to aſ-
cend to *Ieruſalem*, to confer the Goſpell,
which he preached, with the other Apoſtles; leſt, perhaps, the Church might not
receiue the authority of his preaching: &
that, conſequently, his preaching ſhould
be in vaine. Now the Proteſtants haue v-
ſed, & do vſe a contrary manner, not only
in that their firſt Euangeliſt *Luther*, neither did leerne (as himſelfe cofeſſeth) the
new Goſpell which he preached, of any
man; neither was lawfully called, appointed, & ſent to preach this new Goſpel, by
the then liuing Paſtors of Gods Church :
who rather reproued, and contradicted
him for his audacious & temerarious fact:
but alſo in that they gaue liberty to euery
one to teach themſelues, only by reading
or hearing the Bible; ſeeming alſo to permit euery one, learned and vnlearned, to
examine and judge their Paſtors doctrine
by Scripture, & to imbrace that doctrine,

Act.9.15.
Gal.2.2.

Luther tom.4. fol. 186. & 280.

E   which

which by the reading or hearing of Scripture, shalbe suggested by their priuat spirit, to be true and conformable to Scripture; without respect or care, whether that which is suggested by their Spirit, be, or be not agreeable to that, which is, or hath bin formerly taught (by the ordinary Pastors of Gods Church) to be conformable to Scripture: which cānot chuse but breed great vncertainty, and so much variety of opinions, in matters of Faith, as there are diuersities of priuate spirits; the which to be true, daily experience maketh manifest to the world.

Another obseruation, vsed by the Apostles & Apostolike Pastors, to breed and continue certainty, and vnity of Faith in Christians, was, that when any important Cōtrouersie of religion did arise; they did not send men to *onely* Scriptures, or to euery ones priuate spirit; but (as we may *Act.* 15.28 learne in the Acts of the Apostles, and in Ecclesiasticall Histories) they assembled Councels, and did by their infallible Decree (of *Visum est spiritui sancto, & Nobis:*) end the Cōtrouersies. But Protestants do send men for finall resolution of Cōtrouersies of Faith, *to only Scripture,* & thinke

it

it fitter to haue Controuerſies continue,
then to be tied to the Decrees of generall
Councels, made by the common Spirit of
the Church. Secondly (by affirming all
neceſſary matters, to be ſufficiently deci-
ded *by only Scripture*) they ſeeme to hold
Councels to be needleſſe; & conſequently, they controule the practiſe of the Apoſtles themſelues, who thought it, in ſome *Act.* 15.28
ſort, needfull to aſſemble a Councell, to
determine a Controuerſie about matters,
ſome of which they concluded to be neceſſary. They controule alſo the practiſe
of the ancient Fathers, who would neuer
haue aſſembled ſo many general Coũcels
with ſo much trouble & coſt, if they had See this
not thought the matters to be neceſſary : more at
and that this meanes of a generall Coun- large in
cell, was, in ſome ſort, needfull in theſe ca- *Caluino-*
ſes, to breed & cõtinue certainty, & vnity *turciſmo.*
of true belief in the Church. Thirdly, whẽ *lib.*1.*cap.*3
Cõtrouerſies of Religiõ riſe among Pro-
teſtants, ſuch is their Spirit, that it is impoſſible to end them by a general Coũcel.

For firſt, they are neuer able to gather a
general Councel of Proteſtants, in regard
they wil neuer agree, who are, & whõ are
not to be accounted true Proteſtants; &

conſe-

consequently who are to be admitted in the Councel. Secondly, admit the Coūcel were gathered, they would neuer agree who should be Actors, & who should be Iudges, or what means should be accoūted sufficient, to find out the truth: or if they should agree, that onely Scripture should be the means, Actor, & Iudge, yet there should be controuersie, how many books, and which particuler translations should be accounted true Scripture. And when all were done, the question would yet remain, which side of the Controuersie were fauoured by the Scripture, if no meanes were vsed, to finde out the right sense, besides the bare words of Scripture which both parties had read before, and which each party would expound in fauour of his own side. Now if they did admit other meanes; either this should be ancient Councels, & Fathers; or els euery ones priuat Spirit. If Councels & Fathers; they would neuer agree, which, and how far they were, in particuler doctrines, to be admitted. And as for priuate Spirits, euery one seeth, that they would agree no better, then they did before they came to the Councell, since neuer a one would

submit

ſubmit that which he firmely thought,to be ſuggeſted by the Spirit, to any, or all the men in the world. Thirdly, admit the Councell had concluded one thing; what nearer were they to retaine vnity, in that matter, whē their Spirit telleth them, that it is ſtil free for euery one of them, to examine & to judge, whether this definition of their Councell, were rightly made, or not, according to Scripture, with power in euery priuate man to reuerſe it, if to his Spirit it ſeeme not rightly made.

A third obſeruation, both of the Apoſtles and Fathers, (originally deſcending frō the expreſſe ordinance of Chriſt himſelfe) was to acknowledge Eccleſiaſticall ſuperiority and authority; namely, of one viſible Head, and chiefe Paſtor, in ſtead of Chriſt: *vt Capite conſtituto ſchiſmatis tolleretur occaſio*; that a Head being appointed, occaſion of Schiſme might be taken away; it being wel enough knowne vnto them, that, not onely in a particuler Church, but much more in the vniuerſall multitude of Chriſtiās, diſperſed through the world, it was very hard, if not impoſſible, to keep vnity, if there were not ſome one Head, whoſe ſentence were to bee

Iob,21.17.

Hier.cont.
Iouinian.

heard,

heard, & obeyed by al, in stead of Christ; as it was also to them very well knowne (which is now adaies euidently by experience seene) that from nothing so much did Heresies and Schismes spring, as from want of due practise of this obseruation. Now the Protestant Spirit abhorreth nothing so much, as the practise of this obseruation, and therfore no maruel though there are, & daily more & more wil grow among thē, so many different sects, without any means of vnity or reconciliation.

Thus we see, how vnlike the Spirit of Protestants is vnlike to the Spirit of the Apostles & ancient Fathers; whom, notwithstanding, they cannot deny to haue had the Spirit of God. Perhaps they may ascribe this variety and difference of their Spirit from the Apostles and ancient Fathers, to the diuersity of times, saying, then was then, and now is now. If they say so (as they cannot but absurdly, in regard the Spirit of God is stil one ard the same, and doth not, in this manner varie from it selfe, according to the varietie of times) yet, at least, we must looke to find it like, & to agree well with those whom at this very time theimselues think to haue

the

the true Spirit. But this we shall not find
to bee so ; for the *Sacramentary* Protestants will admit the *Lutherans* for their
brethren; and consequently may not deny them to haue the true Spirit. But what
good agreemēt is betwixt the *Sacramen-*
tary, and the *Lutheran* Spirit, I referre me
to their bitter inuectiues one against another, about points of Faith, euen of great
importance : about which also, euen *Sa-*
cramentaries with other *Sacramentaries*,
& *Lutherans* with other *Lutherans*, haue
no such excellēt agreemēt, as were fit for
men that had the same Spirit, as I might
easily shew out of diuers good * Authors.

Well, to conclude this point, if one
Protestant had one and the same Spirit,
which others (euen Protestants) haue, he
should be as apt to beleeue in matters of
Faith, that, which is suggested to others
by their Spirit, as that which is suggested
to himselfe, by his own priuate Spirit. But
this wee shall neuer finde among Protestants of the hotter spirited sort, who,
when once they settle firmely a conceit
vpon any thing, which being suggested
by their owne priuate Spirit, they thinke
to be conformable to Scripture they will

not

* See be-
sides *V-*
lenberge,
Coccius.
Caluino-
turcismo,
aboue ci-
ted.
The Pro-
testants
Apology,
which
setteth
out a Ta-
ble of
their bit-
ter books
written
one a-
gainst an-
other.

not beleeue any one , nor neuer so great
a multitude of others , although more
learned , and wise, although better stu-
died in Scripture ; although saying and
swearing , that they feele the contrary, suggested by their Spirit, to bee
conformable to Scripture. And as one
noteth well there is one point, to wit
(that euery one must beleeue the certaintie of his own Election, Iustification,and
Saluation) which no other (beside himselfe) doth beleeue by infallible faith,but
onely probable hope. So as in this point
which by Protestants is esteemed a most
materiall , fundamentall and necessary
point. There is not any one Protestant
whose Spirit doth agree with the Spirit
of another. Therefore since the Spirit of
God inclineth men to agree with others
in beleefe, the Protestant Spirit is not the
Spirit of God.

F I N I S.

A

COMPARISON OF A
TRVE ROMAN CATHO-
LIKE WITH A PROTESTANT,
whereby may be discouered the difference of their Spirits, not only in things
belonging to faith and beleefe, but also
concerning their liues, conuersation
and manners : taken out of a more
ample discourse of this subiect,
made by that worthy and reue-
rend Father, F. Parsons, *in*
the 20. *Chapter of his Ex-*
amen of Fox *his Ca-*
lendar, the last six
Moneths.

FIRST the Roman Catholike (whom *Fox* calleth Papist) tou-ching matters of Faith and be-leefe, composeth himselfe to that humi-litie, as whether he bee learned or vn-learned, or what arguments soeuer hee hath on the one or other side : yet pre-sumeth hee to determine nothing of himselfe, but remitteth that determi-nation (if any thing be doubtfull or vndetermined) vnto the judgement

A comparison of a true Roman Catho-like with a Prote-stant in matter of doctrine.

A   and

and decree of the vniuerfall Church,
and Gouernours thereof. And hence
proceedeth the agreements and vnitie
of Faith, which they haue held and con-
serued in so large a body, for so many
ages, as haue passed since Christ and
his Apostles. Whereas Protestants in
this behalfe following another Spirit
of selfe-will, and selfe judgement, and
loosing the raynes of libertie to the
pregnancie of each mans wit, doe hold
and determine what their owne judgements for the time doe thinke to bee
true, or most probable, and are subject
to no authoritie in this behalfe, but to
their owne Spirit; which is variable,
according to the varietie of arguments
and probabilities that doe occurre. And
hereof doe ensue the great varietie of
sects and opinions among them, euen
in this one age since they began, as you
may see by that which is set downe in
the third and seuenteenth Chapters of
the fourth part of the three Conuersi-
ons of England.

Next to this, for so much as appertaineth to life and actions; the Catholike man holdeth that wee can doe nothing

thing at all of our selues, no not so much as to thinke a good thought, but we must be preuented and assisted by Gods holy grace, as may bee shewed out of the Councell of Trent, which *Concil.* teacheth with Saint *Paul*, that our suf- *Trid. Seff.* ficiencie is of Christ; yet is the force of *6. cap. 16.* this grace so tempered notwithstanding, as it vseth no violence, nor excludeth the free concurrance of mans wil, preuented and stirred vp by the foresaid grace of our Sauiour, and motion of the holy Ghost: So as freely by this helpe, we yeeld to the said good motions, and doe beleeue in God, and his promises: and this act of Faith (as you may learne out of the said Councel) is *Seff.6.s.8.* the first foundation and root of all our justification: but yet not sufficient of it selfe, except Charitie and Hope (two other Theologicall vertues) doe accompany the same; so as we dee both loue and hope in him, in whom we beleeue. And out of these, and by direction of these, doe flow againe other Christian vertues, called morall; for that they appertaine to the direction of life and manners, which vertues doe

A 2   consist

consist principally in the inward habits
and actes of the mind, and from thence
doe proceede to the externall actions
and operations, whereby wee exercise
our selues in keeping Gods Commandements, and exercising workes of pietie toward our neighbour, as cloathing
the naked, feeding the hungry, visiting
the sicke, and the like. In workes of
deuotion in like maner, as singing, and
praying to God, kneeling, knocking
our breasts, mortifying our bodies, by
fasting, watching, and other such like.
All which exteriour actions are so farre
forth commendable and meritorious,
as they proceed from the inward vertues and motions of Gods Spirit.

External
actions
flowing
of inter-
nall ver-
tues.

S. *Tho.* 1.
2. q. 20.
art. 4.
And albeit (as Saint *Thomas* saith)
these exteriour actes doe adde nothing
in substantiall goodnesse to the inward
acts, but haue their merit from thence;
yet, for that man consisteth both of spirit and flesh, it was reason that hee
should bee bound to honor God with
both, that is to say, both with inward
acts of vertue, proceeding from Gods
grace and motion, and with outward
vertuous actes, testifying the inward,
                                    where-

whereby wee see what an excellent Christian Common-wealth the Catholike Religion doth appoint, if it were executed according to her doctrine, to wit, that all mens minds should be replenished with all sort of vertues, towards both God & our neighbor, and that their actions should be full of all righteousnesse, pietie and charitie in exteriour behauiour, so as neither in thought, word, nor deede they should offend either of them both. And thus much for the Catholike man, concerning his actions, life and manners.

But this Catholike Religion doth not stay heere, nor teach onely in generall what actions a Christian man should haue, and from what internall principles of grace and vertue they should flow, but doth offer vs diuers particular means also how to procure, and conserue, and increase this grace, which is the fountaine of al goodnesse: for first, it exhibiteth vnto vs, besides all other meanes of prayer, and particular indeauours of our part, seuen generall meanes and instruments left vs to that purpose, by the institution of

The Catholike doctrine of seuen Sacraments, and their vse.

A 3   Christ

Chrift himfelfe, which are feuen Sacraments, that being receiued with due difpofition of the receiuer, doe alwaies bring grace by the vertue and force of Chrifts merit and inftitution, without dependance of the merit, or demerit of the Minifter that adminiftreth them. By vfe of which Sacraments, infinite grace is deriued daily by Chrift our Sauiour vnto his Church, and particular members thereof, in euery ftate and degree of men.

Moreouer, Catholike Religion not contented with thefe generalities, doth come yet more in particular to frame direct, and helpe a Chriftian man in the way of his faluation, euen from the firft houre of his birth in Chrift, vntill his foule, departing from this world, be rendered vp againe into his Creators hands. For firft, he hauing all his fins forgiuen clearely and freely by the grace of Chrift receiued in *Baptifme*, hee is ftrengthened to the fight and courfe of a true Chriftian life, by the Sacrament of *Confirmation*, and impofition of hands : his foule alfo is fed, and nourifhed fpiritually by the facred food

The particular direction of a Chriftian man from his Baptifme vntill his death, by helpe of diuers Sacraments.
Baptifme.
Confirmation.

food of our Sauiours bodie in the *En-* *Eucharist.*
charist : two seuerall states of Christian
life are peculiarly assisted with grace of
two particular Sacraments, Priests and
Clergie-men by the Sacrament of *Ho-* *Holy Or-*
ly Orders; and maried people by the *der.*
Sacrament of *Matrimony*. And for *Mariage.*
that in this large race and course of life
(as Saint *Paul* calleth it) we often fall
and offend God by reason of our infir-
mitie ; there is a most soueraigne Sacrament of *Penance*, for remedie here- *Penance.*
of appointed by our prouident Saui-
our, founded in the merits of his sacred
Passion, called *Secunda tabula post nau-* *Hier. in*
fragium, by holy Fathers, that is, the *cap.3.Esa.*
second table or planke, whereon wee *& ep.8.ad*
may lay hands, and escape drowning, *Demetr.*
after the shipwracke of our pardon, *Pacian.ep.*
1. ad Sym-
grace and iustification receiued in our *pron.*
Baptisme, which was the first table : by
which second table of *Penance*, all sorts
may rise againe how often soeuer they
fall ; which Sacrament consisteth of
three parts, sorrow for our sinnes, and *Contrition*
confessing the same, for the remission *Confession*
of the guilt, and some kinde of satisfa- *Satisfa-*
ction on our behalfe, for remouing the *ction.*

A 4   tem-

temporall punifhment remaining : the true vfe whereof bringeth fuch exceeding helpe and comfort to a Chriftian foule, as it is vnfpeakable. For that by the firft two parts a man is oft brought fweetly to forrow for his fins, to thinke vpon them, to deteft them, aske pardon of God for them, to make new purpofes of better life for the time to come, to examine his confcience more particularly, and other fuch heauenly effects as no man can tell the comfort thereof, but he that receiueth them.

The force of Satisfaction.
By the third part alfo, which is *Satisfaction*, though a man performe neuer fo little thereof in this life, yet doth it greatly auaile him, not onely in refpect of the grateful acceptation thereof at Gods hands, for that it commeth freely of his owne good will, but alfo for that it humbleth euen the proudeft minde in the fight of almightie God : it reftraineth alfo greatly our wicked appetites from fin for the time to come, when we know wee muft giue a particular account, and fatisfie alfo for our fenfualities fomewhat euen in this world. And finally, it is the very chiefe
sinew

sinew of Christian conuersation and behauiour one towards another : for when the rich man knoweth (for example sake) that he must satisfie one way or another, and be bound by his ghostly father to make restitution so farre, as hee is able, of whatsoeuer hee hath wrongfully taken from the poor, when the poore also are taught that they must doe the like towards the rich, the sonne towards his father, the seruant towards his master, if bee haue deceiued him ; when the murmurer in like manner knoweth that he must make actuall restitution of fame (if he haue defamed any) this Catholike doctrine, I say, and practise, must needs be a strong hedge to all vertuous and pious conuersation among men, that beleeue and follow the same.

And finally, not to passe to more particularities, whereas Catholike doctrine teacheth vs, that all or most disorders of this life in a sensuall man (to omit the infirmities of our higher powers in like manner) doe proceede originally from the fountaine of *Concupiscence*, and law of the flesh remaining

The war ning in vs after our baptisme, and, *ad*
of Con- *certamen*, as holy Fathers do tearme it,
cupiscece that is to say, for our conflict and com-
and helpe bate, to the end our life may be a true
of Gods warfare, as the holy Scripture calleth
grace for it. This Concupiscence, I say, or sen-
the same. suall motion, being the ground of our
temptations, though it be not sinne of
it selfe, except we consent vnto it, yet
is shee busie in stirring vs daily to wickednesse; as a Christian mans principall
exercise, and diligence, ought to be in
resisting her, which he may doe by the
helpe and assistance of Christs grace,
(merited by his sacred Passion) wherein he extinguished the guilt of this ori-
ginall corruption, though hee left still
the sting and prouocation for our greater merit, and continuall victory by his
holy grace, in them that will striue and
fight, as they may and ought to doe.

But yet, for that this fight is com-
bersome, and fastidious in it selfe, and
deadly also to many, that suffer themselues to be ouercome; the Catholike
Religion doth teach a man how he shal
fight in this conflict, what armes, and
defence he may vse in particular to defend

fend himfelfe, and to gaine victorie.
And to this head or branch are reduced
all our fpirituall bookes and volumes
about mortification, as well of our wil,
judgement, and affections of minde,
as all other parts alfo of our inferiour
fenfualitie, to wit, how you may refift
this and that temptation, what preuen-
tion you may make, what bulwarke
you may raife, what defence you may
reft vpō, wherin do enter all particular
directiōs, of fafting, prayer, watching,
haire-cloath, lying on the ground, and
other bodily afflictions fo much vfed
by olde Saints, and may bee vfed alfo now by all (if they will) for gaining
of this important victorie : there entreth alfo among other defences, that
great and foueraigne remedie of flying
the world wholly, and retyring to the
port of a religious life, for fuch as o-
therwife fee themfelues either weake,
or in danger to bee wholly ouercome
by this venimous beaft of Concupi-
fcence, or elfe doe defire to merit more
aboundantly at Gods hands, by offering themfelues wholly and entirely to
his feruice, and to the more neere imi-
tation

tation of their Lord and Sauiour. By all which helpes, assistances, and directions deliuered in this behalfe by Catholike doctrine, to euery mans state and degree of life, a Catholike Christian passeth on more securely during his life, and at his last going out of this world, receiueth finally the grace and comfort of the last Sacrament of *Extreame vnction*, instituted by Christ, and recommended vnto vs by Saint *Iames* his Apostle; and from thence passeth to receiue that eternall joy and kingdome at his Sauiours hands, which hee hath prepared for them that beleeue in him, and striue and fight for him in this life against sinne and iniquitie.

Extreame vnction.
Iames 5.

And thus haue we described briefly, but seriously and truely, the state and condition of a Roman Catholike man, to oppose the same against a ridiculous vaine definition, or rather fiction of IOHN FOX. But now if wee would paragon the same with the Protestants Doctrine and practise, in all these points before mentioned, we shal quickly see the difference. And as for the first point of all, concerning Faith and

and beleefe in generall, the difference is ſo palpably ſet downe in that which hath bin alreadie ſaid, as it is needleſſe to ſay any more.

In the ſecond point concerning the inward principles of our outward actions: truth it is, that they agree with vs in ſomewhat, to wit, that all good commeth originally from Gods holy grace and motion; but preſently they diſagree againe, for that they hold our grace of Iuſtification to be no inherent qualitie, but onely an externall imputation, and that Gods motion to our minde is ſuch, as it excludeth wholly all concourſe and cooperation of our Free-will, whereby they cut off at one blow, all endeauours of our part to do any goodneſſe at all, and leaue vs as a ſtone or blocke to be moued by God onely, whereof alſo enſueth, that hee muſt needs be author of our ſins, and other blaſphemies, and infinite incon-ueniences, not only in matter of Faith, but in life and actions alſo; for that this principle being once receiued, that our Free-will, though it be preuented, mooued and ſtrengthened by Gods grace,

The comparison of the foreſaid Catholike doctrine, with that of the Proteſtants.

grace, can doe nothing at all, nor cooperate to any good worke, or refist any euill: who will haue care afterward to endeauour, labour, ftriue, or wearie himfelfe about any thing that is difficult, or difpleafant vnto him?

Next to this, concerning the vertues Theologicall, of Faith, Hope and Charity, Proteftants are content with Faith only to our juftification, as you fee by *Iohn Fox*, who faith that the Scriptures doe exprefly exclude both Hope and Charitie. And albeit fome other of his fect will feeme to couer the matter, by faying, that Hope and Charitie do follow Faith as fruits thereof, if it be true Faith; yet in practife is there no man of thē indeed, that will permit his faith to this triall: but whether he haue thefe fruits or noe, he will defend his faith to be good, and that himfelfe is juftified thereby. So as from hence you fee another gappe opened to all prefumption and liberty of life: for howfoeuer a Proteftant liueth, yet will he not yeeld thereby that his faith is nought (and indeed the argument inforceth it not) and then followeth it, that his faith being

Fox. p.22.

cap. proced,

ing good, hee is justified, and consequently, howsoeuer he liue, yet is hee
a just man, and who will trouble himselfe with the labour of a good life, if
beleeuing onely be sufficient. And this
for internall vertues.

But as for externall actions, euen
those of the Law and ten Commandements commanded by Christ himselfe,
Fox derideth them in our people, as
may be seene in his Definition, and requireth onely two exteriour actions in
his people, to wit, *Baptizing* and sup-
ping, or celebrating the *Lords Supper*,
for all other matters, hee saith, no one
thing is necessary for the exercise of his
new Gospell, or to make a perfect
Christian after his definition. So as if
you lay before you two sorts of people, the one labouring and wholly oc-
cupying themselues in all godly life,
fructificantes in omni bono opere, fructi- Coloss. 1.
fying in all good workes (as the Apo- vers.10.
stles words are, who also in the same
place calleth this worke, The true wisdome and right vnderstanding of Gods
heauenly will, and worthie walking
before him:) you may behold, I say,
the

The continuall exercises of Catholikes in good workes.

the one sort of these people, which *Fox* calleth Papists, not onely endued with inward good desires, but externally also busied altogether in good deeds, shewing the same by the fruits of their inward vertues, to wit, in building of Churches, Hospitals, Monasteries, Colledges, giuing almes, maintaining Orphanes, Widdowes and Pupills, receiuing Pilgrimes, and other such Christian exercises, as also meeting at Churches, praying on their knees, sighing and sobbing for their sinnes, and confessing the same to Gods substitute, to wit, their ghostly father, asking pardon also of their neighbours, and making restitution, if any thing with euill conscience they haue taken or withholden, &c. Whiles in the meane space, the other sort accounted Saints of the new making by *Fox*, doe walke vp and downe, talking of their beleefe, but lay their hands vpon no good external worke at all by obligation, if wee beleeue *Fox*, except onely the *Lords Supper*, nor is it incident to their vocation. And hereby also may we consider, how great a difference there is betweene these

theſe two ſorts of people in a Common-wealth, where they liue together,
and what an infinite gate is laid open
by this looſſe new doctrine, to idlenes
and laſie behauiour in Chriſtian conuerſation , quite oppoſite not onely to
the doctrine and practiſe of ancient
Fathers, and the Primitiue Church, but
to the whole courſe of Scriptures, in
like manner, which euery where doe
inculcate with all ſollicitude, the continual performance of externall good
works , and that thereby indeed true
Chriſtians are knowne, in exerciſing
themſelues in Chriſts Cõmandements.

And as for Sacraments, which according to our doctrine, are heauenly
conduites and moſt excellent inſtru-
ments, appointed by God, for deriuing
of gráce vnto vs in euery ſtate and condition of Chriſtian men; theſe fellowes
doe firſt cut off fiue of the ſeuen , and
the other two they doe ſo weaken and
debaſe; as they are ſcarce worthy the
receiuing: for they doe not hold , that
either their *Baptiſme*, or the *Lords Supper*, doth giue any grace at all to him
that receiueth them, though hee pre-
B pare

The dif-
ference
about
Sacra-
ments
and ef-
fects
thereof.

pare himselfe neuer so well thereunto,
but onely that they are certaine signes
of their election & iustification, which
signes notwithstanding , hauing no
more certaintie in them, then themselues list to apprehend by their special
faith, concerning their owne iustification, and the matter standing in their
owne hands to shew themselues iustified, when they will ; by these signes it
seemeth indeed to be a very iest or co-
medie, but yet breaketh down a maine
bank of Christiã discipline, care & sollicitude, that is to be seene in our men,
when they receiue any Sacrament, for
that beleeuing (as Catholique Faith
teacheth them) that all Sacraments
bring grace to them, that receiue them
with due preparation, and of their own
part, put no let by their indisposition ;
they doe labour and endeauour to pre-
pare themselues worthily, to the said
receiuing therof, by Penance, Fasting,
Prayer, Almes-deeds, and other like
holy endeauours, assuring themselues
also on the contrary side, that negligent
receiuing of Sacraments doth not onely not bring grace, but encreaseth rather

The dif-
ferent
prepara-
tion to
receiue
Sacra-
ments.

ther their owne offence. So as this preparation of Catholike people to the receiuing of Sacraments, is a continuall
kinde of spurre to good purposes, vertue and renouation of life: whereas
this other sort of good fellowes, perswading themselues that their Sacraments are onely bare signes of things
already past; and as it were, a continuall representation of justification alreadie receiued, there needeth not any
such laborsome indeauour for due preparation, nor yet care or sollicitude of
life or manners; for that alreadie they
haue the thing, which they desire, and
that those are but signes, tokens and
testimonies that they haue receiued it
indeed, which yet, as I said, hath no
more assurance, then euery mans owne
perswasion and apprehension will afford.

　　Lastly, concerning the foresaid
fountaine of temptation in our flesh
and sensualitie, called *Concupiscence*:
they differ from vs in two essentiall
points: first, that they hold this concupiscence, not for a tempter onely, but
rather for a conqueror, for so much as

　　　　　　B 2　　　　　　　they

they teach that euery motion of her to
senſualitie in vs, is a ſinne, whether it
bee yeelded vnto by our will or noe.
The ſecond point following neceſſarily of this firſt, is, that all reſiſtance of
our part to the motions of this concupiſcence, is either needleſſe or boot-
leſſe; for that the motion it ſelfe being
ſinne without our conſent, it followeth
conſequently, that the matter is not
remediable by our endeauours; and
heere now breaketh in a whole ſea of
diſorders to Chriſtian life, for that ſuppoſing firſt, that which is moſt true,
that euery Chriſtian man hath this aſ-
ſault of concupiſcence within him; and
ſecondly, by this new doctrine, that no
man can auoid to ſinne thereby vpon
euery motion that is offered, what nee-
neth, or what auaileth any reſiſtance of
ours, or any conflict to the contrary?
ſinne it is, though we reſiſt neuer ſo
much, and but ſinne it is, if we yeelde.
And ſeeing that by another principle
of this new doctrine, all ſinnes are e-
qually mortall, what is gained by ſtri-
uing, or what is loſt by yeelding? And
to what end are all thoſe large Treati-
ſes

The dif-
ference
about
mortify-
ing and
reſiſting
of our
Concu-
piſcence.

ſes of ancient Fathers, about fighting againſt this concupiſcence, and mortification of her appetites and motions? What doe auaile all their exhortations to this purpoſe, as alſo thoſe of the Scriptures, to continencie, chaſtitie, virginitie, abſtinence, ſobrietie, and other like vertues; for ſo much as euery firſt motion of our concupiſcence to the contrary (which firſt motion wee cannot auoid) is ſin in it ſelfe, to what purpoſe (I ſay) are we perſwaded and animated, to fight and ſtriue againſt this enemie, ſeeing there is no hope of victorie, but that at euery blow ſhee conquereth and ouerthroweth vs, as the Proteſtants teach?

Wherefore to proceed no further in this compariſon, you may eaſily by this, that is ſaid, conſider the differences betweene theſe two people, and in particular, you may with griefe and teares contemplate among other points, fiue generall inundations of looſeneſſe and wicked liberty, brought into Chriſtian conuerſation, by the foreſaid fiue principles of theſe mens doctrine, to wit: Firſt, in taking away wholly all con-

Fiue principal inundations of licentiouſneſſe, brought in by Proteſtants doctrine.

I

B 3 currance,

currance, and good endeauors of mans will to any vertuous action whatsoeuer, though neuer so much preuented or assisted by the helpe of Gods grace.

2   Secondly, in ascribing all iustificatiō to onely Faith, and thereby moouing the concurrance of Hope, Charitie, Piety,

3   Deuotion, and other vertues. Thirdly, in disgracing and denying the necessity of the exercise of externall good workes, proceeding from those internall vertues, and commended vnto vs to walke therein. Fourthly, in deba

4   sing the force, dignity, and number of Sacraments, appointed for instruments and conduites of Gods holy grace vn

5   to all sorts of men. And lastly, in attributing a kingdome of sinne irresistable to our concupiscence, in fauour of temptations and sensuall motions, and discomforting thereby all people from fighting against the same.

Which fiue principles being well weighed & considered, together with the practise and successe that haue ensued vpon them throughout Christendome, where this new doctrine hath preuailed; no indifferent man can bee

so

ſo ſimple, but that he will eaſily diſco-
uer the true difference betweene theſe
two people, and their Religions; as alſo betweene *Fox* his lying fond Definition of a Catholike, and this our De-
ſcription of Catholikes & Proteſtants,
containing the moſt ſubſtantiall points
of Faith, and life, both of the one and
the other.

AN ADDITION MADE
by the Collecter.

NOW *becauſe I haue mentioned*
I O H N F O X, *I would deſire thee*
(*good Reader*) *to reade that learned*
Treatiſe of Three Conuerſions, *eſpeci-*
ally the third part, wherein I O H N F O X   The 17.
his booke of Martyrs (*ſo called*) *is par-*   Chapter
ticularly examined and confuted, *where*   of the
thou mayeſt clearely deſcrie the erroneous   fix laſt
and falſe ſpirit of the Proteſtants, *for ſo*   Months,
much as they make choice of any ſort of   §. 6. in
people whatſoeuer, *bearing the name of*   the be-
Chriſtians, to be of their Church and fra-   ginning,
ternitie, notwithſtanding that they held   to the
and beleeued many moſt damnable errors   §. 8.

B 4   *and*

*and heresies ; but howsoeuer, if they spake
freely against the Pope, or stoutly denied
but one article of the Catholike Faith, for
which they haue been condemned for Heretikes by our Church, they were presently
accounted for right good Protestants, and
fit for* IOHN FOX *to Canonize and
make Martyrs. Of this that worthy Author in the foresaid Treatise sheweth
briefely in a Consideration which hee maketh, what sort of people be put by* IOHN
FOX *into his Kalendar.*

Three
Conuers.
part.3.
chap.17.
n.6.

    *It is then to be noted (saith hee) that
in the Kalendar and story thereof (to wit,*
FOX *his* Actes *and* Monuments) *are
comprised all the heads of Factions and
Sects that haue been different from the
knowne Catholike Religion, and among
themselues for these three or foure last
hundred yeares, as* Waldo *of* Lyons, *and
his* Waldensians, *the Earle of* Tholosa,
and his Albigensians, Iohn Wickliffe *of*
England, *and his* Wickliffians, Iohn
Husse *of* Bemeland, *and his* Hussites,
Iohn Zisca *of the same Nation, and his*
Thaborites, Walter Lollard *in Germanie, and his* Lolardians: *and in our daies,*
Martin Luther, *and his* Lutherans, *both
sects,*

sects, Molles *and* Rigidi Vldericus,
Zuinglius, *and his* Zuinglians, Iohn
Caluin, *and his* Caluinists *both mingled,
and* Puritans; *and other the like: All
which are allowed and commended by*
Fox, *eyther in his Kalendar or Historie,
though they did not a little disagree, as
well among themselues, as with the Catholike Church, both in words and actions,
manner of life, preachings and writings,
as before hath been shewed.*

*And whereas we that follow Catholike
doctrine, are so exact for holding vnitie
therein, as we reiect and hold for wicked
(according to the Creed of Saint* Athanasius, *and first Councell of* Nice*) whosoeuer doth not beleeue inuiolably the said
Catholike Faith, and intirely in euery
point, and doe sometimes condemne euen to
death, and burne some for dissenting in
one only point of Faith, (as* Iohn Fox
*himselfe hath diuers times complained)
how can it be, that he and his Church can
gather vp and tye together in one vnion of
Faith, and communion of Saints, all these
different and opposite heads, together with
their members and followers? Truely no
other way, but onely as* Samson *tyed his*
Foxes

Foxes together by the tayles, though their heads and faces were opposite, and contrarie one to another, which serued him not to plow nor sow, plant nor tyll, but only to set a fire, waste, and destroy the corne which others haue sowed before, which is the only office and peculiar worke, that these wrangling opposit hereticall heads do bring forth in the Church of God, to wit, pull downe, digge vp, destroy, discredit and disgrace that which was sowen, planted, and established before them, and thereby to bring all to misdoubt, vnbeleefe, and atheisme. So F. PARSONS.

And because peraduenture euery one, desirous to know more of this matter, cannot so easily procure to see or reade that discussion or examination of *Iohn Fox* his Saints, and of their different spirits from the Catholike; I will let you see the summe of both Kalendars, as it is set downe by the fore-named Author in the end of the Kalendar, both in the first and last sixe Moneths of that his Examen.

The

The summe of all Saints named in
both Kalendars.

In the Catholike Kalendar.

The number of all mentioned 1704.
whereof are Popes Martyrs 27.
Popes Confessors 8. Bishops Martyrs 37. Bishops Confessors 63.
Virgins Martyrs 76. (besides the
11000. slaine with Saint *Ursula*)
Virgins Confessors 11. Kings and
Queenes Martyrs 3. Kings and
Queenes Confessors 8. other holy men and women 3429. other
men and women Confessors 42.
All these were of one Faith and Religion
agreable to the Roman at this day.

In the Foxian Kalendar.

The number of all mentioned 456.
Bishops Pseudomartyrs 5. Bishops
Confessors 1. Virgin Martyrs 000.
Mayd Martyrs 2. Kings & Queenes
Martyrs and Confessors 1. other
men & women Martyrs 393. other
men and women Confessors 53.
                                These

These were of diuers sects and opinions;
and contrary in many points the one
to the other: as for example.

Waldensians and Albegensians 13.
Lollards and Wickliffians 36. Huf-
fites and Lutherans 78. Zuinglians
and Caluinifts 268. Anabaptifts,
Puritans, and doubtfull of what
fect 59.

Againe of these were

Husbandmen, Weauers, Sawyers,
Shoo-makers, Curriers, Smithes,
and other such like occupations
282. Poore women and Spinfters,
64. Apoftata Monks and Friers 25.
Apoftata Prieftts 38. Minifters 10.
Publike Malefactors, and condemned by the Lawes for such, 19.

The greateft Disputers of this ranke a-
gaiuft the Catholike Bifhops and
learned men, were

Men.   *George Tankerfield* a Cooke, Auguft
13. *Iohn Mandrell* a Cowheard,
March 27. *Richard Chrafhfield* a
yong

yong Artificer, March 28. *Raph Al-
lerton* a Tayler, September 19. *Iohn
Fortune* a Black-smith, September
30. *Richard Woodman* an Iron ma-
ker, Iune 23.

Ellen Erwing a Millers wife, August *Women,*
23. *Ioane Lashford* a maried maide,
Ianuary 18. *Isabell Foster*, a Cut-
lers wife, Ianuary 17. *Anne Ale-
bright*, a poore woman of Canter-
bury, Ianuary 19. *Alice Potkins*,
Spinster, Nouember 15. *Alice dri-
uer*, a famous Doctrice, Nouember 22.

And to giue you some particular taste
of this roauing spirit which raigned in
some of Master *Fox* his principall
Protestant Martyrs; Master *Iohn Bradford*, whom *Fox* most highly extolleth See this
in many leaues, and stileth him Prea- in the
cher-Martyr; was accustomed much to Examen
bragge of his singuler assurance that *of Fox his*
he had of the right course hee was in, Kalendar
which he said was so *cleare and euident* chap. 11.
to him, that there could be no more doubt num. 18.
thereof, then whether the Sunne did shine 29.
vpon a faire day: and when the Bishops
asked

asked him *How he came to so great a certainty*, he answered, *I am certaine of my saluation and religion by the Scriptures:* but when they posed him further, how hee could bee sure of Scriptures themselues, and of their true meaning without the testimony of the Church; hee had no other shift, but to runne to the assurance of his owne spirit, telling them, that albeit he receiued the knowledge of the Scriptures by the testimonie of the Church (as those of the Citie of Sychar did the notice of Christ by the woman from the Well) yet that when he once had them, then could he vse them well enough, for vnderstanding them; and for shew hereof, when a little after hee had occasion to interpret some peeces of Scriptures, he did it so absurdly as a man might well see, how much might be builded vpon the assurance of that his particular and priuate spirit, as for example, among other places, hee tooke vpon him to proue by Scripture that the Pope was Antichrist, and cited for it onely those words of the Apostle to the Thessalonians, That *Antichrist shall sit in the Temple*

Iohn 4.

Temple of God, &c. which though it proue nothing, as you see, for that wee deny not but that Antichrist when hee commeth, shall sit in the Temple of God, yea and pretend to be God him-selfe, (which no Popes euer did or shal doe;) yet to *Bradford* the allegation of this place seemed much to the pur-pose, and to *Iohn Fox,* that admireth all which the other vttered, it appeareth so full a proofe, as he maketh this note in the margent: *The Pope proued to bee Antichrist by Scriptures.* But this proofe (as you see) standeth only vpon *Brad-fords* interpretation, which interpreta-tion is not onely not conforme to any ancient Fathers exposition whatsoeuer, but is manifestly also contrary to the text it selfe, where immediatly before the words alledged, That *he shall sit in the Temple of God,* are these words, *Extolletur supra omne quod dicitur Deus, aut quod colitur,* That Antichrist (when he commeth) shall bee extolled aboue all that is called God, or that is wor-shipped for God, so as he shall not call him Gods seruant (as the Pope doth) nor the seruant of his seruants, but chiefe

chiefe God himselfe, which no Pope, as is said, euer did or will, and consequently these words cannot possibly agree to the Pope, and yet forsooth the spirit of *Bradford,* that cannot erre or be deceiued, doth expound it so, and thereby you see the certaintie of his spirit.

After this, againe he went about to perswade the two Bishops, who examined him, that he agreed with them, and with their Church in substance of Faith and beleefe, and consequently might bee saued with them, notwithstanding this deniall of two articles, for which only he said he was condemned: to wit, *Transubstantiation, and that the euill men doe not receiue the body of Christ,* when they communicate, which two articles *Bradford* affirmed not to appertaine to the substance of faith, or foundation of Christ, and consequently, that he was vnjustly cast out of the Church for them, for so much as hee firmely beleeued all the articles of the Creede with them : whereunto, when the Bishops smiling replied say_ ing, Yea, *Is this your Diuinitie?* B R A D-
FORD

FORD anſwered *Noe*; it is PAVLS, which ſaith, That *if men hold the foundation Chriſt, though they build vpon him ſtraw and ſtubble, yet they ſhall be ſaued.* 1.Cor.3. 11.

So he, whereby you ſee that this great learned Cleake would proue by Saint *Paul*, that both Proteſtants and all other Sectaries, that in words doe profeſſe to beleeue all the Articles of the Creede (though each one in ſeuerall ſenſe to himſelfe) ſhall be ſaued together with Catholikes, and that all theſe our contentions with them, and other Sectaries are but ſtraw and ſtubble, and touch not the foundation of Chriſt at all : This was his ſpirit, and doe you thinke that this ſpirit could be deceiued, or will our Engliſh Proteſtants at this day, allow this ſpirit, or joyne with *Bradford* in this paradox ? I know they will not, and would bee aſhamed to interpret the place of Saint *Paul* in that ſenſe, for ſo much as it is euident, that he meaneth of the ſtraw and ſtubble of workes, and not doctrine, or at leaſt ſuch principall points of doctrine as thoſe are, which

C   *Bradford*

Bradford did professe contrary to the
Catholique truth.   Notwithstanding
there bee some principall Protestant
Doctors, who, howsoeuer they interpret the foresaid place of Saint *Paul,*
1. *Cor.*3. and vpon what other place
soeuer of Scripture they pretend to
builde, yet doe they holde and maintaine the same Paradox in Christian
Religion (as I may call it)and the same
exorbitant grosse errour, which the
phanaticall spirit of *Iohn Bradford* suggested vnto him for an assured truth,
to wit, that all, euen Heretikes, as well
as Catholikes, may bee saued, so long
as they hold the foundation Christ.

Morton in
his Trea-
tise of the
Kingdom
of Israel,
pag.91.

For so Master Doctor *Morton* (now
called a Bishop) saith, *Wheresoeuer a*
company of men doe ioyntly and publikely
by worshipping the true God in Christ,
professe the substance of Christian Reli-
gion, which is Faith in Iesus Christ , the
Sonne of God, and Sauiour of the world,
that there is a true Church , notwithstan-
ding any corruption whatsoeuer. And,
giuing this title to one section in his

Ibidem .

booke, *That Heretikes are members of*
the

the Catholike Church. In proofe hereof
he faith further, *Who professe* IESVS
CHRIST *to bee the Sauiour of the
world, &c. although they doe indirectly
by wickednesse of life, or heresie in doctrine deny their owne profession, yet are
they to be accounted Christians, and true
members of the Church:* by whofe account you fee all Heretikes whatfoeuer
are to be accounted for true members
of the Church, feeing all doe confesse
Iefus Chrift to bee the Sauiour of the *Supra*
world, and therefore hee holdeth the *pag. 94.*
Arrians, who deny the God-head of
Chrift, to bee alfo of the Church of
God. The like doth Doctor *Field,*concerning the Greeke Churches, though
they erre againft the holy Ghoft ; faying in his Treatife of the Church: *Wee* Field
cannot condemne the Grecians as Here- of the
tikes : And againe, before that pag.70. Church,
It no way appeareth that the Churches of pag. 210.
*Greece are hereticall, or in damnable
Schifme.* Which opinion and judgement of thefe principall new Minifters
in our Proteftant Kingdome of Ifrael,
if it were found and good,and procee-

ded from the true Spirit ; wee might
easily grant and beleeue that all sort of
Heretikes whatsoeuer are, or euer haue
been, may be saued, notwithstanding
their abominable and blasphemous
heresies, which they haue taught and
beleeued, concerning God, the blessed
Trinitie, the Incarnation of our Sauiour, or in a word, against any, or almost all the Articles of our Creede :
which strange paradox how contrary
it is vnto the whole current of holy
Scripture, which saith expressely, That
an hereticall man is damned; let any
indifferent man consider and judge,
surely the whole streame of all Antiquitie, the graue, holy, and wise judgement of holy men that haue liued in
Gods Church throughout all ages,
were of another beleefe and opinion,
and of a quite contrary spirit to this of
Protestant Doctors : you shall heare
one or two speake for the rest. Saint
Cyprian saith, ***Whosoeuer is seperated
from the Church, and ioyneth himselfe to
an adulteresse conuenticle*** (which euery
Heretike doth) *is seperated also from the
promises*

Tit. 3.

*Cyprian.
lib. de
Simpl.
prælat.*

promises of the Church, nor euer shall hee come to enioy the rewards thereof, if hee leaue her; he is an alien, a prophane per-son, an enemie, he cannot haue God for his Father, that hath not the Church for his Mother: yea though hee should bee slaine for the confessing of Chrifts name, yet can he not be saued; Macula ifta nec fangui-næ abluitur, *this crime of feperating him-felfe from the Church cannot bee washed away with blood:* Inexpiabilis culpa nec passione purgatur, *It is a fault vnexpia-ble* (suppoling one continue in it) *nor can it be purged by death it felfe.* Saint *Augustine* also, *Neither is Baptisme* (faith he) *profitable to an Heretike being out of the Church, nor yet if for the confes-sion of Chrift he should be put to death, for that hee is conuinced to want charitie*, whereof the Apostle faith, *Though I should deliuer my body fo that I burn, and haue not charity, it doth profit me nothing.* The fame hath S. *Austen* in many pla-ces of his Workes, and the fame is the conftant and common opinion of all holy Fathers: and therefore whether thefe holy ancient Fathers, or our late moderne

Much lesse may Protestants flatter & deceiue them-felues, by thinking they liue well, and may bee faued.

Aug. l. 4. de Bapt. cont. Do-nat. c. 17.

C 3

moderne Proteſtant Doctors are moſt
likely to be guided by the true ſpirit of
God, as well in this, as in many moſt
important points of our Chriſtian beleefe, wherein they differ as much as
light from darkneſſe, truth from falſe-
hood ; I leaue vnto euery Chriſtian man, who hath a true and earneſt care of his eternall ſaluation, ſeriouſly and diligently to weigh and con-
ſider.

AN-

ANOTHER DIFFERENCE

worthy of obseruation betweene
the Catholike and Protestant spirit,
consisting in the willingnes of the
one, and vnwillingnesse of the
*other to admit publike and in-
different triall of their
Doctrine.*

HEREAS one principal mark
by which a good Spirit may be
discerned from a bad, is that
the good Spirit loueth light, and willingly commeth to the light, admitting
any reasonable and indifferent meanes
of triall. But the bad Spirit hateth
light, and commeth not to the light,
but flyeth all publike and indifferent
meanes, by which it may be examined.
I wish the gentle Reader duely to consider how this propertie of the good
spirit agreeth to the Catholike Church
and the propertie of the bad spirit a-
greeth to the Protestants Congregation.

On the one side it may easily bee
seene how much the Catholike Church
loueth light, in that the Doctors there-

C 4   of

of in their publike writings ordinarily vse to explicate and set downe clearely and sincerely, the state of the question in controuersie. Secondly, They truly set downe the opinions and arguments of their Aduersaries, and this sometimes more fully then is done by their Aduersaries themselues. Thirdly, They explicate the Catholike doctrine, confirming it with cleare testimonies of holy Scriptures, Councels, Fathers, and Reasons, and answering fully all, or the strongest Obiections. Fourthly, They are ready both in their publike Schools and in their Prouinciall and Generall Councels to admit, yea inuite, their greatest Aduersaries to speake freely whatsoeuer they thinke good, for triall of the truth in all matters of Controuersie. This to be true, appeareth partly by the learned and methodicall books of our Catholike Authors, namely, *Bellarmine, Stapleton, Valentia,* and others; partly by the practise of our publike Schooles, where any may freely make whatsoeuer arguments they will, for disputation sake, partly by some especiall examples of free disputation

tation permitted to be made in Catholike Countries, euen by knowne Heretikes: as for ancient times, wee reade how the Councell of Carthage inuited the Donatists to a publike and free Conference or disputation, saying, *Eligatis ex vobis ipsis*, &c. Choose some among your selues who may vndergoe this businesse to proue your cause, that we also may do the like, and that some from among this Councell may be appointed, who may at the same time and place agree vpon, examine or trie together with those which shal be chosen among you, whatsoeuer controuersie it is which hindereth vs from communicating with you, &c. For if you doe brotherly admit thereof (to wit, of this conference) the truth will easily appeare. But if you refuse to accept of this, your infidelitie (or false faith) will presently be made knowne. Thus this ancient Councell did inuite Heretikes to a triall, also in latter times in our owne Countrey, to wit, in the raigne of Queene *Mary*, there were permitted seuerall open disputations, once in *Pauls* Church in *London* for sixe daies, and

and after at *Oxford*, and again secondly at *Oxford* with liberty to make election of Notaries vpon their part, and
with offer of books and libertie of further time to amend their answeres, all
which is affirmed and granted by *Fox*
in his booke of *Actes and Monuments*,
and clearely conuinceth the Catholike
Spirit to bee a good Spirit, which ad-
mitteth so willingly, and offereth so
freely such publike triall of the truth.
But chiefely this which I said appeareth to be true, by the most ample free
offer, and Inuitement, and safe conduct made and granted by the holy generall Councell of Trent to all Protestants, both of *Germany* and other places, the tenor of which is as followeth.

　*Salvus conductus concessus Germanicæ
　　Nationi :*
　The Safe-conduct granted vnto the
　　German Nation.
　In the generall Congregation the
　　fourth day of March, *MDLXII.*

　　　　　　　　　　　　　Sacro

Sacro sancta œcumenica & generalis Tridentina Synodus, &c.

THe most Sacred œcumenicall and generall Councell of Trent most lawfully gathered together in the holy Ghost the Legates of the holy Sea Apostolike, president in the same, doth make knowne vnto all men, that it doth graunt vnto all and euery one, Priests, Electors, Princes, Dukes, Marquesses, Counts, Barons, Nobles, Knights, Commons, and to all other whatsoeuer, of whatsoeuer state and condition, or qualitie they bee of the Prouince and Nation of *Germany,* to all Cities and other places thereof, and to all other Ecclesiastical and Secular persons, especially those of the Confession of *Augusta,* who shall come, or any who together with them shall come or be sent, or whosoeuer haue hitherto come vnto this Generall Councell of Trent, by what name soeuer they bee called, or may be called by the tenour of these presents, doth grant by publike promise a most full & true security, which is called *A safe Conduct,* freely

to

to come vnto the Citie of *Trent*, and
there to remaine, ftay, abide, propofe,
fpeake, treate, examine together with
the Councell, and difcourfe of what
bufineffe foeuer, and freely to offer vp
and publifh whatfoeuer it ·fhall pleafe
them, and whatfoeuer Articles, as well
in writing, as by word of mouth, and
to declare, maintaine, confirme, and
proue the fame by the holy Scriptures,
and by the words and fentences of holy Fathers, and by reafons; and if need
require, euen to anfwere vnto the objections of the Generall Councel, and
to difpute with thofe who fhall be appointed by the Councell, or peaceably
to conferre without any impediment,
all approbrious fpeeches, reuilings, and
contumelies wholly laid afide, and in
particular, that the matters in controuerfie fhall be handled in the forefaid
Councell, according to the holy Scriptures, and traditions of the Apoftles,
approued Councels, the confent of the
Catholike Church, and the Authoritie
of the holy Fathers, adding this moreouer, that it doth yeeld and abfolutely
grant, that they fhall not be punifhed
                                              vnder

vnder the pretext of Religion, or of
any offences committed, or to be committed againſt the ſame, ſo as by reaſon of their preſence, none ſhall in any
caſe need to ceaſe from performing the
diuine ſeruice either in journey or in
going, abiding, or returning from any
place, noe, not in the Citie of Trent it
ſelfe:& that theſe buſineſſes being finiſhed or not finiſhed, whenſoeuer they
ſhal pleaſe, or by commãdment & conſent of their Superiors they ſhal deſire,
or any one of thẽ ſhal deſire to returne
to their owne dwellings; preſently,
without any let, hinderance, or delay,
their goods, their honour likewiſe and
perſons preſerued, they may freely and
ſecurely returne at their pleaſure, as
often as they will, with the knowledge
notwithſtanding of ſuch as ſhall bee
appointed by the Councell, to the end
that prouiſion may bee made in due
time for their ſecuritie, without fraud
or deceit.

Moreouer, the holy Councell will,
that in this publike promiſe and Safe-
Conduct bee included and contained,
and to be held for included all clauſes
what-

whatfoeuer, which fhall bee neceffarie
and conuenient for their full effectuall
and fufficient fecuritie in their going,
ftaying, and returning : expreffing this
moreouer, for their greater fecuritie,
and for the good of peace and agreement, that if any of them either in jorney comming vnto *Trent*, or whileſt
they abide there, or in returning thēce,
fhould doe or commit (which God forbid) any enormous crime, whereby the
benefit of this publike fidelity and aſ-
fecuration might bee annullated or
made voide, that it is the Councels
will, and it doth grant that fuch as are
found to haue committed fuch offence,
be prefently punifhed by thofe of the
Confeffion of *Augusta* themfelues only, and not by any other, with fuch
condigne penaltie and fufficient fatiffaction as may bee well liked of, and
approued by fome part of the Councel,
the forme, conditions, and manner of
their affecuration (or fecuritie) remaining ftill vnuiolated.

In like manner alfo, the Councels
pleafure is, that if one or more of the
Councell fhall either in their jorney or
abiding,

abiding, or returning, doe or commit (which God forbid) any enormous crime, whereby the benefite of this publike fidelity and affecuration might be violated, or in any fort broken, they who are taken in fuch offence, are to bee punifhed by the Councell it felfe alone, and not by any other, with fuch condigne penaltie & fufficient amendment, as may rightly be well liked of by the Lords of *Germany*, of the Confeffion of *Augufta* , being at the fame time heere prefent, the forme, conditions, and manner of their affecuration (or fecuritie) remaining ftill vnuiolated.

It is moreouer the will of the Councell, that it may be lawfull for the Embaffadors, all and euery one to goe abroad out of the Citie of *Trent*, fo often as they fhall thinke fit or needfull to take the ayre, and to returne into the fame : as alfo freely to appoint or fend their meffenger or meffengers, as alfo to receiue meffengers or any meffenger, fent as often as they fhall think expedient: fo that fome one or more of fuch as are deputed (and appointed)by

the

the Councell, doe accompany them,
who may prouide for their securitie.

Which Safe-Conduct and securitie
ought to stand and continue from the
time, and during the time that it shall
happen they be receiued into the care
of the protection of the Councel and
Officers thereof, and be brought vnto
Trent, and all the time of their abode
there : and againe, when they shall
haue had sufficient audience, then after
the space of twentie dayes, when they
shall require it, or the Councell after
such audience had, shall giue order vnto them to depart, they shall bee con-
ducted from *Trent*, vntill they be (God
willing) restored vnto that secure place
where euery one shal choose vnto himselfe, and this without all fraud and
deceit.

All which the Councell doth promise, and with assured fidelitie doth
professe shall bee inuiolately obserued
(and kept) for and in the name of euery
faithfull Christian, all Princes whatsoeuer, as well Ecclesiasticall as Temporall, and all other Ecclesiasticall and
Secular persons, of what degree or
                                    condition

condition ſoeuer they be of, or by what
name ſoeuer they be called.

Moreouer, without all fraud and
deceit, it doth truely and faithfully
promiſe, that the Councel will neither
openly nor couertly ſeek any occaſion,
or in any ſort vſe, or permit any to vſe
any authoritie, power, right, ordinance
or priuiledge of the Lawes or Canons,
or of any Councel whatſoeuer, eſpecially of *Conſtance* and *Seenes,* in what
forme of words ſoeuer expreſſed, vnto
any prejudice of this publike fidelitie
and ful aſſecuration, & publike and free
audience graunted vnto them by the
Councell, all which (authority, power,
&c.) it doth abrogate in this behalfe,
and for this time.

And if the Holy Councell, or any
one thereof, or of their adherents, of
whatſoeuer condition or ſtate, or dig-
nitie they be, ſhal in any point or cauſe
violate (which neuertheleſſe wee be-
ſeech God forbid) the forme and manner of the aboue written aſſecuration
and Safe Conduct, and that ſufficient
amendment be not preſently made, yea
and ſuch as in the judgements of thoſe

D   of

of the Cōfeſſion of *Auguſta*, ſhall rightly be approued and well liked of, let them account, and it ſhall be lawful for them to account the Councell it ſelfe to haue incurred al the penalties, which either of the Law, of the Law of God and man, or cuſtome, the violators of ſuch Safe-conducts can incurre (& this) without all excuſe, or any gain-ſaying in this behalfe.

The extenting of the former Safe-conduct vnto all other Nations.

THe ſame moſt ſacred Synod, being moſt lawfully gathered together in the holy Ghoſt, the ſaid Legates *de-latere* (ſo called) of the Sea Apoſtolike preſiding, doth grant the publike fidelity or Safe-conduct vnder the ſame forme, and with the ſame words, wherwith it is granted vnto the *Germans*, vnto all and euery one who doe not participate with vs in matters belonging to Faith, of whatſoeuer Kingdom, Nation, Prouince, Citie or place where is publikely & freely preached, or taught, or beleeued, contrary vnto that which the holy Church of Rome doth teach.

A

A SPEECH OF CARDI-
nall BARONIVS placed in the
beginning of the second Tome
of his Annals.

I thinke it fitte to adioyne in this place a
Speech of that worthily renowned and
learned Cardinal Baronius, directed vn-
to all Heretikes; shewing how assured the
faithfull children of Gods Church are,
and euer haue been, concerning the vn-
doubted truth of their holy Catholike
and Apostolike Roman Religion, & how
prompt and ready they haue euer been to
admitte of any indifferent triall of the
same. The Speech or Admonition he en-
tituleth thus :

An Appendix or Addition vnto the Reader,
who is out of the Catholike Church.

AT *nec te dispiscimus,* &c. We contemne not thee (I speake to the
Reader much auerted from the Catholike Faith) nor set vpon thee with re-
bukes, prouoke thee with reproaches,
loade thee with contumelies; because
we are not moued with any perturba-

tion of mind against the persons, when
we reprehend mens errours, wee deale
most kindly with thee, to the end thou
mayest vnderstand that the Truth it
selfe, rather then the Patron thereof,
fighteth against thee : yea we will bee
most liberall to thee, so farre forth, as
that we will not feare, with all lenitie
and submission of minde, to allow thy
selfe perusing diligently these our
workes, and desiring to finde forth the
truth, as a just arbitrator. We hauing
a confidence in the goodnesse of our
cause, will yeeld so much vnto thee, as
not to disdaine to vndergoe thy judgement, concerning the truth of those
things we speake of, prouided that thy
reason, as it were, equally ballanced,
be placed betweene, but aboue both
parties, that is, supposing thee to be of
a sound and sincere judgement, voyd of
all perturbation, wanting particular
affections, and so inclining to neither
partie. If thou bee ready to shew thy
selfe such a judge, I appeale from thy
selfe, when at other times thou haddest
thy minde troubled, vnto thine owne
selfe, now examining things more ex-
actly

actly with the cleared eye of thy vnderstanding, the which power of mans
soule is most vigorous,if being vnchai-
ned and free, it bee suffered freely to
discourse. This consideration enforced our Auncestors, relying vpon the
truth of their doctrine, when they had
occasion to deale with most obstinate
Heretikes, refusing and contemning
the Church her judgement, to conde-
scend so much vnto them, as to permit
their cause to the arbitrement of Hea-
thens, and demand their sentence in
the same. These being Iudges, the
Iews after much contention ouercame
the Samaritans. In like manner,*Origen*   *Ioseph. An-*
choosing by consent of his aduersaries   *tiq.lib.13.*
a Gentile for Vmpire, ouerthrew fiue   *cap.6.*
most peruerse Heretikes, and conuerted him who sate as Vmpire in their
dispute. Likewise the holy Mesopota-   *Epiphan.*
nian Bishop, *Archelaus,* confuted the   *Heref. 66.*
most impious Arch-heretike *Manes,*
by the arbitrement of *Gentiles,* chosen
to decide by common consent of both
disputants. There are many other like
examples,by which it appears the pro-
fessors of the truth to haue refused no

mans judgement or sentence, no not so much as of those who seeme to be condemned by our Lord himselfe, saying: *Hee that beleeueth not, is alreadie iudged.* All these we seeme to ouergo in our maner of free dealing with thee, because wee seeke no other arbitrator then thy selfe, if thou follow the rules of reason, most certainly assuring our selues, that thou wilt giue sentence for, and agree with vs , if thy reason of it owne nature most affecting equitie, do willingly heare the truth. One thing wee expect as the sole reward for our labours, that is, to see thee at length so condemned by thy selfe, judging most justly, as that thou mayest be quitte of thy errours. God grant we may once joyfully meete thee rectified in judgement, embrace and *kiffe thee as our brother, fucking the brefts of our Mother:* at this present although it be vnlawful for vs, because of the prohibition of the Apostle (we speake it not without a most hearty sorrow) to salute thee, or to say so much as all haile vnto thee, notwithstanding there is none that will forbid vs, to beg of almightie God by earnest

prayer

Iohn 3.

Cant. 8.

prayer thy faluation, which wee moſt earneſtly deſire.

By this it appeareth how much the Catholike Spirit loueth light, & wiſh-eth to haue a full and free triall of the truth. Contrariwiſe, the Proteſtants Spirit ſheweth it ſelfe to hate light,firſt in that ordinarily their profeſſors write confuſedly of Controuerſies, ſeldome ſetting downe ſincerely and clearely the ſtate of the queſtion,but often per-uerting it,making that ſeeme to be the queſtion, which is not, alſo ordinarily wronging the Catholike ſentence, in making it ſeeme to ſay what it ſayeth not, alſo vſually concealing,or not ful-ly vrging the arguments of Scriptures, Fathers,Councels, & Reaſons brought by Catholikes in their publike wri-tings. Their owne ſentence and opini-on alſo they ſet downe ſo darkely and obſcurely,as that oftentimes they ſcarſe vnderſtand themſelues, and much leſſe is it vnderſtood by others, what they hold,or would ſay. The arguments alſo which they bring for confirmation of their opinion.as likewiſe their anſwers to our objections are ſo light and vn-

D 4   ſound,

found, yea fometimes fo farre fetched
and ill framed,as it is wonder that men
of witte and learning can fuffer fuch
ftuffe to paffe from them.

I omit to fpeake of their falfification
and corruption of Scriptures and Fathers,whereof a tafte may be taken by
that which is fet downe in M. *Walfing-
ham* his Search into matters of Religion. I omit alfo their flying the judgement of ancient Fathers and Councels,
and their retiring themfelues into the
mift of their owne priuat fantafies, couered with the fpacious titles of onely
Scripture and Gods Spirit.

That which chiefly fheweth Proteftants Spirit to loue darknes, is that by
any meanes they will not be drawne
to permitte Catholikes liuing in their
quarters,to come to fuch a publike,free
and indifferent triall of the truth (euen
by fuch grounds as Proteftants themfelues doe admit, or which by force of
argumét Catholikes wil foundly proue
ought to be admitted) as Proteftants
haue bin permitted,yea inuited,yea vehemently vrged vnto by the Catholike
part: How ofteu haue euen our Englifh

lifh Catholikes Challēged Proteftants
to fuch a publike triall of truth ? Heare
I befeech you the the words of one of Defenee
them, writing about this point, againft of the
a Minifter called Mafter *Charke* : And in the E-
heere (M.*Charke* faith he) becaufe we piftle to
are fallen into this matter, I am in the M.*Charke.*
name of my fellow Catholikes to re-
new our publike Challenge, of equall
Difputation to you, and to all your
brother Minifters againe. M. *Campian*
is gone, whom you name in this matter to be our onely Champion, you fee
that Mafter *Sherwin* is made away with
him, whom you are wont to fay (for
more abafement of the other) to haue
been far better learned then M. *Campian* himfelfe. But howfoeuer that was,
both of them haue you difpatched, and
thereby (in your opinion) greatly wea-
kened our caufe; yet notwithftanding
we are the fame men that we were before: yea much more defirous of this
triall then before. Wherefore wee requeft you now at length, yea we con-
jure you either for the truth fake, if you
feeke it, or for your owne credit fake,
if you will reteine it, that you yeeld vs
after

after so much suite and supplication, some equall triall, either by writing, preaching, or disputing. There is no reason in the world (but onely feare) that may mooue you to deny vs this our request. For the reason (of State) which you alledge (M. *Charke*) in the reply, is most vaine. For what can a peaceable disputation, granted to vs for Religion, indanger the State? but only (that you would say) that this disputation may chance to discouer your errors, and so make the hearers detest the state of your heresie, for other danger there can be none to your State. And if you had the truth with you (as you pretend) whose property is, the more to shew her selfe, the more shee is examined, you should much increase your State by this publike triall: for that you should both gaine more to your part, by opening the said truth, and also confirme many of your owne side, that now justly doe wauer vpon this open discouery of your feare in triall.

Wherefore once againe, I say vnto you Ministers, obtaine vs this disputation,

tion, though it be only but for a fhew,
thereby onely to hold and maintaine
your credit : we proteft before God,
that we feeke it onely for the triall of
Chrifts truth, for fearch whereof, wee
offer our felues to this labour, charges,
and perill of life, we aske for our fafe-
ties, but only fuch a warrant from her
Majefty, as the late Councell of *Trent*
did offer vnto all Proteftants in the
world, wherof you haue the copy with
you : we will come in what kinde and
number, at what time, to what place
you will appoint.

If you wil haue your own Countrimen, they are ready to come. If you wil
haue ftrangers to difpute in your Vni-
uerfities before the learned only, there
fhal not want. For your felues, we giue
you leaue to call all the learned Proteftants of *Europe* for your defence ; wee
wil take only our owne Country-men,
if you permit vs. We giue you leaue to
oppofe or defend, to appoint queftiós,
to choofe cótrouerfies, to begin or end
at your pleafure, and to vfe any other
prerogatiues that you pleafe , fo that
they impugne not the indifferencie of
Triall :

Triall: What can you alledge why you
fhould not accept this?

If you had rather make trial in other
Countries, then at home before your
own people, as perhaps you had, chufe
you what Proteftant ftate you lift, and
procure vs therein the forefaid fafetie
from the Prince, and wee will neither
fpare labour nor coft to meet you therin alfo. Or if this feeme hard, and like
you not, then take you but the paines
fome number of you, to come into any
Catholike Kingdom or Coūtry where
you pleafe, and we will procure what
fecurity foeuer reafonably you fhal demand for your perfons. And more then
that, we will beare your expences alfo,
rather then fo good a worke fhall remaine vnattempted. And if you can
deuife any other condition to bee performed on our parts, which I haue left
out, do you adde the fame, and we will
agree (by the grace of God) to fulfil it.
If we offer you reafon, then deale fom-
what reafonably with vs againe. For al
the world wil crie fhame, and begin to
difcredit you, if you will neither giue
nor take vpon fo great oddes as are
　　　　　　　　　　　　　　　　heere

heere offered you. If you dare not venture with Difputations, yet grant vs at the leaft certaine Sermons to encounter with you vpon this matter: or if that alfo be fo dangerous, procure vs but a little paffage for our bookes.

Now wheras the *Denfence of the Cenfure,* wherein the fore-rehearfed Challenge made by our learned Countrymen is fet downe, was publifhed *Anno Dom.* 1582. the fame Challenge vnto the Minifters of England, with humble fuit and earneft petition to the Prince for the fame, hath bin continually euer fince made, during the late Queenes dayes, and the fame alfo more often reitterated and vrged fince the raigne of his Majeftie, vnto whom the graue and learned Doctor *Kellifon* prefented the fame petition in the name of al Catholikes, yea and after that intreated for the fame in his Epiftle Dedicatorie to the Kings Majeftie, prefixed before his learned booke called *The Suruey of the new Religion.* The fame petition alfo for difputation & triall (to omit many others) was made vnto his Majeftie by that learned Prieft M.*Brierley,* in his

vn-

vnanſwerable booke entituled, *The
Proteſtants Apollogie for the Romane
Church*, where hauing directed the
whole current of his diſcourſe vnto his
learned Majeſtie, hee cloſeth vp the
ſame with a finall petition and humble
intreatie for ſome open and equall triall of diſputation. For the obtaining
whereof (ſaith he) we preſume hereby
to become moſt humble and earneſt
petitioners vnto your Majeſtie. The
euident and neceſſary incertaintie of
our Aduerſaries judgemēts in doctrine
may well ſeeme to need it. The weight
and conſequence of the cauſe (being
no leſſe then the matter of Faith and
Religion) deſerueth. Our Aduerſaries
rule of reducing all things to examination and triall, appointeth it. Our earneſt deſire of their conuerſion thirſteth
greatly after it. Their full perſwaſion
of our pretended erring, and like charitable care of our reformation, ſhould
in all reaſon be no leſſe willing of it.
Our often admitting, or rather prouo-
king of them to open and equal diſpu-
tations had in Queene *Maries* time,
doth as now againe by way of requi-
tall

Tract.3.
Sect.7.

tall anfwerably requite it. The ferious
and refolued confidence of our Catholike Diuines, men confeffedly no leffe
able to performe, thē willing to vnder-
take the fame, doth with moſt graue,
and not to be neglected folicitation,
prouoke and challenge it. The feueral
examples of the fame courfe, heretofore obferued and practifed in fundrie
Nations, and by our very Aduerfaries
prefcribed, doe as it were conduct and
lead vs to it. The venerable and confeffed antiquitie of Catholike Faith
eſtabliſhed, but neuer hitherto condemned in any Generall Councell(and
therfore vnworthy to be now rejected
without fome indifferencie of triall)
prefumeth very confidently to obtaine
it. And laſtly, your Highneffe mature
and ripe judgement, able to moderate
and cenfure the fame, maketh vs fo
much the rather to become moſt humbly defirous and earneſt for it.

Thus you fee with what confidence
in the truth of their caufe, and with
what feruent defire of difputation, and
publike trial of their Spirits, thefe learned Catholikes in the name of the reſt
defire

desire it. With the same earnestnesse
doe our learned Catholikes abroad call
vpon the Protestant Ministers, in all
such places where they beare sway, to
come vnto some publike triall of their
cause: Witnesse Sir *Edwine Sands*, who
in his Relation of the Religion vsed in
the West parts of the world, reporteth
of our Catholike disputers, that they
crie out mainely in all places for triall
by disputations. This saith he, *Campian*
did many yeares since with vs. This as
I passed through *Turrick*, did the Car-
dinall of *Constance* and his Iesuits, with
their Ministers, being by ancient right
within the Diocesse. Not long before, the same was done to them
of *Geneua*. And very lately the
Capuchines renewed the
challenge: so this Knight
a Protestant.

***

FINIS.